Cuba a "Spy" Guide

Just The facts101
Textbook Key Facts

by Cram101
Textbook NOT Included

Table of Contents

Title Page

Copyright

Foundations of Business

Management

Business law

Finance

Human resource management

Information systems

Marketing

Manufacturing

Commerce

Business ethics

Accounting

Index: Answers

Just The Facts101

Exam Prep for

Cuba a "Spy" Guide

Just The Facts101 Exam Prep is your link from
the textbook and lecture to your exams.

**Just The Facts101 Exam Preps are unauthorized and comprehensive reviews
of your textbooks.**

All material provided by CTI Publications (c) 2019

Textbook publishers and textbook authors do not participate in or contribute to these reviews.

Just The Facts101 Exam Prep

Copyright © 2019 by CTI Publications. All rights reserved.

eAIN 444447

Foundations of Business

A business, also known as an enterprise, agency or a firm, is an entity involved in the provision of goods and/or services to consumers. Businesses are prevalent in capitalist economies, where most of them are privately owned and provide goods and services to customers in exchange for other goods, services, or money.

:: Consumer theory ::

A _____ is a technical term in psychology, economics and philosophy usually used in relation to choosing between alternatives. For example, someone prefers A over B if they would rather choose A than B.

Exam Probability: **Medium**

1. *Answer choices:*
(see index for correct answer)

- a. Supply and demand
- b. Marginal rate of substitution
- c. Convex preferences
- d. Hicksian demand function

Guidance: level 1

:: Problem solving ::

In other words, _____ is a situation where a group of people meet to generate new ideas and solutions around a specific domain of interest by removing inhibitions. People are able to think more freely and they suggest as many spontaneous new ideas as possible. All the ideas are noted down and those ideas are not criticized and after _____ session the ideas are evaluated. The term was popularized by Alex Faickney Osborn in the 1953 book Applied Imagination.

Exam Probability: **High**

2. *Answer choices:*
(see index for correct answer)

- a. Curiosity
- b. Creativity techniques
- c. Brainstorming
- d. Proof by exhaustion

Guidance: level 1

:: Debt ::

_____ is the trust which allows one party to provide money or resources to another party wherein the second party does not reimburse the first party immediately, but promises either to repay or return those resources at a later date. In other words, _____ is a method of making reciprocity formal, legally enforceable, and extensible to a large group of unrelated people.

Exam Probability: **High**

3. *Answer choices:*
(see index for correct answer)

- a. Credit
- b. Default trap
- c. Creditor
- d. Borrowing base

Guidance: level 1

:: ::

A _____ is any person who contracts to acquire an asset in return for some form of consideration.

Exam Probability: **Medium**

4. *Answer choices:*

(see index for correct answer)

- a. deep-level diversity
- b. Buyer
- c. imperative
- d. levels of analysis

Guidance: level 1

:: Labour relations ::

_____ is a field of study that can have different meanings depending on the context in which it is used. In an international context, it is a subfield of labor history that studies the human relations with regard to work – in its broadest sense – and how this connects to questions of social inequality. It explicitly encompasses unregulated, historical, and non-Western forms of labor. Here, _____ define "for or with whom one works and under what rules. These rules determine the type of work, type and amount of remuneration, working hours, degrees of physical and psychological strain, as well as the degree of freedom and autonomy associated with the work."

Exam Probability: **Medium**

5. *Answer choices:*

(see index for correct answer)

- a. Worker center
- b. Employee voice
- c. Broad left
- d. Delta Board Council

Guidance: level 1

:: Treaties ::

An _____ is a relationship among people, groups, or states that have joined together for mutual benefit or to achieve some common purpose, whether or not explicit agreement has been worked out among them. Members of an _____ are called allies. _____s form in many settings, including political _____s, military _____s, and business _____s. When the term is used in the context of war or armed struggle, such associations may also be called allied powers, especially when discussing World War I or World War II.

Exam Probability: **Medium**

6. *Answer choices:*

(see index for correct answer)

- a. Alliance
- b. Investor state dispute settlement
- c. Reservation
- d. Bilateral treaty

Guidance: level 1

:: Project management ::

Some scenarios associate "this kind of planning" with learning "life skills". _____s are necessary, or at least useful, in situations where individuals need to know what time they must be at a specific location to receive a specific service, and where people need to accomplish a set of goals within a set time period.

Exam Probability: **Medium**

7. *Answer choices:*

(see index for correct answer)

- a. Schedule
- b. Project blog
- c. Assumption-based planning
- d. DICE framework

Guidance: level 1

:: Fraud ::

In law, _____ is intentional deception to secure unfair or unlawful gain, or to deprive a victim of a legal right. _____ can violate civil law, a criminal law, or it may cause no loss of money, property or legal right but still be an element of another civil or criminal wrong. The purpose of _____ may be monetary gain or other benefits, for example by obtaining a passport, travel document, or driver's license, or mortgage _____, where the perpetrator may attempt to qualify for a mortgage by way of false statements.

Exam Probability: **High**

8. *Answer choices:*
(see index for correct answer)

- a. Workers Resistance
- b. Wangiri
- c. Parcel mule scam
- d. Phone cloning

Guidance: level 1

:: Production economics ::

_____ is the joint use of a resource or space. It is also the process of dividing and distributing. In its narrow sense, it refers to joint or alternating use of inherently finite goods, such as a common pasture or a shared residence. Still more loosely, "_____" can actually mean giving something as an outright gift: for example, to "share" one's food really means to give some of it as a gift. _____ is a basic component of human interaction, and is responsible for strengthening social ties and ensuring a person's well-being.

Exam Probability: **Low**

9. *Answer choices:*
(see index for correct answer)

- a. Post-Fordism
- b. The labor problem
- c. Productive capacity
- d. Sectoral output

Guidance: level 1

:: Accounting terminology ::

_____ is a legally enforceable claim for payment held by a business for goods supplied and/or services rendered that customers/clients have ordered but not paid for. These are generally in the form of invoices raised by a business and delivered to the customer for payment within an agreed time frame. _____ is shown in a balance sheet as an asset. It is one of a series of accounting transactions dealing with the billing of a customer for goods and services that the customer has ordered. These may be distinguished from notes receivable, which are debts created through formal legal instruments called promissory notes.

Exam Probability: **Low**

10. *Answer choices:*
(see index for correct answer)

- a. Accrued liabilities
- b. Statement of financial position
- c. Accounts receivable
- d. Fund accounting

Guidance: level 1

:: Cash flow ::

_____ s are narrowly interconnected with the concepts of value, interest rate and liquidity. A _____ that shall happen on a future day tN can be transformed into a _____ of the same value in t0.

Exam Probability: **Medium**

11. *Answer choices:*
(see index for correct answer)

- a. Free cash flow
- b. Cash flow forecasting
- c. Cash flow
- d. Cash flow loan

Guidance: level 1

:: ::

_____ is the administration of an organization, whether it is a business, a not-for-profit organization, or government body. _____ includes the activities of setting the strategy of an organization and coordinating the efforts of its employees to accomplish its objectives through the application of available resources, such as financial, natural, technological, and human resources. The term " _____ " may also refer to those people who manage an organization.

Exam Probability: **Low**

12. *Answer choices:*
(see index for correct answer)

- a. information systems assessment
- b. hierarchical
- c. Management
- d. personal values

Guidance: level 1

:: Business ethics ::

_____ is a type of harassment technique that relates to a sexual nature and the unwelcome or inappropriate promise of rewards in exchange for sexual favors. _____ includes a range of actions from mild transgressions to sexual abuse or assault. Harassment can occur in many different social settings such as the workplace, the home, school, churches, etc. Harassers or victims may be of any gender.

Exam Probability: **Medium**

13. *Answer choices:*
(see index for correct answer)

- a. Sexual harassment
- b. Accounting scandals
- c. Earnings quality
- d. Perfect Relations

Guidance: level 1

:: Legal terms ::

_____, a form of alternative dispute resolution, is a way to resolve disputes outside the courts. The dispute will be decided by one or more persons, which renders the "_____ award". An _____ award is legally binding on both sides and enforceable in the courts.

Exam Probability: **Medium**

14. *Answer choices:*
(see index for correct answer)

- a. Enacted law
- b. Arbitration
- c. Champerty and maintenance
- d. respondent

Guidance: level 1

:: Stock market ::

A shareholder is an individual or institution that legally owns one or more shares of stock in a public or private corporation. _____ may be referred to as members of a corporation. Legally, a person is not a shareholder in a corporation until their name and other details are entered in the corporation's register of _____ or members.

Exam Probability: **Low**

15. *Answer choices:*
(see index for correct answer)

- a. CEE Stock Exchange Group
- b. Chip
- c. Profit warning
- d. Shareholders

Guidance: level 1

:: Business ::

A _____ is a mathematical object used to count, measure, and label. The original examples are the natural _____ s 1, 2, 3, 4, and so forth. A written symbol like "5" that represents a _____ is called a numeral. A numeral system is an organized way to write and manipulate this type of symbol, for example the Hindu–Arabic numeral system allows combinations of numerical digits like "5" and "0" to represent larger _____ s like 50. A numeral in linguistics can refer to a symbol like 5, the words or phrase that names a _____ , like "five hundred", or other words that mean a specific _____ , like "dozen". In addition to their use in counting and measuring, numerals are often used for labels , for ordering , and for codes . In common usage, _____ may refer to a symbol, a word or phrase, or the mathematical object.

Exam Probability: **High**

16. *Answer choices:*

_(see index for correct answer)

- a. Architecture of Interoperable Information Systems
- b. Co-creation
- c. Number
- d. Local multiplier effect

Guidance: level 1

:: Generally Accepted Accounting Principles ::

In accounting, _____ is the income that a business have from its normal business activities, usually from the sale of goods and services to customers. _____ is also referred to as sales or turnover.Some companies receive _____ from interest, royalties, or other fees. _____ may refer to business income in general, or it may refer to the amount, in a monetary unit, earned during a period of time, as in "Last year, Company X had _____ of $42 million". Profits or net income generally imply total _____ minus total expenses in a given period. In accounting, in the balance statement it is a subsection of the Equity section and _____ increases equity, it is often referred to as the "top line" due to its position on the income statement at the very top. This is to be contrasted with the "bottom line" which denotes net income .

Exam Probability: **High**

17. *Answer choices:*

(see index for correct answer)

- a. Depreciation
- b. Long-term liabilities
- c. French generally accepted accounting principles
- d. Gross sales

Guidance: level 1

:: Public relations ::

_____ is the public visibility or awareness for any product, service or company. It may also refer to the movement of information from its source to the general public, often but not always via the media. The subjects of _____ include people, goods and services, organizations, and works of art or entertainment.

Exam Probability: **Medium**

18. *Answer choices:*

(see index for correct answer)

- a. Mobile Public Affairs Detachment
- b. Media monitoring service
- c. Flaunt
- d. Publicity

Guidance: level 1

:: Finance ::

_____ is a field that is concerned with the allocation of assets and liabilities over space and time, often under conditions of risk or uncertainty. _____ can also be defined as the art of money management. Participants in the market aim to price assets based on their risk level, fundamental value, and their expected rate of return. _____ can be split into three sub-categories: public _____, corporate _____ and personal _____.

Exam Probability: **Low**

19. *Answer choices:*

(see index for correct answer)

- a. Lease-option
- b. Primary deficit
- c. Finance
- d. Operating partner

Guidance: level 1

:: Infographics ::

A _____ is a symbolic representation of information according to visualization technique. _____ s have been used since ancient times, but became more prevalent during the Enlightenment. Sometimes, the technique uses a three-dimensional visualization which is then projected onto a two-dimensional surface. The word graph is sometimes used as a synonym for _____ .

Exam Probability: **High**

20. *Answer choices:*

(see index for correct answer)

- a. U.S. Route shield
- b. Webdings
- c. Diagram
- d. Four Square Writing Method

Guidance: level 1

:: ::

_____ is the study and management of exchange relationships. _____ is the business process of creating relationships with and satisfying customers. With its focus on the customer, _____ is one of the premier components of business management.

Exam Probability: **Low**

21. *Answer choices:*

(see index for correct answer)

- a. Marketing
- b. similarity-attraction theory
- c. open system
- d. personal values

Guidance: level 1

:: Financial markets ::

A _____ is a financial market in which long-term debt or equity-backed securities are bought and sold. _____ s channel the wealth of savers to those who can put it to long-term productive use, such as companies or governments making long-term investments. Financial regulators like the Bank of England and the U.S. Securities and Exchange Commission oversee _____ s to protect investors against fraud, among other duties.

Exam Probability: **Medium**

22. *Answer choices:*
(see index for correct answer)

- a. Internal financing
- b. Floor trading
- c. Earnings guidance
- d. Capital market

Guidance: level 1

:: Industry ::

_____ describes various measures of the efficiency of production. Often, a _____ measure is expressed as the ratio of an aggregate output to a single input or an aggregate input used in a production process, i.e. output per unit of input. Most common example is the labour _____ measure, e.g., such as GDP per worker. There are many different definitions of _____ and the choice among them depends on the purpose of the _____ measurement and/or data availability. The key source of difference between various _____ measures is also usually related to how the outputs and the inputs are aggregated into scalars to obtain such a ratio-type measure of _____ .

Exam Probability: **High**

23. *Answer choices:*
(see index for correct answer)

- a. Private sector
- b. Takt time

- c. Energy policy
- d. Productivity

Guidance: level 1

:: Currency ::

A _____ , in the most specific sense is money in any form when in use or circulation as a medium of exchange, especially circulating banknotes and coins. A more general definition is that a _____ is a system of money in common use, especially for people in a nation. Under this definition, US dollars, pounds sterling, Australian dollars, European euros, Russian rubles and Indian Rupees are examples of currencies. These various currencies are recognized as stores of value and are traded between nations in foreign exchange markets, which determine the relative values of the different currencies. Currencies in this sense are defined by governments, and each type has limited boundaries of acceptance.

Exam Probability: **Medium**

24. *Answer choices:*
(see index for correct answer)

- a. York rating
- b. Nomisma
- c. Commodity currency
- d. Demurrage

Guidance: level 1

:: Infographics ::

A _____ is a graphical representation of data, in which "the data is represented by symbols, such as bars in a bar _____ , lines in a line _____ , or slices in a pie _____ ". A _____ can represent tabular numeric data, functions or some kinds of qualitative structure and provides different info.

Exam Probability: **Medium**

25. *Answer choices:*
(see index for correct answer)

- a. Funnel chart

- b. Chart
- c. Table
- d. Rhizome Navigation

Guidance: level 1

:: National accounts ::

_____ is a monetary measure of the market value of all the final goods and services produced in a period of time, often annually. GDP per capita does not, however, reflect differences in the cost of living and the inflation rates of the countries; therefore using a basis of GDP per capita at purchasing power parity is arguably more useful when comparing differences in living standards between nations.

Exam Probability: **Low**

26. *Answer choices:*
(see index for correct answer)

- a. Fixed capital
- b. capital formation
- c. National Income

Guidance: level 1

:: Marketing ::

_____ is the percentage of a market accounted for by a specific entity. In a survey of nearly 200 senior marketing managers, 67% responded that they found the revenue- "dollar _____" metric very useful, while 61% found "unit _____" very useful.

Exam Probability: **Medium**

27. *Answer choices:*
(see index for correct answer)

- a. Market share
- b. Decoy effect
- c. push and pull
- d. Kronos Effect

Guidance: level 1

:: International trade ::

In finance, an _____ is the rate at which one currency will be exchanged for another. It is also regarded as the value of one country's currency in relation to another currency. For example, an interbank _____ of 114 Japanese yen to the United States dollar means that ¥114 will be exchanged for each US$1 or that US$1 will be exchanged for each ¥114. In this case it is said that the price of a dollar in relation to yen is ¥114, or equivalently that the price of a yen in relation to dollars is $1/114.

Exam Probability: **High**

28. *Answer choices:*
(see index for correct answer)

- a. Cross-border cooperation
- b. International Association for Technology Trade
- c. Bimetallism
- d. Exchange rate

Guidance: level 1

:: Planning ::

_____ is a high level plan to achieve one or more goals under conditions of uncertainty. In the sense of the "art of the general," which included several subsets of skills including tactics, siegecraft, logistics etc., the term came into use in the 6th century C.E. in East Roman terminology, and was translated into Western vernacular languages only in the 18th century. From then until the 20th century, the word "_____" came to denote "a comprehensive way to try to pursue political ends, including the threat or actual use of force, in a dialectic of wills" in a military conflict, in which both adversaries interact.

Exam Probability: **High**

29. *Answer choices:*
(see index for correct answer)

- a. Commercial area
- b. Reproductive life plan
- c. School timetable
- d. Strategy

Guidance: level 1

:: Evaluation ::

_____ is the practice of being honest and showing a consistent and uncompromising adherence to strong moral and ethical principles and values. In ethics, _____ is regarded as the honesty and truthfulness or accuracy of one's actions. _____ can stand in opposition to hypocrisy, in that judging with the standards of _____ involves regarding internal consistency as a virtue, and suggests that parties holding within themselves apparently conflicting values should account for the discrepancy or alter their beliefs. The word _____ evolved from the Latin adjective integer, meaning whole or complete. In this context, _____ is the inner sense of "wholeness" deriving from qualities such as honesty and consistency of character. As such, one may judge that others "have _____" to the extent that they act according to the values, beliefs and principles they claim to hold.

Exam Probability: **Medium**

30. *Answer choices:*

(see index for correct answer)

- a. International Association for the Evaluation of Educational Achievement
- b. Academic equivalency evaluation
- c. Ecological indicator
- d. Integrity

Guidance: level 1

:: Accounting software ::

_____ is any item or verifiable record that is generally accepted as payment for goods and services and repayment of debts, such as taxes, in a particular country or socio-economic context. The main functions of _____ are distinguished as: a medium of exchange, a unit of account, a store of value and sometimes, a standard of deferred payment. Any item or verifiable record that fulfils these functions can be considered as _____.

Exam Probability: **Medium**

31. *Answer choices:*

(see index for correct answer)

- a. FinanceWorks
- b. Quicken
- c. Boeing Calc
- d. Money

Guidance: level 1

:: Actuarial science ::

_____ is the possibility of losing something of value. Values can be gained or lost when taking _____ resulting from a given action or inaction, foreseen or unforeseen. _____ can also be defined as the intentional interaction with uncertainty. Uncertainty is a potential, unpredictable, and uncontrollable outcome; _____ is a consequence of action taken in spite of uncertainty.

Exam Probability: **High**

32. *Answer choices:*

(see index for correct answer)

- a. Experience modifier
- b. Risk
- c. RiskMetrics
- d. Age stratification

Guidance: level 1

:: Project management ::

In political science, an _____ is a means by which a petition signed by a certain minimum number of registered voters can force a government to choose to either enact a law or hold a public vote in parliament in what is called indirect _____, or under direct _____, the proposition is immediately put to a plebiscite or referendum, in what is called a Popular initiated Referendum or citizen-initiated referendum).

Exam Probability: **Low**

33. *Answer choices:*

(see index for correct answer)

- a. Project management process

- b. Initiative
- c. Deliverable
- d. Project Management South Africa

Guidance: level 1

:: Telecommunication theory ::

In reliability theory and reliability engineering, the term _____ has the following meanings.

Exam Probability: **High**

34. *Answer choices:*
(see index for correct answer)

- a. Demand Assigned Multiple Access
- b. Root-raised-cosine filter
- c. Balance return loss
- d. Field strength in free space

Guidance: level 1

:: ::

A _____ is an organization, usually a group of people or a company, authorized to act as a single entity and recognized as such in law. Early incorporated entities were established by charter. Most jurisdictions now allow the creation of new _____ s through registration.

Exam Probability: **High**

35. *Answer choices:*
(see index for correct answer)

- a. surface-level diversity
- b. deep-level diversity
- c. Sarbanes-Oxley act of 2002
- d. Corporation

Guidance: level 1

:: Contract law ::

A _____ is a legally-binding agreement which recognises and governs the rights and duties of the parties to the agreement. A _____ is legally enforceable because it meets the requirements and approval of the law. An agreement typically involves the exchange of goods, services, money, or promises of any of those. In the event of breach of _____ , the law awards the injured party access to legal remedies such as damages and cancellation.

Exam Probability: **Medium**

36. *Answer choices:*
(see index for correct answer)

- a. Principles of European Contract Law
- b. Principles of International Commercial Contracts
- c. Cover
- d. Contract

Guidance: level 1

:: Legal terms ::

An _____ is an action which is inaccurate or incorrect. In some usages, an _____ is synonymous with a mistake. In statistics, " _____ " refers to the difference between the value which has been computed and the correct value. An _____ could result in failure or in a deviation from the intended performance or behaviour.

Exam Probability: **Low**

37. *Answer choices:*
(see index for correct answer)

- a. Petitioner
- b. Error
- c. Obiter dictum
- d. Principal case

Guidance: level 1

:: ::

In regulatory jurisdictions that provide for it, _____ is a group of laws and organizations designed to ensure the rights of consumers as well as fair trade, competition and accurate information in the marketplace. The laws are designed to prevent the businesses that engage in fraud or specified unfair practices from gaining an advantage over competitors. They may also provides additional protection for those most vulnerable in society. _____ laws are a form of government regulation that aim to protect the rights of consumers. For example, a government may require businesses to disclose detailed information about products—particularly in areas where safety or public health is an issue, such as food.

Exam Probability: **High**

38. *Answer choices:*

(see index for correct answer)

- a. Consumer Protection
- b. co-culture
- c. interpersonal communication
- d. imperative

Guidance: level 1

:: Business process ::

A _____ or business method is a collection of related, structured activities or tasks by people or equipment which in a specific sequence produce a service or product for a particular customer or customers. _____ es occur at all organizational levels and may or may not be visible to the customers. A _____ may often be visualized as a flowchart of a sequence of activities with interleaving decision points or as a process matrix of a sequence of activities with relevance rules based on data in the process. The benefits of using _____ es include improved customer satisfaction and improved agility for reacting to rapid market change. Process-oriented organizations break down the barriers of structural departments and try to avoid functional silos.

Exam Probability: **Low**

39. *Answer choices:*

(see index for correct answer)

- a. Business process
- b. IBM Blueworks Live
- c. Business process outsourcing to India
- d. Signavio

Guidance: level 1

:: Alchemical processes ::

In chemistry, a _____ is a special type of homogeneous mixture composed of two or more substances. In such a mixture, a solute is a substance dissolved in another substance, known as a solvent. The mixing process of a _____ happens at a scale where the effects of chemical polarity are involved, resulting in interactions that are specific to solvation. The _____ assumes the phase of the solvent when the solvent is the larger fraction of the mixture, as is commonly the case. The concentration of a solute in a _____ is the mass of that solute expressed as a percentage of the mass of the whole _____ . The term aqueous _____ is when one of the solvents is water.

Exam Probability: **Low**

40. *Answer choices:*
(see index for correct answer)

- a. Fixation
- b. Projection
- c. Fermentation in food processing
- d. Ceration

Guidance: level 1

:: Management ::

_____ is the process of thinking about the activities required to achieve a desired goal. It is the first and foremost activity to achieve desired results. It involves the creation and maintenance of a plan, such as psychological aspects that require conceptual skills. There are even a couple of tests to measure someone's capability of _____ well. As such, _____ is a fundamental property of intelligent behavior. An important further meaning, often just called " _____ " is the legal context of permitted building developments.

Exam Probability: **Medium**

41. *Answer choices:*

(see index for correct answer)

- a. Professional performances
- b. Overtime rate
- c. Planning
- d. Community of practice

Guidance: level 1

:: Financial accounting ::

_____ is a financial metric which represents operating liquidity available to a business, organisation or other entity, including governmental entities. Along with fixed assets such as plant and equipment, _____ is considered a part of operating capital. Gross _____ is equal to current assets. _____ is calculated as current assets minus current liabilities. If current assets are less than current liabilities, an entity has a _____ deficiency, also called a _____ deficit.

Exam Probability: **Medium**

42. *Answer choices:*

(see index for correct answer)

- a. Carry
- b. Holding gains
- c. Net worth
- d. Accelerated depreciation

Guidance: level 1

:: Production and manufacturing ::

_____ consists of organization-wide efforts to "install and make permanent climate where employees continuously improve their ability to provide on demand products and services that customers will find of particular value." "Total" emphasizes that departments in addition to production are obligated to improve their operations; "management" emphasizes that executives are obligated to actively manage quality through funding, training, staffing, and goal setting. While there is no widely agreed-upon approach, TQM efforts typically draw heavily on the previously developed tools and techniques of quality control. TQM enjoyed widespread attention during the late 1980s and early 1990s before being overshadowed by ISO 9000, Lean manufacturing, and Six Sigma.

Exam Probability: **High**

43. *Answer choices:*
(see index for correct answer)

- a. Total quality management
- b. Reverse engineering
- c. Original design manufacturer
- d. Feeder line

Guidance: level 1

:: Land value taxation ::

_____, sometimes referred to as dry _____, is the solid surface of Earth that is not permanently covered by water. The vast majority of human activity throughout history has occurred in _____ areas that support agriculture, habitat, and various natural resources. Some life forms have developed from predecessor species that lived in bodies of water.

Exam Probability: **High**

44. *Answer choices:*
(see index for correct answer)

- a. Land
- b. Lands Valuation Appeal Court
- c. Henry George
- d. Physiocracy

Guidance: level 1

:: Commercial item transport and distribution ::

A _____ is a commitment or expectation to perform some action in general or if certain circumstances arise. A _____ may arise from a system of ethics or morality, especially in an honor culture. Many duties are created by law, sometimes including a codified punishment or liability for non-performance. Performing one's _____ may require some sacrifice of self-interest.

Exam Probability: **Low**

45. *Answer choices:*
(see index for correct answer)

- a. Sea protest
- b. Delivery order
- c. Duty
- d. Tank chassis

Guidance: level 1

:: ::

_____ is a marketing communication that employs an openly sponsored, non-personal message to promote or sell a product, service or idea. Sponsors of _____ are typically businesses wishing to promote their products or services. _____ is differentiated from public relations in that an advertiser pays for and has control over the message. It differs from personal selling in that the message is non-personal, i.e., not directed to a particular individual. _____ is communicated through various mass media, including traditional media such as newspapers, magazines, television, radio, outdoor _____ or direct mail; and new media such as search results, blogs, social media, websites or text messages. The actual presentation of the message in a medium is referred to as an advertisement, or "ad" or advert for short.

Exam Probability: **High**

46. *Answer choices:*
(see index for correct answer)

- a. co-culture
- b. hierarchical perspective
- c. similarity-attraction theory
- d. Advertising

Guidance: level 1

:: Quality management ::

_____ ensures that an organization, product or service is consistent. It has four main components: quality planning, quality assurance, quality control and quality improvement. _____ is focused not only on product and service quality, but also on the means to achieve it. _____ , therefore, uses quality assurance and control of processes as well as products to achieve more consistent quality. What a customer wants and is willing to pay for it determines quality. It is written or unwritten commitment to a known or unknown consumer in the market . Thus, quality can be defined as fitness for intended use or, in other words, how well the product performs its intended function

Exam Probability: **High**

47. *Answer choices:*
(see index for correct answer)

- a. Quality management
- b. Institute of Standards and Industrial Research of Iran
- c. PQASSO
- d. Informal Methods

Guidance: level 1

:: Foreign direct investment ::

A _____ is an investment in the form of a controlling ownership in a business in one country by an entity based in another country. It is thus distinguished from a foreign portfolio investment by a notion of direct control.

Exam Probability: **High**

48. *Answer choices:*
(see index for correct answer)

- a. Dutch disease
- b. Foreign direct investments in Kosovo
- c. Immigrant investor programs
- d. Expropriation

Guidance: level 1

:: ::

_____ is the collection of techniques, skills, methods, and processes used in the production of goods or services or in the accomplishment of objectives, such as scientific investigation. _____ can be the knowledge of techniques, processes, and the like, or it can be embedded in machines to allow for operation without detailed knowledge of their workings. Systems applying _____ by taking an input, changing it according to the system's use, and then producing an outcome are referred to as _____ systems or technological systems.

Exam Probability: **High**

49. *Answer choices:*
(see index for correct answer)

- a. corporate values
- b. Character
- c. co-culture
- d. Technology

Guidance: level 1

:: Systems theory ::

A _____ is a group of interacting or interrelated entities that form a unified whole. A _____ is delineated by its spatial and temporal boundaries, surrounded and influenced by its environment, described by its structure and purpose and expressed in its functioning.

Exam Probability: **Low**

50. *Answer choices:*
(see index for correct answer)

- a. decentralized system
- b. Viable System Model
- c. System
- d. transient state

Guidance: level 1

:: ::

_____ is the means to see, hear, or become aware of something or someone through our fundamental senses. The term _____ derives from the Latin word perceptio, and is the organization, identification, and interpretation of sensory information in order to represent and understand the presented information, or the environment.

Exam Probability: **High**

51. *Answer choices:*

(see index for correct answer)

- a. Perception
- b. cultural
- c. Sarbanes-Oxley act of 2002
- d. corporate values

Guidance: level 1

:: Majority–minority relations ::

_____, also known as reservation in India and Nepal, positive discrimination / action in the United Kingdom, and employment equity in Canada and South Africa, is the policy of promoting the education and employment of members of groups that are known to have previously suffered from discrimination. Historically and internationally, support for _____ has sought to achieve goals such as bridging inequalities in employment and pay, increasing access to education, promoting diversity, and redressing apparent past wrongs, harms, or hindrances.

Exam Probability: **Low**

52. *Answer choices:*

(see index for correct answer)

- a. positive discrimination
- b. cultural Relativism
- c. cultural dissonance

Guidance: level 1

:: Money ::

In economics, _____ is money in the physical form of currency, such as banknotes and coins. In bookkeeping and finance, _____ is current assets comprising currency or currency equivalents that can be accessed immediately or near-immediately. _____ is seen either as a reserve for payments, in case of a structural or incidental negative _____ flow or as a way to avoid a downturn on financial markets.

Exam Probability: **Low**

53. *Answer choices:*
(see index for correct answer)

- a. Ideal money
- b. History of money
- c. Love of money
- d. Cash

Guidance: level 1

:: Strategic alliances ::

A _____ is an agreement between two or more parties to pursue a set of agreed upon objectives needed while remaining independent organizations. A _____ will usually fall short of a legal partnership entity, agency, or corporate affiliate relationship. Typically, two companies form a _____ when each possesses one or more business assets or have expertise that will help the other by enhancing their businesses. _____ s can develop in outsourcing relationships where the parties desire to achieve long-term win-win benefits and innovation based on mutually desired outcomes.

Exam Probability: **Medium**

54. *Answer choices:*
(see index for correct answer)

- a. Cross-licensing
- b. Strategic alliance
- c. Defensive termination
- d. Bridge Alliance

Guidance: level 1

:: Management occupations ::

_____ is the process of designing, launching and running a new business, which is often initially a small business. The people who create these businesses are called entrepreneurs.

Exam Probability: **Medium**

55. *Answer choices:*
(see index for correct answer)

- a. Ceco
- b. Director of nursing
- c. Comprador
- d. Entrepreneurship

Guidance: level 1

:: Occupations ::

An _____ is a person who has a position of authority in a hierarchical organization. The term derives from the late Latin from officiarius, meaning "official".

Exam Probability: **Medium**

56. *Answer choices:*
(see index for correct answer)

- a. Carpentry
- b. Officer
- c. Copyist
- d. Vintner

Guidance: level 1

:: ::

_____ is the collection of mechanisms, processes and relations by which corporations are controlled and operated. Governance structures and principles identify the distribution of rights and responsibilities among different participants in the corporation and include the rules and procedures for making decisions in corporate affairs. _____ is necessary because of the possibility of conflicts of interests between stakeholders, primarily between shareholders and upper management or among shareholders.

Exam Probability: **High**

57. *Answer choices:*

(see index for correct answer)

- a. co-culture
- b. interpersonal communication
- c. Sarbanes-Oxley act of 2002
- d. Corporate governance

Guidance: level 1

:: Property ::

The right to property or right to own property is often classified as a human right for natural persons regarding their possessions. A general recognition of a right to private property is found more rarely and is typically heavily constrained insofar as property is owned by legal persons and where it is used for production rather than consumption.

Exam Probability: **Low**

58. *Answer choices:*

(see index for correct answer)

- a. Property rights
- b. Gross annual value
- c. Ownership society
- d. Croft

Guidance: level 1

:: Meetings ::

An _____ is a group of people who participate in a show or encounter a work of art, literature, theatre, music, video games, or academics in any medium. _____ members participate in different ways in different kinds of art; some events invite overt _____ participation and others allowing only modest clapping and criticism and reception.

Exam Probability: **Low**

59. *Answer choices:*
(see index for correct answer)

- a. Official function
- b. Prayer meeting
- c. Audience
- d. Committee

Guidance: level 1

Management

Management is the administration of an organization, whether it is a business, a not-for-profit organization, or government body. Management includes the activities of setting the strategy of an organization and coordinating the efforts of its employees (or of volunteers) to accomplish its objectives through the application of available resources, such as financial, natural, technological, and human resources.

:: Electronic feedback ::

_____ occurs when outputs of a system are routed back as inputs as part of a chain of cause-and-effect that forms a circuit or loop. The system can then be said to feed back into itself. The notion of cause-and-effect has to be handled carefully when applied to _____ systems.

Exam Probability: **Medium**

1. *Answer choices:*
(see index for correct answer)

- a. Feedback
- b. feedback loop

Guidance: level 1

:: Scientific method ::

In the social sciences and life sciences, a _____ is a research method involving an up-close, in-depth, and detailed examination of a subject of study, as well as its related contextual conditions.

Exam Probability: **Low**

2. *Answer choices:*

(see index for correct answer)

- a. Causal research
- b. pilot project
- c. Case study
- d. explanatory research

Guidance: level 1

:: Supply chain management terms ::

In business and finance, _____ is a system of organizations, people, activities, information, and resources involved in moving a product or service from supplier to customer. _____ activities involve the transformation of natural resources, raw materials, and components into a finished product that is delivered to the end customer. In sophisticated _____ systems, used products may re-enter the _____ at any point where residual value is recyclable. _____ s link value chains.

Exam Probability: **Low**

3. *Answer choices:*
(see index for correct answer)

- a. Most valuable customers
- b. Supply chain
- c. Consumable
- d. Consumables

Guidance: level 1

:: Leadership ::

_____ /Management is a part of a style of leadership that focuses on supervision, organization, and performance; it is an integral part of the Full Range Leadership Model. _____ is a style of leadership in which leaders promote compliance by followers through both rewards and punishments. Through a rewards and punishments system, transactional leaders are able to keep followers motivated for the short-term. Unlike transformational leaders, those using the transactional approach are not looking to change the future, they look to keep things the same. Leaders using _____ as a model pay attention to followers' work in order to find faults and deviations.

4. *Answer choices:*
(see index for correct answer)

- a. Love leadership
- b. Transformational leadership
- c. Three levels of leadership model
- d. Transactional leadership

Guidance: level 1

:: Survey methodology ::

An _____ is a conversation where questions are asked and answers are given. In common parlance, the word "_____" refers to a one-on-one conversation between an _____ er and an _____ ee. The _____ er asks questions to which the _____ ee responds, usually so information may be transferred from _____ ee to _____ er. Sometimes, information can be transferred in both directions. It is a communication, unlike a speech, which produces a one-way flow of information.

Exam Probability: **Low**

5. *Answer choices:*
(see index for correct answer)

- a. Group concept mapping
- b. Interview
- c. American Association for Public Opinion Research
- d. Self-report study

Guidance: level 1

:: Project management ::

A _____ is a professional in the field of project management. _____ s have the responsibility of the planning, procurement and execution of a project, in any undertaking that has a defined scope, defined start and a defined finish; regardless of industry. _____ s are first point of contact for any issues or discrepancies arising from within the heads of various departments in an organization before the problem escalates to higher authorities. Project management is the responsibility of a _____ . This individual seldom participates directly in the activities that produce the end result, but rather strives to maintain the progress, mutual interaction and tasks of various parties in such a way that reduces the risk of overall failure, maximizes benefits, and minimizes costs.

Exam Probability: **High**

6. *Answer choices:*

(see index for correct answer)

- a. Integrated product team
- b. Project manufacturing
- c. The Transformation Project
- d. International Project Management Association

Guidance: level 1

:: ::

_____ refers to the confirmation of certain characteristics of an object, person, or organization. This confirmation is often, but not always, provided by some form of external review, education, assessment, or audit. Accreditation is a specific organization's process of _____ . According to the National Council on Measurement in Education, a _____ test is a credentialing test used to determine whether individuals are knowledgeable enough in a given occupational area to be labeled "competent to practice" in that area.

Exam Probability: **Low**

7. *Answer choices:*

(see index for correct answer)

- a. personal values
- b. process perspective
- c. Certification

- d. surface-level diversity

Guidance: level 1

:: Marketing ::

_____ or stock is the goods and materials that a business holds for the ultimate goal of resale.

Exam Probability: **High**

8. *Answer choices:*
(see index for correct answer)

- a. Inventory
- b. Sales contest
- c. Law of primacy in persuasion
- d. Gladvertising

Guidance: level 1

:: Organizational theory ::

Decentralisation is the process by which the activities of an organization, particularly those regarding planning and decision making, are distributed or delegated away from a central, authoritative location or group. Concepts of _____ have been applied to group dynamics and management science in private businesses and organizations, political science, law and public administration, economics, money and technology.

Exam Probability: **High**

9. *Answer choices:*
(see index for correct answer)

- a. Organizational communication
- b. Organization development
- c. Decentralization
- d. Cooperation

Guidance: level 1

:: Marketing ::

_____, in marketing, manufacturing, call centres and management, is the use of flexible computer-aided manufacturing systems to produce custom output. Such systems combine the low unit costs of mass production processes with the flexibility of individual customization.

Exam Probability: **Medium**

10. *Answer choices:*
(see index for correct answer)

- a. Mass customization
- b. Gladvertising
- c. Brandjacking
- d. Online research community

Guidance: level 1

:: Television commercials ::

_____ is a phenomenon whereby something new and somehow valuable is formed. The created item may be intangible or a physical object.

Exam Probability: **Low**

11. *Answer choices:*
(see index for correct answer)

- a. Pretty
- b. Terry Tate: Office Linebacker
- c. Reassuringly Expensive
- d. Eyebrows

Guidance: level 1

:: ::

A _____ is an individual or institution that legally owns one or more shares of stock in a public or private corporation. _____ s may be referred to as members of a corporation. Legally, a person is not a _____ in a corporation until their name and other details are entered in the corporation's register of _____ s or members.

Exam Probability: **Low**

12. *Answer choices:*
(see index for correct answer)

- a. co-culture
- b. Shareholder
- c. corporate values
- d. empathy

Guidance: level 1

:: Organizational behavior ::

_____ is the term now used more commonly in business management, particularly human resource management. _____ refers to the number of subordinates a supervisor has.

Exam Probability: **High**

13. *Answer choices:*
(see index for correct answer)

- a. Organizational behavior management
- b. Self-policing
- c. Nut Island effect
- d. Span of control

Guidance: level 1

:: Leadership ::

_____ Theory, or the _____ Model, is a model created by Paul Hersey and Ken Blanchard, developed while working on Management of Organizational Behavior. The theory was first introduced in 1969 as "life cycle theory of leadership". During the mid-1970s, life cycle theory of leadership was renamed "_____ Theory."

Exam Probability: **High**

14. *Answer choices:*
(see index for correct answer)

- a. Situational leadership
- b. Coro
- c. Consideration and Initiating Structure

- d. The Saint, the Surfer, and the CEO

Guidance: level 1

:: ::

_____ refers to the overall process of attracting, shortlisting, selecting and appointing suitable candidates for jobs within an organization. _____ can also refer to processes involved in choosing individuals for unpaid roles. Managers, human resource generalists and _____ specialists may be tasked with carrying out _____ , but in some cases public-sector employment agencies, commercial _____ agencies, or specialist search consultancies are used to undertake parts of the process. Internet-based technologies which support all aspects of _____ have become widespread.

Exam Probability: **High**

15. *Answer choices:*
(see index for correct answer)

- a. process perspective
- b. open system
- c. Recruitment
- d. interpersonal communication

Guidance: level 1

:: Quality management ::

_____ ensures that an organization, product or service is consistent. It has four main components: quality planning, quality assurance, quality control and quality improvement. _____ is focused not only on product and service quality, but also on the means to achieve it. _____ , therefore, uses quality assurance and control of processes as well as products to achieve more consistent quality. What a customer wants and is willing to pay for it determines quality. It is written or unwritten commitment to a known or unknown consumer in the market . Thus, quality can be defined as fitness for intended use or, in other words, how well the product performs its intended function

Exam Probability: **High**

16. *Answer choices:*
(see index for correct answer)

- a. Quality policy
- b. Quality management
- c. Registro Italiano Navale
- d. Product quality risk in supply chain

Guidance: level 1

:: Management ::

A _____ is a formal written document containing business goals, the methods on how these goals can be attained, and the time frame within which these goals need to be achieved. It also describes the nature of the business, background information on the organization, the organization's financial projections, and the strategies it intends to implement to achieve the stated targets. In its entirety, this document serves as a road map that provides direction to the business.

Exam Probability: **Low**

17. *Answer choices:*
(see index for correct answer)

- a. Industrial forensics
- b. Business plan
- c. Productive efficiency
- d. Business process improvement

Guidance: level 1

:: ::

_____ is the amount of time someone works beyond normal working hours. The term is also used for the pay received for this time. Normal hours may be determined in several ways.

Exam Probability: **Medium**

18. *Answer choices:*
(see index for correct answer)

- a. cultural
- b. co-culture
- c. functional perspective
- d. corporate values

Guidance: level 1

:: ::

_____ is the stock of habits, knowledge, social and personality attributes embodied in the ability to perform labor so as to produce economic value.

Exam Probability: **High**

19. *Answer choices:*

(see index for correct answer)

- a. levels of analysis
- b. cultural
- c. hierarchical
- d. open system

Guidance: level 1

:: ::

_____ is the means to see, hear, or become aware of something or someone through our fundamental senses. The term _____ derives from the Latin word perceptio, and is the organization, identification, and interpretation of sensory information in order to represent and understand the presented information, or the environment.

Exam Probability: **High**

20. *Answer choices:*

(see index for correct answer)

- a. hierarchical perspective
- b. surface-level diversity
- c. Sarbanes-Oxley act of 2002
- d. Perception

Guidance: level 1

:: Social psychology ::

In social psychology, _____ is the phenomenon of a person exerting less effort to achieve a goal when he or she works in a group than when working alone. This is seen as one of the main reasons groups are sometimes less productive than the combined performance of their members working as individuals, but should be distinguished from the accidental coordination problems that groups sometimes experience.

Exam Probability: **Medium**

21. *Answer choices:*
(see index for correct answer)

- a. Cross-cultural leadership
- b. Social loafing
- c. Social penetration
- d. externalization

Guidance: level 1

:: Budgets ::

A _____ is a financial plan for a defined period, often one year. It may also include planned sales volumes and revenues, resource quantities, costs and expenses, assets, liabilities and cash flows. Companies, governments, families and other organizations use it to express strategic plans of activities or events in measurable terms.

Exam Probability: **Low**

22. *Answer choices:*
(see index for correct answer)

- a. Railway Budget
- b. Budget
- c. Budgeted cost of work scheduled
- d. Budget set

Guidance: level 1

:: Cognitive biases ::

The _____ is a type of immediate judgement discrepancy, or cognitive bias, where a person making an initial assessment of another person, place, or thing will assume ambiguous information based upon concrete information. A simplified example of the _____ is when an individual noticing that the person in the photograph is attractive, well groomed, and properly attired, assumes, using a mental heuristic, that the person in the photograph is a good person based upon the rules of that individual's social concept. This constant error in judgment is reflective of the individual's preferences, prejudices, ideology, aspirations, and social perception. The _____ is an evaluation by an individual and can affect the perception of a decision, action, idea, business, person, group, entity, or other whenever concrete data is generalized or influences ambiguous information.

Exam Probability: **High**

23. *Answer choices:*
(see index for correct answer)

- a. Conjunction fallacy
- b. Empathy gap
- c. Reactive devaluation
- d. Forer effect

Guidance: level 1

:: Operations research ::

_____ is a method to achieve the best outcome in a mathematical model whose requirements are represented by linear relationships. _____ is a special case of mathematical programming.

Exam Probability: **Medium**

24. *Answer choices:*
(see index for correct answer)

- a. Decision analysis
- b. Interdisciplinary Center for Organizational Architecture
- c. Linear programming
- d. Extended newsvendor model

Guidance: level 1

:: Project management ::

_____ and Theory Y are theories of human work motivation and management. They were created by Douglas McGregor while he was working at the MIT Sloan School of Management in the 1950s, and developed further in the 1960s. McGregor's work was rooted in motivation theory alongside the works of Abraham Maslow, who created the hierarchy of needs. The two theories proposed by McGregor describe contrasting models of workforce motivation applied by managers in human resource management, organizational behavior, organizational communication and organizational development. _____ explains the importance of heightened supervision, external rewards, and penalties, while Theory Y highlights the motivating role of job satisfaction and encourages workers to approach tasks without direct supervision. Management use of _____ and Theory Y can affect employee motivation and productivity in different ways, and managers may choose to implement strategies from both theories into their practices.

Exam Probability: **Low**

25. *Answer choices:*
(see index for correct answer)

- a. Product description
- b. Costab
- c. Opportunity management
- d. Theory X

Guidance: level 1

:: Systems thinking ::

In business management, a _____ is a company that facilitates the learning of its members and continuously transforms itself. The concept was coined through the work and research of Peter Senge and his colleagues.

Exam Probability: **Low**

26. *Answer choices:*
(see index for correct answer)

- a. Club of Rome
- b. Future history
- c. Learning organization
- d. Ray Hammond

Guidance: level 1

:: Elementary mathematics ::

_____ is a numerical measurement of how far apart objects are. In physics or everyday usage, _____ may refer to a physical length or an estimation based on other criteria. In most cases, "_____ from A to B" is interchangeable with "_____ from B to A". In mathematics, a _____ function or metric is a generalization of the concept of physical _____. A metric is a function that behaves according to a specific set of rules, and is a way of describing what it means for elements of some space to be "close to" or "far away from" each other.

Exam Probability: **Medium**

27. *Answer choices:*
(see index for correct answer)

- a. Elementary mathematics
- b. Argument of a function
- c. Constant function
- d. Distance

Guidance: level 1

:: Industrial Revolution ::

The _____, now also known as the First _____, was the transition to new manufacturing processes in Europe and the US, in the period from about 1760 to sometime between 1820 and 1840. This transition included going from hand production methods to machines, new chemical manufacturing and iron production processes, the increasing use of steam power and water power, the development of machine tools and the rise of the mechanized factory system. The _____ also led to an unprecedented rise in the rate of population growth.

Exam Probability: **High**

28. *Answer choices:*
(see index for correct answer)

- a. Bernat Mill
- b. Herman Ossian Armour
- c. Leawood Pump House
- d. Industrial Revolution

Guidance: level 1

:: ::

According to Torrington, a _____ is usually developed by conducting a job analysis, which includes examining the tasks and sequences of tasks necessary to perform the job. The analysis considers the areas of knowledge and skills needed for the job. A job usually includes several roles. According to Hall, the _____ might be broadened to form a person specification or may be known as "terms of reference". The person/job specification can be presented as a stand-alone document, but in practice it is usually included within the _____ . A _____ is often used by employers in the recruitment process.

Exam Probability: **High**

29. *Answer choices:*
(see index for correct answer)

- a. imperative
- b. Job description
- c. similarity-attraction theory
- d. hierarchical perspective

Guidance: level 1

:: Project management ::

Contemporary business and science treat as a _____ any undertaking, carried out individually or collaboratively and possibly involving research or design, that is carefully planned to achieve a particular aim.

Exam Probability: **High**

30. *Answer choices:*
(see index for correct answer)

- a. Bill of quantities
- b. Identifying and Managing Project Risk
- c. Soft Costs
- d. Project manager

Guidance: level 1

:: Human resource management ::

_____ is a family of procedures to identify the content of a job in terms of activities involved and attributes or job requirements needed to perform the activities. _____ provides information of organizations which helps to determine which employees are best fit for specific jobs. Through _____, the analyst needs to understand what the important tasks of the job are, how they are carried out, and the necessary human qualities needed to complete the job successfully.

Exam Probability: **Low**

31. *Answer choices:*
(see index for correct answer)

- a. Open plan
- b. Autonomous work group
- c. Employment testing
- d. Resource-based view

Guidance: level 1

:: ::

_____ is both a research area and a practical skill encompassing the ability of an individual or organization to "lead" or guide other individuals, teams, or entire organizations. Specialist literature debates various viewpoints, contrasting Eastern and Western approaches to _____, and also United States versus European approaches. U.S. academic environments define _____ as "a process of social influence in which a person can enlist the aid and support of others in the accomplishment of a common task".

Exam Probability: **High**

32. *Answer choices:*
(see index for correct answer)

- a. Leadership
- b. deep-level diversity
- c. imperative
- d. personal values

Guidance: level 1

:: Commercial item transport and distribution ::

In commerce, supply-chain management, the management of the flow of goods and services, involves the movement and storage of raw materials, of work-in-process inventory, and of finished goods from point of origin to point of consumption. Interconnected or interlinked networks, channels and node businesses combine in the provision of products and services required by end customers in a supply chain. Supply-chain management has been defined as the "design, planning, execution, control, and monitoring of supply-chain activities with the objective of creating net value, building a competitive infrastructure, leveraging worldwide logistics, synchronizing supply with demand and measuring performance globally." SCM practice draws heavily from the areas of industrial engineering, systems engineering, operations management, logistics, procurement, information technology, and marketing and strives for an integrated approach. Marketing channels play an important role in supply-chain management. Current research in supply-chain management is concerned with topics related to sustainability and risk management, among others. Some suggest that the "people dimension" of SCM, ethical issues, internal integration, transparency/visibility, and human capital/talent management are topics that have, so far, been underrepresented on the research agenda.

Exam Probability: **Medium**

33. *Answer choices:*

(see index for correct answer)

- a. Counter-to-counter package
- b. Toll Global Logistics
- c. Semi-trailer
- d. Supply chain management

Guidance: level 1

:: Organizational theory ::

_____ refers to both a body of non-elective government officials and an administrative policy-making group. Historically, a _____ was a government administration managed by departments staffed with non-elected officials. Today, _____ is the administrative system governing any large institution, whether publicly owned or privately owned. The public administration in many countries is an example of a _____, but so is the centralized hierarchical structure of a business firm.

Exam Probability: **Medium**

34. *Answer choices:*

(see index for correct answer)

- a. Bureaucracy
- b. Resource dependence theory
- c. Organization theory
- d. Exit-Voice-Loyalty-Neglect Model

Guidance: level 1

:: Critical thinking ::

An _____ is a set of statements usually constructed to describe a set of facts which clarifies the causes, context, and consequences of those facts. This description of the facts et cetera may establish rules or laws, and may clarify the existing rules or laws in relation to any objects, or phenomena examined. The components of an _____ can be implicit, and interwoven with one another.

Exam Probability: **Medium**

35. *Answer choices:*

(see index for correct answer)

- a. Explanation
- b. Topical logic
- c. Inquiry: Critical Thinking Across the Disciplines
- d. Argumentation theory

Guidance: level 1

:: Product design ::

_____ as a verb is to create a new product to be sold by a business to its customers. A very broad coefficient and effective generation and development of ideas through a process that leads to new products. Thus, it is a major aspect of new product development.

Exam Probability: **High**

36. *Answer choices:*

(see index for correct answer)

- a. Rolf Fehlbaum
- b. Product design
- c. Sara Little Turnbull
- d. Peter Opsvik

Guidance: level 1

:: Business models ::

_____es are privately owned corporations, partnerships, or sole proprietorships that have fewer employees and/or less annual revenue than a regular-sized business or corporation. Businesses are defined as "small" in terms of being able to apply for government support and qualify for preferential tax policy varies depending on the country and industry. _____es range from fifteen employees under the Australian Fair Work Act 2009, fifty employees according to the definition used by the European Union, and fewer than five hundred employees to qualify for many U.S. _____ Administration programs. While _____es can also be classified according to other methods, such as annual revenues, shipments, sales, assets, or by annual gross or net revenue or net profits, the number of employees is one of the most widely used measures.

Exam Probability: **Low**

37. *Answer choices:*

(see index for correct answer)

- a. Small business
- b. Technology push
- c. InnovationXchange
- d. Utility computing

Guidance: level 1

:: Evaluation methods ::

In social psychology, _____ is the process of looking at oneself in order to assess aspects that are important to one's identity. It is one of the motives that drive self-evaluation, along with self-verification and self-enhancement. Sedikides suggests that the _____ motive will prompt people to seek information to confirm their uncertain self-concept rather than their certain self-concept and at the same time people use _____ to enhance their certainty of their own self-knowledge. However, the _____ motive could be seen as quite different from the other two self-evaluation motives. Unlike the other two motives through _____ people are interested in the accuracy of their current self view, rather than improving their self-view. This makes _____ the only self-evaluative motive that may cause a person's self-esteem to be damaged.

Exam Probability: **High**

38. *Answer choices:*
(see index for correct answer)

- a. Logic model
- b. Test management
- c. Self-assessment
- d. Ethnography

Guidance: level 1

:: Types of marketing ::

In microeconomics and management, _____ is an arrangement in which the supply chain of a company is owned by that company. Usually each member of the supply chain produces a different product or service, and the products combine to satisfy a common need. It is contrasted with horizontal integration, wherein a company produces several items which are related to one another. _____ has also described management styles that bring large portions of the supply chain not only under a common ownership, but also into one corporation.

Exam Probability: **High**

39. *Answer choices:*
(see index for correct answer)

- a. Relationship marketing

- b. Vertical integration
- c. Community marketing
- d. Influencer marketing

Guidance: level 1

:: Business law ::

A _____ is a business entity created by two or more parties, generally characterized by shared ownership, shared returns and risks, and shared governance. Companies typically pursue _____ s for one of four reasons: to access a new market, particularly emerging markets; to gain scale efficiencies by combining assets and operations; to share risk for major investments or projects; or to access skills and capabilities.

Exam Probability: **Low**

40. *Answer choices:*
(see index for correct answer)

- a. Partnership
- b. Oppression remedy
- c. Bulk transfer
- d. Joint venture

Guidance: level 1

:: Outsourcing ::

_____ is the relocation of a business process from one country to another—typically an operational process, such as manufacturing, or supporting processes, such as accounting. Typically this refers to a company business, although state governments may also employ _____. More recently, technical and administrative services have been offshored.

Exam Probability: **Medium**

41. *Answer choices:*
(see index for correct answer)

- a. Offshoring
- b. Strategic sourcing
- c. Global sourcing
- d. Extengineering

Guidance: level 1

:: Time management ::

_____ is the process of planning and exercising conscious control of time spent on specific activities, especially to increase effectiveness, efficiency, and productivity. It involves a juggling act of various demands upon a person relating to work, social life, family, hobbies, personal interests and commitments with the finiteness of time. Using time effectively gives the person "choice" on spending/managing activities at their own time and expediency.

Exam Probability: **Medium**

42. *Answer choices:*
(see index for correct answer)

- a. Maestro concept
- b. waiting room
- c. Time allocation
- d. Getting Things Done

Guidance: level 1

:: ::

_____ is the moral stance, political philosophy, ideology, or social outlook that emphasizes the moral worth of the individual. Individualists promote the exercise of one's goals and desires and so value independence and self-reliance and advocate that interests of the individual should achieve precedence over the state or a social group, while opposing external interference upon one's own interests by society or institutions such as the government. _____ is often defined in contrast to totalitarianism, collectivism, and more corporate social forms.

Exam Probability: **High**

43. *Answer choices:*
(see index for correct answer)

- a. empathy
- b. Individualism
- c. functional perspective
- d. corporate values

Guidance: level 1

:: Human resource management ::

_____ , executive management, upper management, or a management team is generally a team of individuals at the highest level of management of an organization who have the day-to-day tasks of managing that organization — sometimes a company or a corporation.

Exam Probability: **Low**

44. *Answer choices:*
(see index for correct answer)

- a. Senior management
- b. Person specification
- c. Human resource accounting
- d. Job sharing

Guidance: level 1

:: ::

An _____ in international trade is a good or service produced in one country that is bought by someone in another country. The seller of such goods and services is an _____ er; the foreign buyer is an importer.

Exam Probability: **High**

45. *Answer choices:*
(see index for correct answer)

- a. hierarchical
- b. Export
- c. co-culture
- d. levels of analysis

Guidance: level 1

:: Project management ::

_____ is a process of setting goals, planning and/or controlling the organizing and leading the execution of any type of activity, such as.

Exam Probability: **High**

46. *Answer choices:*
(see index for correct answer)

- a. Management process
- b. Scope statement
- c. Deliverable
- d. Multidisciplinary approach

Guidance: level 1

:: ::

_____ involves decision making. It can include judging the merits of multiple options and selecting one or more of them. One can make a _____ between imagined options or between real options followed by the corresponding action. For example, a traveler might choose a route for a journey based on the preference of arriving at a given destination as soon as possible. The preferred route can then follow from information such as the length of each of the possible routes, traffic conditions, etc. The arrival at a _____ can include more complex motivators such as cognition, instinct, and feeling.

Exam Probability: **High**

47. *Answer choices:*
(see index for correct answer)

- a. personal values
- b. co-culture
- c. Choice
- d. corporate values

Guidance: level 1

:: E-commerce ::

_____ is the activity of buying or selling of products on online services or over the Internet. Electronic commerce draws on technologies such as mobile commerce, electronic funds transfer, supply chain management, Internet marketing, online transaction processing, electronic data interchange , inventory management systems, and automated data collection systems.

Exam Probability: **Medium**

48. *Answer choices:*

(see index for correct answer)

- a. Online Revolution
- b. E-commerce
- c. Social commerce
- d. Mobile ticketing

Guidance: level 1

:: ::

_____ is an evaluative or corrective exercise that can occur in any area of human life. _____ can therefore take many different forms . How people go about criticizing, can vary a great deal. In specific areas of human endeavour, the form of _____ can be highly specialized and technical; it often requires professional knowledge to appreciate the _____ . For subject-specific information, see the Varieties of _____ page.

Exam Probability: **High**

49. *Answer choices:*

(see index for correct answer)

- a. hierarchical perspective
- b. corporate values
- c. open system
- d. deep-level diversity

Guidance: level 1

:: ::

In communications and information processing, _____ is a system of rules to convert information—such as a letter, word, sound, image, or gesture—into another form or representation, sometimes shortened or secret, for communication through a communication channel or storage in a storage medium. An early example is the invention of language, which enabled a person, through speech, to communicate what they saw, heard, felt, or thought to others. But speech limits the range of communication to the distance a voice can carry, and limits the audience to those present when the speech is uttered. The invention of writing, which converted spoken language into visual symbols, extended the range of communication across space and time.

Exam Probability: **Low**

50. *Answer choices:*
(see index for correct answer)

- a. functional perspective
- b. open system
- c. deep-level diversity
- d. cultural

Guidance: level 1

:: Statistical terminology ::

_____ is the magnitude or dimensions of a thing. _____ can be measured as length, width, height, diameter, perimeter, area, volume, or mass.

Exam Probability: **High**

51. *Answer choices:*
(see index for correct answer)

- a. Size
- b. Endogeneity
- c. Statistical error
- d. Neutral vector

Guidance: level 1

:: Free trade agreements ::

A _____ is a wide-ranging taxes, tariff and trade treaty that often includes investment guarantees. It exists when two or more countries agree on terms that helps them trade with each other. The most common _____ s are of the preferential and free trade types are concluded in order to reduce tariffs, quotas and other trade restrictions on items traded between the signatories.

Exam Probability: **High**

52. *Answer choices:*

(see index for correct answer)

- a. CISFTA
- b. Regional Comprehensive Economic Partnership
- c. Trade agreement
- d. New West Partnership

Guidance: level 1

:: Business models ::

A _____ , _____ company or daughter company is a company that is owned or controlled by another company, which is called the parent company, parent, or holding company. The _____ can be a company, corporation, or limited liability company. In some cases it is a government or state-owned enterprise. In some cases, particularly in the music and book publishing industries, subsidiaries are referred to as imprints.

Exam Probability: **High**

53. *Answer choices:*

(see index for correct answer)

- a. Pay to play
- b. Fractional ownership
- c. Technology push
- d. Subsidiary

Guidance: level 1

:: Project management ::

A _____ is a team whose members usually belong to different groups, functions and are assigned to activities for the same project. A team can be divided into sub-teams according to need. Usually _____ s are only used for a defined period of time. They are disbanded after the project is deemed complete. Due to the nature of the specific formation and disbandment, _____ s are usually in organizations.

Exam Probability: **High**

54. *Answer choices:*

(see index for correct answer)

- a. Product description
- b. Resource
- c. Expected commercial value
- d. Time limit

Guidance: level 1

:: Employment discrimination ::

A _____ is a metaphor used to represent an invisible barrier that keeps a given demographic from rising beyond a certain level in a hierarchy.

Exam Probability: **Low**

55. *Answer choices:*

(see index for correct answer)

- a. United Kingdom employment equality law
- b. Glass ceiling
- c. LGBT employment discrimination in the United States
- d. Employment discrimination law in the European Union

Guidance: level 1

:: Training ::

_____ is teaching, or developing in oneself or others, any skills and knowledge that relate to specific useful competencies. _____ has specific goals of improving one's capability, capacity, productivity and performance. It forms the core of apprenticeships and provides the backbone of content at institutes of technology. In addition to the basic _____ required for a trade, occupation or profession, observers of the labor-market recognize as of 2008 the need to continue _____ beyond initial qualifications: to maintain, upgrade and update skills throughout working life. People within many professions and occupations may refer to this sort of _____ as professional development.

Exam Probability: **High**

56. *Answer choices:*
(see index for correct answer)

- a. Korean Standards Association
- b. Boardcast
- c. Training
- d. National sports team

Guidance: level 1

:: Human resource management ::

_____ means increasing the scope of a job through extending the range of its job duties and responsibilities generally within the same level and periphery. _____ involves combining various activities at the same level in the organization and adding them to the existing job. It is also called the horizontal expansion of job activities. This contradicts the principles of specialisation and the division of labour whereby work is divided into small units, each of which is performed repetitively by an individual worker and the responsibilities are always clear. Some motivational theories suggest that the boredom and alienation caused by the division of labour can actually cause efficiency to fall. Thus, _____ seeks to motivate workers through reversing the process of specialisation. A typical approach might be to replace assembly lines with modular work; instead of an employee repeating the same step on each product, they perform several tasks on a single item. In order for employees to be provided with _____ they will need to be retrained in new fields to understand how each field works.

Exam Probability: **High**

57. *Answer choices:*

(see index for correct answer)

- a. Progress, plans, problems
- b. IDS HR in Practice
- c. Workforce management
- d. Job enlargement

Guidance: level 1

:: Workplace ::

A _____ , also referred to as a performance review, performance evaluation, development discussion, or employee appraisal is a method by which the job performance of an employee is documented and evaluated. _____ s are a part of career development and consist of regular reviews of employee performance within organizations.

Exam Probability: **Medium**

58. *Answer choices:*

(see index for correct answer)

- a. Workplace conflict
- b. Performance appraisal
- c. Workplace phobia
- d. Workplace wellness

Guidance: level 1

:: Business ethics ::

_____ is a type of harassment technique that relates to a sexual nature and the unwelcome or inappropriate promise of rewards in exchange for sexual favors. _____ includes a range of actions from mild transgressions to sexual abuse or assault. Harassment can occur in many different social settings such as the workplace, the home, school, churches, etc. Harassers or victims may be of any gender.

Exam Probability: **High**

59. *Answer choices:*

(see index for correct answer)

- a. Business Ethics Quarterly
- b. Wheelmen
- c. Eating your own dog food
- d. Terror-free investing

Guidance: level 1

Business law

Corporate law (also known as business law) is the body of law governing the rights, relations, and conduct of persons, companies, organizations and businesses. It refers to the legal practice relating to, or the theory of corporations. Corporate law often describes the law relating to matters which derive directly from the life-cycle of a corporation. It thus encompasses the formation, funding, governance, and death of a corporation.

:: Commercial crimes ::

_____ is the process of concealing the origins of money obtained illegally by passing it through a complex sequence of banking transfers or commercial transactions. The overall scheme of this process returns the money to the launderer in an obscure and indirect way.

Exam Probability: **Low**

1. *Answer choices:*

(see index for correct answer)

- a. Money laundering
- b. Copyfraud
- c. Price fixing
- d. Commercial bribery

Guidance: level 1

:: Insurance law ::

_____ exists when an insured person derives a financial or other kind of benefit from the continuous existence, without repairment or damage, of the insured object. A person has an _____ in something when loss of or damage to that thing would cause the person to suffer a financial or other kind of loss. Normally, _____ is established by ownership, possession, or direct relationship. For example, people have _____ s in their own homes and vehicles, but not in their neighbors' homes and vehicles, and almost certainly not those of strangers.

Exam Probability: **High**

2. *Answer choices:*
(see index for correct answer)

- a. Insurable interest
- b. Loss of use
- c. Assigned risk
- d. Motor vehicle insurance law in India

Guidance: level 1

:: ::

_____ is an abstract concept of management of complex systems according to a set of rules and trends. In systems theory, these types of rules exist in various fields of biology and society, but the term has slightly different meanings according to context. For example.

Exam Probability: **Medium**

3. *Answer choices:*
(see index for correct answer)

- a. information systems assessment
- b. co-culture
- c. Regulation
- d. imperative

Guidance: level 1

:: ::

The words "_____" and "testify" both derive from the Latin word testis, referring to the notion of a disinterested third-party witness.

Exam Probability: **Low**

4. *Answer choices:*
(see index for correct answer)

- a. Testimony
- b. co-culture
- c. corporate values
- d. similarity-attraction theory

Guidance: level 1

:: ::

An _____ is a contingent motivator. Traditional _____ s are extrinsic motivators which reward actions to yield a desired outcome. The effectiveness of traditional _____ s has changed as the needs of Western society have evolved. While the traditional _____ model is effective when there is a defined procedure and goal for a task, Western society started to require a higher volume of critical thinkers, so the traditional model became less effective. Institutions are now following a trend in implementing strategies that rely on intrinsic motivations rather than the extrinsic motivations that the traditional _____ s foster.

Exam Probability: **High**

5. *Answer choices:*
(see index for correct answer)

- a. imperative
- b. Character
- c. Incentive
- d. corporate values

Guidance: level 1

:: ::

The _____ to the United States Constitution prevents the government from making laws which respect an establishment of religion, prohibit the free exercise of religion, or abridge the freedom of speech, the freedom of the press, the right to peaceably assemble, or the right to petition the government for redress of grievances. It was adopted on December 15, 1791, as one of the ten amendments that constitute the Bill of Rights.

Exam Probability: **Medium**

6. *Answer choices:*

(see index for correct answer)

- a. Character
- b. corporate values
- c. levels of analysis
- d. surface-level diversity

Guidance: level 1

:: ::

Competition law is a law that promotes or seeks to maintain market competition by regulating anti-competitive conduct by companies. Competition law is implemented through public and private enforcement. Competition law is known as " _____ law" in the United States for historical reasons, and as "anti-monopoly law" in China and Russia. In previous years it has been known as trade practices law in the United Kingdom and Australia. In the European Union, it is referred to as both _____ and competition law.

Exam Probability: **Medium**

7. *Answer choices:*

(see index for correct answer)

- a. Antitrust
- b. levels of analysis
- c. hierarchical perspective
- d. similarity-attraction theory

Guidance: level 1

:: ::

Advertising is a marketing communication that employs an openly sponsored, non-personal message to promote or sell a product, service or idea. Sponsors of advertising are typically businesses wishing to promote their products or services. Advertising is differentiated from public relations in that an advertiser pays for and has control over the message. It differs from personal selling in that the message is non-personal, i.e., not directed to a particular individual.Advertising is communicated through various mass media, including traditional media such as newspapers, magazines, television, radio, outdoor advertising or direct mail; and new media such as search results, blogs, social media, websites or text messages. The actual presentation of the message in a medium is referred to as an _____ , or "ad" or advert for short.

Exam Probability: **Low**

8. *Answer choices:*

(see index for correct answer)

- a. surface-level diversity
- b. deep-level diversity
- c. empathy
- d. Advertisement

Guidance: level 1

:: Meetings ::

A _____ is a body of one or more persons that is subordinate to a deliberative assembly. Usually, the assembly sends matters into a _____ as a way to explore them more fully than would be possible if the assembly itself were considering them. _____ s may have different functions and their type of work differ depending on the type of the organization and its needs.

Exam Probability: **Low**

9. *Answer choices:*

(see index for correct answer)

- a. Carlton Club meeting
- b. Annual Georgia European Union Summit
- c. Committee
- d. Popular assembly

Guidance: level 1

:: ::

The _____ of 1977 is a United States federal law known primarily for two of its main provisions: one that addresses accounting transparency requirements under the Securities Exchange Act of 1934 and another concerning bribery of foreign officials. The Act was amended in 1988 and in 1998, and has been subject to continued congressional concerns, namely whether its enforcement discourages U.S. companies from investing abroad.

Exam Probability: **Low**

10. *Answer choices:*

(see index for correct answer)

- a. interpersonal communication
- b. similarity-attraction theory
- c. imperative
- d. Foreign Corrupt Practices Act

Guidance: level 1

:: Contract law ::

A _____ cannot be enforced by law. _____ s are different from voidable contracts, which are contracts that may be nullified. However, when a contract is being written and signed, there is no automatic mechanism available in every situation that can be utilized to detect the validity or enforceability of that contract. Practically, a contract can be declared to be void by a court of law. So the main question is that under what conditions can a contract be deemed as void

Exam Probability: **High**

11. *Answer choices:*

(see index for correct answer)

- a. Handshake deal
- b. Void contract
- c. Letter of comfort
- d. Requirements contract

Guidance: level 1

:: ::

A _____ is a request to do something, most commonly addressed to a government official or public entity. _____ s to a deity are a form of prayer called supplication.

Exam Probability: **Medium**

12. *Answer choices:*
(see index for correct answer)

- a. Character
- b. Petition
- c. levels of analysis
- d. information systems assessment

Guidance: level 1

:: Majority–minority relations ::

_____ , also known as reservation in India and Nepal, positive discrimination / action in the United Kingdom, and employment equity in Canada and South Africa, is the policy of promoting the education and employment of members of groups that are known to have previously suffered from discrimination. Historically and internationally, support for _____ has sought to achieve goals such as bridging inequalities in employment and pay, increasing access to education, promoting diversity, and redressing apparent past wrongs, harms, or hindrances.

Exam Probability: **Medium**

13. *Answer choices:*
(see index for correct answer)

- a. cultural dissonance
- b. cultural Relativism
- c. positive discrimination

Guidance: level 1

:: ::

Employment is a relationship between two parties, usually based on a contract where work is paid for, where one party, which may be a corporation, for profit, not-for-profit organization, co-operative or other entity is the employer and the other is the employee. Employees work in return for payment, which may be in the form of an hourly wage, by piecework or an annual salary, depending on the type of work an employee does or which sector she or he is working in. Employees in some fields or sectors may receive gratuities, bonus payment or stock options. In some types of employment, employees may receive benefits in addition to payment. Benefits can include health insurance, housing, disability insurance or use of a gym. Employment is typically governed by employment laws, regulations or legal contracts.

Exam Probability: **Medium**

14. *Answer choices:*
(see index for correct answer)

- a. Personnel
- b. surface-level diversity
- c. information systems assessment
- d. open system

Guidance: level 1

:: Real property law ::

A _____ is the grant of authority or rights, stating that the granter formally recognizes the prerogative of the recipient to exercise the rights specified. It is implicit that the granter retains superiority , and that the recipient admits a limited status within the relationship, and it is within that sense that _____ s were historically granted, and that sense is retained in modern usage of the term.

Exam Probability: **Medium**

15. *Answer choices:*
(see index for correct answer)

- a. United States Court of Private Land Claims
- b. Charter
- c. Reversionary lease
- d. Tidelands

Guidance: level 1

:: Contract law ::

_____ , in human interactions, is a sincere intention to be fair, open, and honest, regardless of the outcome of the interaction. While some Latin phrases lose their literal meaning over centuries, this is not the case with bona fides; it is still widely used and interchangeable with its generally accepted modern-day English translation of _____ . It is an important concept within law and business. The opposed concepts are bad faith, mala fides and perfidy . In contemporary English, the usage of bona fides is synonymous with credentials and identity. The phrase is sometimes used in job advertisements, and should not be confused with the bona fide occupational qualifications or the employer's _____ effort, as described below.

Exam Probability: **High**

16. *Answer choices:*
(see index for correct answer)

- a. Neo-classical contract
- b. Good faith
- c. Nudum pactum
- d. Right of first refusal

Guidance: level 1

:: ::

Business is the activity of making one's living or making money by producing or buying and selling products . Simply put, it is "any activity or enterprise entered into for profit. It does not mean it is a company, a corporation, partnership, or have any such formal organization, but it can range from a street peddler to General Motors."

Exam Probability: **Low**

17. *Answer choices:*
(see index for correct answer)

- a. surface-level diversity
- b. Firm
- c. corporate values
- d. Character

Guidance: level 1

:: Legal doctrines and principles ::

In the common law of torts, _____ loquitur is a doctrine that infers negligence from the very nature of an accident or injury in the absence of direct evidence on how any defendant behaved. Although modern formulations differ by jurisdiction, common law originally stated that the accident must satisfy the necessary elements of negligence: duty, breach of duty, causation, and injury. In _____ loquitur, the elements of duty of care, breach, and causation are inferred from an injury that does not ordinarily occur without negligence.

Exam Probability: **High**

18. *Answer choices:*
(see index for correct answer)

- a. Act of state
- b. Acquiescence
- c. Assumption of risk
- d. Respondeat superior

Guidance: level 1

:: Fair use ::

_____ is a doctrine in the law of the United States that permits limited use of copyrighted material without having to first acquire permission from the copyright holder. _____ is one of the limitations to copyright intended to balance the interests of copyright holders with the public interest in the wider distribution and use of creative works by allowing as a defense to copyright infringement claims certain limited uses that might otherwise be considered infringement.

Exam Probability: **Medium**

19. *Answer choices:*
(see index for correct answer)

- a. Fair Use: The Story of the Letter U and the Numeral 2
- b. Fair use
- c. Toward a Fair Use Standard
- d. Derivative work

Guidance: level 1

:: Personal property law ::

> Bailment describes a legal relationship in common law where physical possession of personal property, or a chattel, is transferred from one person to another person who subsequently has possession of the property. It arises when a person gives property to someone else for safekeeping, and is a cause of action independent of contract or tort.

Exam Probability: **Low**

20. *Answer choices:*
(see index for correct answer)

- a. bailment
- b. bailor

Guidance: level 1

:: Shareholders ::

> A _____ is a payment made by a corporation to its shareholders, usually as a distribution of profits. When a corporation earns a profit or surplus, the corporation is able to re-invest the profit in the business and pay a proportion of the profit as a _____ to shareholders. Distribution to shareholders may be in cash or, if the corporation has a _____ reinvestment plan, the amount can be paid by the issue of further shares or share repurchase. When _____ s are paid, shareholders typically must pay income taxes, and the corporation does not receive a corporate income tax deduction for the _____ payments.

Exam Probability: **Medium**

21. *Answer choices:*
(see index for correct answer)

- a. Dividend
- b. Australian Shareholders Association
- c. Shotgun clause
- d. Say on pay

Guidance: level 1

:: Competition law ::

In competition law, a _____ is a market in which a particular product or service is sold. It is the intersection of a relevant product market and a relevant geographic market. The European Commission defines a _____ and its product and geographic components as follows.

Exam Probability: **Low**

22. *Answer choices:*

(see index for correct answer)

- a. Legal Services Board
- b. Competition law
- c. The Competition Act, 2002
- d. Relevant market

Guidance: level 1

:: Business law ::

A _____ is a group of people who jointly supervise the activities of an organization, which can be either a for-profit business, nonprofit organization, or a government agency. Such a board's powers, duties, and responsibilities are determined by government regulations and the organization's own constitution and bylaws. These authorities may specify the number of members of the board, how they are to be chosen, and how often they are to meet.

Exam Probability: **Medium**

23. *Answer choices:*

(see index for correct answer)

- a. Apparent authority
- b. Board of directors
- c. Registered agent
- d. Undervalue transaction

Guidance: level 1

:: Contract law ::

In jurisprudence, _____ is an equitable doctrine that involves one person taking advantage of a position of power over another person. This inequity in power between the parties can vitiate one party's consent as they are unable to freely exercise their independent will.

Exam Probability: **Medium**

24. *Answer choices:*
(see index for correct answer)

- a. Offer and acceptance
- b. Secured transaction
- c. Undue influence
- d. Quantum meruit

Guidance: level 1

:: Real property law ::

_____ is an area of criminal law or tort law broadly divided into three groups: _____ to the person, _____ to chattels and _____ to land.

Exam Probability: **Medium**

25. *Answer choices:*
(see index for correct answer)

- a. Trespass
- b. Lateral and subjacent support
- c. Jural relationship
- d. Ultimogeniture

Guidance: level 1

:: Commercial item transport and distribution ::

A _____ in common law countries is a person or company that transports goods or people for any person or company and that is responsible for any possible loss of the goods during transport. A _____ offers its services to the general public under license or authority provided by a regulatory body. The regulatory body has usually been granted "ministerial authority" by the legislation that created it. The regulatory body may create, interpret, and enforce its regulations upon the _____ with independence and finality, as long as it acts within the bounds of the enabling legislation.

Exam Probability: **Medium**

26. *Answer choices:*
(see index for correct answer)

- a. Common carrier
- b. Port centric logistics
- c. Ocean transportation intermediary
- d. Lowboy

Guidance: level 1

:: ::

In financial markets, a share is a unit used as mutual funds, limited partnerships, and real estate investment trusts. The owner of _____ in the corporation/company is a shareholder of the corporation. A share is an indivisible unit of capital, expressing the ownership relationship between the company and the shareholder. The denominated value of a share is its face value, and the total of the face value of issued _____ represent the capital of a company, which may not reflect the market value of those _____.

Exam Probability: **High**

27. *Answer choices:*
(see index for correct answer)

- a. Shares
- b. corporate values
- c. hierarchical perspective
- d. information systems assessment

Guidance: level 1

:: Mereology ::

_____, in the abstract, is what belongs to or with something, whether as an attribute or as a component of said thing. In the context of this article, it is one or more components, whether physical or incorporeal, of a person's estate; or so belonging to, as in being owned by, a person or jointly a group of people or a legal entity like a corporation or even a society. Depending on the nature of the _____, an owner of _____ has the right to consume, alter, share, redefine, rent, mortgage, pawn, sell, exchange, transfer, give away or destroy it, or to exclude others from doing these things, as well as to perhaps abandon it; whereas regardless of the nature of the _____, the owner thereof has the right to properly use it, or at the very least exclusively keep it.

Exam Probability: **Medium**

28. *Answer choices:*
(see index for correct answer)

- a. Property
- b. Mereological nihilism
- c. Gunk
- d. Simple

Guidance: level 1

:: Legal terms ::

_____, or non-absolute contributory negligence outside the United States, is a partial legal defense that reduces the amount of damages that a plaintiff can recover in a negligence-based claim, based upon the degree to which the plaintiff's own negligence contributed to cause the injury. When the defense is asserted, the factfinder, usually a jury, must decide the degree to which the plaintiff's negligence and the combined negligence of all other relevant actors all contributed to cause the plaintiff's damages. It is a modification of the doctrine of contributory negligence that disallows any recovery by a plaintiff whose negligence contributed even minimally to causing the damages.

Exam Probability: **High**

29. *Answer choices:*

(see index for correct answer)

- a. Commanding precedent
- b. Comparative negligence
- c. Bifurcation
- d. As is

Guidance: level 1

:: Business law ::

A _____ , also known as the sole trader, individual entrepreneurship or proprietorship, is a type of enterprise that is owned and run by one person and in which there is no legal distinction between the owner and the business entity. A sole trader does not necessarily work `alone'—it is possible for the sole trader to employ other people.

Exam Probability: **Low**

30. *Answer choices:*

(see index for correct answer)

- a. Negotiable instrument
- b. Tax patent
- c. Chattel mortgage
- d. Contract failure

Guidance: level 1

:: Forgery ::

_____ is a white-collar crime that generally refers to the false making or material alteration of a legal instrument with the specific intent to defraud anyone . Tampering with a certain legal instrument may be forbidden by law in some jurisdictions but such an offense is not related to _____ unless the tampered legal instrument was actually used in the course of the crime to defraud another person or entity. Copies, studio replicas, and reproductions are not considered forgeries, though they may later become forgeries through knowing and willful misrepresentations.

Exam Probability: **Low**

31. *Answer choices:*

(see index for correct answer)

- a. Copy-evident document
- b. Archaeological forgery
- c. Forgery
- d. Forgery of Foreign Bills Act 1803

Guidance: level 1

:: Contract law ::

_____ is a legal process for collecting a monetary judgment on behalf of a plaintiff from a defendant. _____ allows the plaintiff to take the money or property of the debtor from the person or institution that holds that property. A similar legal mechanism called execution allows the seizure of money or property held directly by the debtor.

Exam Probability: **High**

32. *Answer choices:*
(see index for correct answer)

- a. Garnishment
- b. Co-signing
- c. Invitation to treat
- d. Collateral contract

Guidance: level 1

:: United States federal public corruption crime ::

Mail fraud and _____ are federal crimes in the United States that involve mailing or electronically transmitting something associated with fraud. Jurisdiction is claimed by the federal government if the illegal activity crosses interstate or international borders.

Exam Probability: **Medium**

33. *Answer choices:*
(see index for correct answer)

- a. RICO Act
- b. Wire fraud

Guidance: level 1

:: White-collar criminals ::

_____ refers to financially motivated, nonviolent crime committed by businesses and government professionals. It was first defined by the sociologist Edwin Sutherland in 1939 as "a crime committed by a person of respectability and high social status in the course of their occupation". Typical _____ s could include wage theft, fraud, bribery, Ponzi schemes, insider trading, labor racketeering, embezzlement, cybercrime, copyright infringement, money laundering, identity theft, and forgery. Lawyers can specialize in _____ .

Exam Probability: **Low**

34. *Answer choices:*
(see index for correct answer)

- a. Du Jun
- b. Tongsun Park

Guidance: level 1

:: Fraud ::

In law, _____ is intentional deception to secure unfair or unlawful gain, or to deprive a victim of a legal right. _____ can violate civil law, a criminal law, or it may cause no loss of money, property or legal right but still be an element of another civil or criminal wrong. The purpose of _____ may be monetary gain or other benefits, for example by obtaining a passport, travel document, or driver's license, or mortgage _____ , where the perpetrator may attempt to qualify for a mortgage by way of false statements.

Exam Probability: **Medium**

35. *Answer choices:*
(see index for correct answer)

- a. Faked death
- b. Charity fraud
- c. Check kiting
- d. Fraud

Guidance: level 1

:: ::

The _____ of 1933, also known as the 1933 Act, the _____, the Truth in _____, the Federal _____, and the `33 Act, was enacted by the United States Congress on May 27, 1933, during the Great Depression, after the stock market crash of 1929. Legislated pursuant to the Interstate Commerce Clause of the Constitution, it requires every offer or sale of securities that uses the means and instrumentalities of interstate commerce to be registered with the SEC pursuant to the 1933 Act, unless an exemption from registration exists under the law. The term "means and instrumentalities of interstate commerce" is extremely broad and it is virtually impossible to avoid the operation of the statute by attempting to offer or sell a security without using an "instrumentality" of interstate commerce. Any use of a telephone, for example, or the mails would probably be enough to subject the transaction to the statute.

Exam Probability: **Medium**

36. *Answer choices:*
(see index for correct answer)

- a. co-culture
- b. surface-level diversity
- c. deep-level diversity
- d. corporate values

Guidance: level 1

:: ::

The _____ is an intergovernmental organization that is concerned with the regulation of international trade between nations. The WTO officially commenced on 1 January 1995 under the Marrakesh Agreement, signed by 124 nations on 15 April 1994, replacing the General Agreement on Tariffs and Trade , which commenced in 1948. It is the largest international economic organization in the world.

Exam Probability: **Low**

37. *Answer choices:*
(see index for correct answer)

- a. imperative
- b. levels of analysis
- c. World Trade Organization

- d. empathy

Guidance: level 1

:: Contract Clause case law ::

The _____ appears in the United States Constitution, Article I, section 10, clause 1. The clause prohibits a State from passing any law that "impairs the obligation of contracts" or "makes any thing but gold and silver coin a tender in payment of debts". It states.

Exam Probability: **Medium**

38. *Answer choices:*
(see index for correct answer)

- a. Charles River Bridge v. Warren Bridge
- b. Fletcher v. Peck
- c. Smyth v. Ames

Guidance: level 1

:: ::

An _____, for United States federal income tax, is a closely held corporation that makes a valid election to be taxed under Subchapter S of Chapter 1 of the Internal Revenue Code. In general, _____ s do not pay any income taxes. Instead, the corporation's income or losses are divided among and passed through to its shareholders. The shareholders must then report the income or loss on their own individual income tax returns.

Exam Probability: **High**

39. *Answer choices:*
(see index for correct answer)

- a. Sarbanes-Oxley act of 2002
- b. Character
- c. process perspective
- d. corporate values

Guidance: level 1

:: Arbitration law ::

The United States Arbitration Act, more commonly referred to as the _____ or FAA, is an act of Congress that provides for judicial facilitation of private dispute resolution through arbitration. It applies in both state courts and federal courts, as was held constitutional in Southland Corp. v. Keating. It applies where the transaction contemplated by the parties "involves" interstate commerce and is predicated on an exercise of the Commerce Clause powers granted to Congress in the U.S. Constitution.

Exam Probability: **High**

40. *Answer choices:*
(see index for correct answer)

- a. Federal Arbitration Act
- b. Convention on the Recognition and Enforcement of Foreign Arbitral Awards
- c. Uniform Arbitration Act
- d. James A. Graham

Guidance: level 1

:: ::

An _____ is the production of goods or related services within an economy. The major source of revenue of a group or company is the indicator of its relevant _____. When a large group has multiple sources of revenue generation, it is considered to be working in different industries. Manufacturing _____ became a key sector of production and labour in European and North American countries during the Industrial Revolution, upsetting previous mercantile and feudal economies. This came through many successive rapid advances in technology, such as the production of steel and coal.

Exam Probability: **Medium**

41. *Answer choices:*
(see index for correct answer)

- a. personal values
- b. Industry
- c. hierarchical
- d. levels of analysis

Guidance: level 1

:: ::

_____ is a means of protection from financial loss. It is a form of risk management, primarily used to hedge against the risk of a contingent or uncertain loss

Exam Probability: **High**

42. *Answer choices:*
(see index for correct answer)

- a. deep-level diversity
- b. Insurance
- c. functional perspective
- d. information systems assessment

Guidance: level 1

:: Intention ::

_____ is the mental element of a person's intention to commit a crime; or knowledge that one's action or lack of action would cause a crime to be committed. It is a necessary element of many crimes.

Exam Probability: **Medium**

43. *Answer choices:*
(see index for correct answer)

- a. bona fide
- b. Letter of Intent

Guidance: level 1

:: Euthenics ::

_____ is an ethical framework and suggests that an entity, be it an organization or individual, has an obligation to act for the benefit of society at large. _____ is a duty every individual has to perform so as to maintain a balance between the economy and the ecosystems. A trade-off may exist between economic development, in the material sense, and the welfare of the society and environment, though this has been challenged by many reports over the past decade. _____ means sustaining the equilibrium between the two. It pertains not only to business organizations but also to everyone whose any action impacts the environment. This responsibility can be passive, by avoiding engaging in socially harmful acts, or active, by performing activities that directly advance social goals. _____ must be intergenerational since the actions of one generation have consequences on those following.

Exam Probability: **High**

44. *Answer choices:*
(see index for correct answer)

- a. Home economics
- b. Social responsibility
- c. Euthenics
- d. Minnie Cumnock Blodgett

Guidance: level 1

:: Contract law ::

Coercion is the practice of forcing another party to act in an involuntary manner by use of threats or force. It involves a set of various types of forceful actions that violate the free will of an individual to induce a desired response, for example: a bully demanding lunch money from a student or the student gets beaten. These actions may include extortion, blackmail, torture, threats to induce favors, or even sexual assault. In law, coercion is codified as a _____ crime. Such actions are used as leverage, to force the victim to act in a way contrary to their own interests. Coercion may involve the actual infliction of physical pain/injury or psychological harm in order to enhance the credibility of a threat. The threat of further harm may lead to the cooperation or obedience of the person being coerced.

Exam Probability: **Medium**

45. *Answer choices:*
(see index for correct answer)

- a. Accommodation
- b. Duress
- c. French contract law
- d. Implied-in-fact contract

Guidance: level 1

:: Abuse of the legal system ::

_____ occurs when a person is restricted in their personal movement within any area without justification or consent. Actual physical restraint is not necessary for _____ to occur. A _____ claim may be made based upon private acts, or upon wrongful governmental detention. For detention by the police, proof of _____ provides a basis to obtain a writ of habeas corpus.

Exam Probability: **Medium**

46. *Answer choices:*
(see index for correct answer)

- a. False imprisonment
- b. Forum shopping
- c. Obstruction of Justice

Guidance: level 1

:: Insurance terms ::

A _____ in the broadest sense is a natural person or other legal entity who receives money or other benefits from a benefactor. For example, the _____ of a life insurance policy is the person who receives the payment of the amount of insurance after the death of the insured.

Exam Probability: **Low**

47. *Answer choices:*
(see index for correct answer)

- a. Beneficiary
- b. Subrogation
- c. Cash value

- d. Recoupment

Guidance: level 1

:: ::

A _____ loan or, simply, _____ is used either by purchasers of real property to raise funds to buy real estate, or alternatively by existing property owners to raise funds for any purpose, while putting a lien on the property being _____ d. The loan is "secured" on the borrower's property through a process known as _____ origination. This means that a legal mechanism is put into place which allows the lender to take possession and sell the secured property to pay off the loan in the event the borrower defaults on the loan or otherwise fails to abide by its terms. The word _____ is derived from a Law French term used in Britain in the Middle Ages meaning "death pledge" and refers to the pledge ending when either the obligation is fulfilled or the property is taken through foreclosure. A _____ can also be described as "a borrower giving consideration in the form of a collateral for a benefit ".

Exam Probability: **High**

48. *Answer choices:*
(see index for correct answer)

- a. cultural
- b. Mortgage
- c. information systems assessment
- d. Sarbanes-Oxley act of 2002

Guidance: level 1

:: ::

_____ is that part of a civil law legal system which is part of the jus commune that involves relationships between individuals, such as the law of contracts or torts , and the law of obligations . It is to be distinguished from public law, which deals with relationships between both natural and artificial persons and the state, including regulatory statutes, penal law and other law that affects the public order. In general terms, _____ involves interactions between private citizens, whereas public law involves interrelations between the state and the general population.

Exam Probability: **Medium**

49. *Answer choices:*
(see index for correct answer)

- a. levels of analysis
- b. Private law
- c. information systems assessment
- d. hierarchical perspective

Guidance: level 1

:: ::

In English law, a _____ or _____ absolute is an estate in land, a form of freehold ownership. It is a way that real estate and land may be owned in common law countries, and is the highest possible ownership interest that can be held in real property. Allodial title is reserved to governments under a civil law structure. The rights of the _____ owner are limited by government powers of taxation, compulsory purchase, police power, and escheat, and it could also be limited further by certain encumbrances or conditions in the deed, such as, for example, a condition that required the land to be used as a public park, with a reversion interest in the grantor if the condition fails; this is a _____ conditional.

Exam Probability: **Low**

50. *Answer choices:*
(see index for correct answer)

- a. Fee simple
- b. information systems assessment
- c. hierarchical perspective
- d. interpersonal communication

Guidance: level 1

:: Debt ::

_____, in finance and economics, is payment from a borrower or deposit-taking financial institution to a lender or depositor of an amount above repayment of the principal sum, at a particular rate. It is distinct from a fee which the borrower may pay the lender or some third party. It is also distinct from dividend which is paid by a company to its shareholders from its profit or reserve, but not at a particular rate decided beforehand, rather on a pro rata basis as a share in the reward gained by risk taking entrepreneurs when the revenue earned exceeds the total costs.

Exam Probability: **High**

51. *Answer choices:*
(see index for correct answer)

- a. External debt
- b. Charge-off
- c. Floating charge
- d. Interest

Guidance: level 1

:: Real property law ::

_____ is the judicial process whereby a will is "proved" in a court of law and accepted as a valid public document that is the true last testament of the deceased, or whereby the estate is settled according to the laws of intestacy in the state of residence [or real property] of the deceased at time of death in the absence of a legal will.

Exam Probability: **Low**

52. *Answer choices:*
(see index for correct answer)

- a. Tenancy Deposit Scheme
- b. Servient estate
- c. Probate
- d. Buyer listing

Guidance: level 1

:: Legal terms ::

_____, or exemplary damages, are damages assessed in order to punish the defendant for outrageous conduct and/or to reform or deter the defendant and others from engaging in conduct similar to that which formed the basis of the lawsuit. Although the purpose of _____ is not to compensate the plaintiff, the plaintiff will receive all or some of the _____ award.

Exam Probability: **Medium**

53. *Answer choices:*
(see index for correct answer)

- a. European Authorized Representative
- b. Punitive damages
- c. Factual basis
- d. Open verdict

Guidance: level 1

:: ::

In international relations, _____ is – from the perspective of governments – a voluntary transfer of resources from one country to another.

Exam Probability: **High**

54. *Answer choices:*
(see index for correct answer)

- a. cultural
- b. information systems assessment
- c. Character
- d. Aid

Guidance: level 1

:: Finance ::

A _____ , in the law of the United States, is a contract that governs the relationship between the parties to a kind of financial transaction known as a secured transaction. In a secured transaction, the Grantor assigns, grants and pledges to the grantee a security interest in personal property which is referred to as the collateral. Examples of typical collateral are shares of stock, livestock, and vehicles. A _____ is not used to transfer any interest in real property , only personal property. The document used by lenders to obtain a lien on real property is a mortgage or deed of trust.

Exam Probability: **Medium**

55. *Answer choices:*
(see index for correct answer)

- a. Pet banks
- b. Security agreement
- c. Single deposit
- d. BIOFIN

Guidance: level 1

:: ::

_____ is the production of products for use or sale using labour and machines, tools, chemical and biological processing, or formulation. The term may refer to a range of human activity, from handicraft to high tech, but is most commonly applied to industrial design, in which raw materials are transformed into finished goods on a large scale. Such finished goods may be sold to other manufacturers for the production of other, more complex products, such as aircraft, household appliances, furniture, sports equipment or automobiles, or sold to wholesalers, who in turn sell them to retailers, who then sell them to end users and consumers.

Exam Probability: **High**

56. *Answer choices:*
(see index for correct answer)

- a. personal values
- b. co-culture
- c. levels of analysis
- d. Manufacturing

Guidance: level 1

:: ::

_____ is the practice of protecting the natural environment by individuals, organizations and governments. Its objectives are to conserve natural resources and the existing natural environment and, where possible, to repair damage and reverse trends.

Exam Probability: **Medium**

57. *Answer choices:*
(see index for correct answer)

- a. information systems assessment
- b. Environmental Protection
- c. Sarbanes-Oxley act of 2002
- d. process perspective

Guidance: level 1

:: ::

Industrial espionage, _____ , corporate spying or corporate espionage is a form of espionage conducted for commercial purposes instead of purely national security. While _____ is conducted or orchestrated by governments and is international in scope, industrial or corporate espionage is more often national and occurs between companies or corporations.

Exam Probability: **Medium**

58. *Answer choices:*
(see index for correct answer)

- a. surface-level diversity
- b. Sarbanes-Oxley act of 2002
- c. Economic espionage
- d. levels of analysis

Guidance: level 1

:: ::

_____ , in United States trademark law, is a statutory cause of action that permits a party to petition the Trademark Trial and Appeal Board of the Patent and Trademark Office to cancel a trademark registration that "may disparage or falsely suggest a connection with persons, living or dead, institutions, beliefs, or national symbols, or bring them into contempt or disrepute." Unlike claims regarding the validity of the mark, a _____ claim can be brought "at any time," subject to equitable defenses such as laches.

Exam Probability: **Medium**

59. *Answer choices:*
(see index for correct answer)

- a. Sarbanes-Oxley act of 2002
- b. Disparagement
- c. levels of analysis
- d. imperative

Guidance: level 1

Finance

Finance is a field that is concerned with the allocation (investment) of assets and liabilities over space and time, often under conditions of risk or uncertainty. Finance can also be defined as the science of money management. Participants in the market aim to price assets based on their risk level, fundamental value, and their expected rate of return. Finance can be split into three sub-categories: public finance, corporate finance and personal finance.

:: Options (finance) ::

In finance, a put or _____ is a stock market device which gives the owner the right, but not the obligation, to sell an asset, at a specified price, by a predetermined date to a given party. The purchase of a _____ is interpreted as a negative sentiment about the future value of theunderlying stock. The term "put" comes from the fact that the owner has the right to "put up for sale" the stock or index.

Exam Probability: **Medium**

1. *Answer choices:*
(see index for correct answer)

- a. Timer Call
- b. Put option
- c. Stock option return
- d. LEAPS

Guidance: level 1

:: Management accounting ::

In _____ or managerial accounting, managers use the provisions of accounting information in order to better inform themselves before they decide matters within their organizations, which aids their management and performance of control functions.

Exam Probability: **Medium**

2. *Answer choices:*

(see index for correct answer)

- a. Dual overhead rate
- b. Standard cost
- c. Management accounting
- d. Process costing

Guidance: level 1

:: Business law ::

A _____, also known as the sole trader, individual entrepreneurship or proprietorship, is a type of enterprise that is owned and run by one person and in which there is no legal distinction between the owner and the business entity. A sole trader does not necessarily work `alone`—it is possible for the sole trader to employ other people.

Exam Probability: **Medium**

3. *Answer choices:*

(see index for correct answer)

- a. Partnership
- b. Teck Corp. Ltd. v. Millar
- c. Double ticketing
- d. Company mortgage

Guidance: level 1

:: Accounting in the United States ::

The _____ is a private-sector, nonprofit corporation created by the Sarbanes–Oxley Act of 2002 to oversee the audits of public companies and other issuers in order to protect the interests of investors and further the public interest in the preparation of informative, accurate and independent audit reports. The PCAOB also oversees the audits of broker-dealers, including compliance reports filed pursuant to federal securities laws, to promote investor protection. All PCAOB rules and standards must be approved by the U.S. Securities and Exchange Commission .

Exam Probability: **High**

4. *Answer choices:*
(see index for correct answer)

- a. Uniform Certified Public Accountant Examination
- b. International Qualification Examination
- c. Public Company Accounting Oversight Board
- d. Revolving fund

Guidance: level 1

:: Bonds (finance) ::

In finance, a _____ or convertible note or convertible debt is a type of bond that the holder can convert into a specified number of shares of common stock in the issuing company or cash of equal value. It is a hybrid security with debt- and equity-like features. It originated in the mid-19th century, and was used by early speculators such as Jacob Little and Daniel Drew to counter market cornering.

Exam Probability: **Medium**

5. *Answer choices:*
(see index for correct answer)

- a. Convertible bond
- b. 360-day calendar
- c. Basis point value
- d. Inflation-indexed bond

Guidance: level 1

:: Financial ratios ::

The _____ is a liquidity ratio that measures whether a firm has enough resources to meet its short-term obligations. It compares a firm's current assets to its current liabilities, and is expressed as follows.

Exam Probability: **Low**

6. *Answer choices:*
(see index for correct answer)

- a. Alpha
- b. Debt-to-equity ratio
- c. Times interest earned
- d. Net income per employee

Guidance: level 1

:: Financial markets ::

For an individual, a _____ is the minimum amount of money by which the expected return on a risky asset must exceed the known return on a risk-free asset in order to induce an individual to hold the risky asset rather than the risk-free asset. It is positive if the person is risk averse. Thus it is the minimum willingness to accept compensation for the risk.

Exam Probability: **Low**

7. *Answer choices:*
(see index for correct answer)

- a. Earnings guidance
- b. Principal trade
- c. Risk premium
- d. Convertible arbitrage

Guidance: level 1

:: Financial ratios ::

_____ is a measure of how revenue growth translates into growth in operating income. It is a measure of leverage, and of how risky, or volatile, a company's operating income is.

Exam Probability: **Low**

8. *Answer choices:*
(see index for correct answer)

- a. return on invested capital
- b. Debt-to-GDP ratio
- c. CASA ratio
- d. Rate of return on a portfolio

Guidance: level 1

:: Generally Accepted Accounting Principles ::

In accounting, an economic item's _____ is the original nominal monetary value of that item. _____ accounting involves reporting assets and liabilities at their _____ s, which are not updated for changes in the items' values. Consequently, the amounts reported for these balance sheet items often differ from their current economic or market values.

Exam Probability: **Medium**

9. *Answer choices:*
(see index for correct answer)

- a. Historical cost
- b. Net income
- c. Indian Accounting Standards
- d. Gross profit

Guidance: level 1

:: Manufacturing ::

_____ costs are all manufacturing costs that are related to the cost object but cannot be traced to that cost object in an economically feasible way.

Exam Probability: **High**

10. *Answer choices:*
(see index for correct answer)

- a. Rubber technology
- b. Manufacturing overhead
- c. Build to stock

- d. Supplier Risk Management

Guidance: level 1

:: Financial ratios ::

The _____ or dividend-price ratio of a share is the dividend per share, divided by the price per share. It is also a company's total annual dividend payments divided by its market capitalization, assuming the number of shares is constant. It is often expressed as a percentage.

Exam Probability: **Low**

11. *Answer choices:*
(see index for correct answer)

- a. Capitalization rate
- b. Dividend yield
- c. EV/GCI
- d. EV/EBITDA

Guidance: level 1

:: Generally Accepted Accounting Principles ::

In accounting, _____, gross margin, sales profit, or credit sales is the difference between revenue and the cost of making a product or providing a service, before deducting overheads, payroll, taxation, and interest payments. This is different from operating profit. Gross margin is the term normally used in the U.S., while _____ is the more common usage in the UK and Australia.

Exam Probability: **High**

12. *Answer choices:*
(see index for correct answer)

- a. Insurance asset management
- b. Paid in capital
- c. Gross profit
- d. Operating profit

Guidance: level 1

:: ::

_____ is the collection of techniques, skills, methods, and processes used in the production of goods or services or in the accomplishment of objectives, such as scientific investigation. _____ can be the knowledge of techniques, processes, and the like, or it can be embedded in machines to allow for operation without detailed knowledge of their workings. Systems applying _____ by taking an input, changing it according to the system's use, and then producing an outcome are referred to as _____ systems or technological systems.

Exam Probability: **Low**

13. *Answer choices:*
(see index for correct answer)

- a. co-culture
- b. Technology
- c. interpersonal communication
- d. personal values

Guidance: level 1

:: Real estate ::

Amortisation is paying off an amount owed over time by making planned, incremental payments of principal and interest. To amortise a loan means "to kill it off". In accounting, amortisation refers to charging or writing off an intangible asset's cost as an operational expense over its estimated useful life to reduce a company's taxable income.

Exam Probability: **Low**

14. *Answer choices:*
(see index for correct answer)

- a. Rent control
- b. Assignment
- c. Lease administration
- d. Amortization

Guidance: level 1

:: Accounting terminology ::

_____ is a legally enforceable claim for payment held by a business for goods supplied and/or services rendered that customers/clients have ordered but not paid for. These are generally in the form of invoices raised by a business and delivered to the customer for payment within an agreed time frame. _____ is shown in a balance sheet as an asset. It is one of a series of accounting transactions dealing with the billing of a customer for goods and services that the customer has ordered. These may be distinguished from notes receivable, which are debts created through formal legal instruments called promissory notes.

Exam Probability: **High**

15. *Answer choices:*
(see index for correct answer)

- a. revenue recognition principle
- b. Absorption costing
- c. outstanding balance
- d. Impairment cost

Guidance: level 1

:: Management accounting ::

_____ is a managerial accounting cost concept. Under this method, manufacturing overhead is incurred in the period that a product is produced. This addresses the issue of absorption costing that allows income to rise as production rises. Under an absorption cost method, management can push forward costs to the next period when products are sold. This artificially inflates profits in the period of production by incurring less cost than would be incurred under a _____ system. _____ is generally not used for external reporting purposes. Under the Tax Reform Act of 1986, income statements must use absorption costing to comply with GAAP.

Exam Probability: **Low**

16. *Answer choices:*
(see index for correct answer)

- a. Financial statement analysis
- b. RCA open-source application
- c. Pre-determined overhead rate
- d. Job costing

Guidance: level 1

:: Data analysis ::

In statistics, the _____ is a measure that is used to quantify the amount of variation or dispersion of a set of data values. A low _____ indicates that the data points tend to be close to the mean of the set, while a high _____ indicates that the data points are spread out over a wider range of values.

Exam Probability: **Low**

17. *Answer choices:*
(see index for correct answer)

- a. Quantile normalization
- b. PERSIANN
- c. Standard deviation
- d. Text mining

Guidance: level 1

:: ::

A _____ is an entity that owes a debt to another entity. The entity may be an individual, a firm, a government, a company or other legal person. The counterparty is called a creditor. When the counterpart of this debt arrangement is a bank, the _____ is more often referred to as a borrower.

Exam Probability: **High**

18. *Answer choices:*
(see index for correct answer)

- a. hierarchical perspective
- b. empathy
- c. personal values
- d. Sarbanes-Oxley act of 2002

Guidance: level 1

:: ::

In production, research, retail, and accounting, a _____ is the value of money that has been used up to produce something or deliver a service, and hence is not available for use anymore. In business, the _____ may be one of acquisition, in which case the amount of money expended to acquire it is counted as _____. In this case, money is the input that is gone in order to acquire the thing. This acquisition _____ may be the sum of the _____ of production as incurred by the original producer, and further _____s of transaction as incurred by the acquirer over and above the price paid to the producer. Usually, the price also includes a mark-up for profit over the _____ of production.

Exam Probability: **Low**

19. *Answer choices:*
(see index for correct answer)

- a. personal values
- b. Cost
- c. hierarchical
- d. cultural

Guidance: level 1

:: E-commerce ::

A _____ is a plastic payment card that can be used instead of cash when making purchases. It is similar to a credit card, but unlike a credit card, the money is immediately transferred directly from the cardholder's bank account when performing a transaction.

Exam Probability: **High**

20. *Answer choices:*
(see index for correct answer)

- a. Silent commerce
- b. Debit card
- c. AsiaPay
- d. TRADACOMS

Guidance: level 1

:: Marketing ::

_____ is a financial mechanism in which a debtor obtains the right to delay payments to a creditor, for a defined period of time, in exchange for a charge or fee. Essentially, the party that owes money in the present purchases the right to delay the payment until some future date. The discount, or charge, is the difference between the original amount owed in the present and the amount that has to be paid in the future to settle the debt.

Exam Probability: **Low**

21. *Answer choices:*
(see index for correct answer)

- a. societal marketing
- b. Cola Wars
- c. Discounting
- d. Back to school

Guidance: level 1

:: ::

A _____ is a fund into which a sum of money is added during an employee's employment years, and from which payments are drawn to support the person's retirement from work in the form of periodic payments. A _____ may be a "defined benefit plan" where a fixed sum is paid regularly to a person, or a "defined contribution plan" under which a fixed sum is invested and then becomes available at retirement age. _____ s should not be confused with severance pay; the former is usually paid in regular installments for life after retirement, while the latter is typically paid as a fixed amount after involuntary termination of employment prior to retirement.

Exam Probability: **Low**

22. *Answer choices:*
(see index for correct answer)

- a. process perspective
- b. Pension
- c. cultural
- d. Sarbanes-Oxley act of 2002

Guidance: level 1

:: Finance ::

_____ is a field that is concerned with the allocation of assets and liabilities over space and time, often under conditions of risk or uncertainty. _____ can also be defined as the art of money management. Participants in the market aim to price assets based on their risk level, fundamental value, and their expected rate of return. _____ can be split into three sub-categories: public _____ , corporate _____ and personal _____ .

Exam Probability: **Low**

23. *Answer choices:*
(see index for correct answer)

- a. Finance
- b. Monetary system
- c. tax asset
- d. Trading the news

Guidance: level 1

:: Fixed income market ::

In finance, the _____ is a curve showing several yields or interest rates across different contract lengths for a similar debt contract. The curve shows the relation between the interest rate and the time to maturity, known as the "term", of the debt for a given borrower in a given currency. For example, the U.S. dollar interest rates paid on U.S. Treasury securities for various maturities are closely watched by many traders, and are commonly plotted on a graph such as the one on the right which is informally called "the _____ ". More formal mathematical descriptions of this relation are often called the term structure of interest rates.

Exam Probability: **High**

24. *Answer choices:*
(see index for correct answer)

- a. Basis point
- b. Pool factor
- c. Bond Exchange of South Africa
- d. Bond market

Guidance: level 1

:: ::

_____ is the withdrawal from one's position or occupation or from one's active working life. A person may also semi-retire by reducing work hours.

Exam Probability: **Medium**

25. *Answer choices:*
(see index for correct answer)

- a. corporate values
- b. functional perspective
- c. hierarchical perspective
- d. open system

Guidance: level 1

:: Auditing ::

_____, as defined by accounting and auditing, is a process for assuring of an organization's objectives in operational effectiveness and efficiency, reliable financial reporting, and compliance with laws, regulations and policies. A broad concept, _____ involves everything that controls risks to an organization.

Exam Probability: **Medium**

26. *Answer choices:*
(see index for correct answer)

- a. Internal control
- b. Management representation
- c. Provided by client
- d. Audit plan

Guidance: level 1

:: Banking ::

A _____ is a financial account maintained by a bank for a customer. A _____ can be a deposit account, a credit card account, a current account, or any other type of account offered by a financial institution, and represents the funds that a customer has entrusted to the financial institution and from which the customer can make withdrawals. Alternatively, accounts may be loan accounts in which case the customer owes money to the financial institution.

Exam Probability: **Low**

27. *Answer choices:*
(see index for correct answer)

- a. Tier 1 capital
- b. Payment order
- c. Capital requirement
- d. Bank account

Guidance: level 1

:: Investment ::

In finance, the benefit from an _____ is called a return. The return may consist of a gain realised from the sale of property or an _____, unrealised capital appreciation, or _____ income such as dividends, interest, rental income etc., or a combination of capital gain and income. The return may also include currency gains or losses due to changes in foreign currency exchange rates.

Exam Probability: **Medium**

28. *Answer choices:*
(see index for correct answer)

- a. Enterprise Investment Scheme
- b. Internal rate of return
- c. Short-term investment fund
- d. Investment

Guidance: level 1

:: Derivatives (finance) ::

_____ is any bodily activity that enhances or maintains physical fitness and overall health and wellness. It is performed for various reasons, to aid growth and improve strength, preventing aging, developing muscles and the cardiovascular system, honing athletic skills, weight loss or maintenance, improving health and also for enjoyment. Many individuals choose to _____ outdoors where they can congregate in groups, socialize, and enhance well-being.

Exam Probability: **Medium**

29. *Answer choices:*
(see index for correct answer)

- a. Exercise
- b. Intrinsic value
- c. Crush spread
- d. Borsa Istanbul

Guidance: level 1

:: Bonds (finance) ::

An _____ is a legal contract that reflects or covers a debt or purchase obligation. It specifically refers to two types of practices: in historical usage, an _____ d servant status, and in modern usage, it is an instrument used for commercial debt or real estate transaction.

Exam Probability: **High**

30. *Answer choices:*
(see index for correct answer)

- a. Indenture
- b. Savings bonds
- c. I-spread
- d. LECOP

Guidance: level 1

:: Costs ::

In economics, _____ is the total economic cost of production and is made up of variable cost, which varies according to the quantity of a good produced and includes inputs such as labour and raw materials, plus fixed cost, which is independent of the quantity of a good produced and includes inputs that cannot be varied in the short term: fixed costs such as buildings and machinery, including sunk costs if any. Since cost is measured per unit of time, it is a flow variable.

Exam Probability: **High**

31. *Answer choices:*
(see index for correct answer)

- a. Total cost
- b. Average cost
- c. Explicit cost
- d. Total cost of acquisition

Guidance: level 1

:: Expense ::

An _____ , operating expenditure, operational expense, operational expenditure or opex is an ongoing cost for running a product, business, or system. Its counterpart, a capital expenditure , is the cost of developing or providing non-consumable parts for the product or system. For example, the purchase of a photocopier involves capex, and the annual paper, toner, power and maintenance costs represents opex. For larger systems like businesses, opex may also include the cost of workers and facility expenses such as rent and utilities.

Exam Probability: **Medium**

32. *Answer choices:*
(see index for correct answer)

- a. Operating expense
- b. Corporate travel
- c. Freight expense
- d. Expense account

Guidance: level 1

:: ::

In accounting, the _____ is a measure of the number of times inventory is sold or used in a time period such as a year. It is calculated to see if a business has an excessive inventory in comparison to its sales level. The equation for _____ equals the cost of goods sold divided by the average inventory. _____ is also known as inventory turns, merchandise turnover, stockturn, stock turns, turns, and stock turnover.

Exam Probability: **Medium**

33. *Answer choices:*
(see index for correct answer)

- a. functional perspective
- b. Inventory turnover
- c. Character
- d. process perspective

Guidance: level 1

:: Financial markets ::

As money became a commodity, the _____ became a component of the financial market for assets involved in short-term borrowing, lending, buying and selling with original maturities of one year or less. Trading in _____ s is done over the counter and is wholesale.

Exam Probability: **Low**

34. *Answer choices:*
(see index for correct answer)

- a. Clearing balance requirement
- b. Internal financing
- c. Faroese Securities Market
- d. Money market

Guidance: level 1

:: Financial regulatory authorities of the United States ::

The _____ is the revenue service of the United States federal government. The government agency is a bureau of the Department of the Treasury, and is under the immediate direction of the Commissioner of Internal Revenue, who is appointed to a five-year term by the President of the United States. The IRS is responsible for collecting taxes and administering the Internal Revenue Code, the main body of federal statutory tax law of the United States. The duties of the IRS include providing tax assistance to taxpayers and pursuing and resolving instances of erroneous or fraudulent tax filings. The IRS has also overseen various benefits programs, and enforces portions of the Affordable Care Act.

Exam Probability: **Low**

35. *Answer choices:*

(see index for correct answer)

- a. Securities Investor Protection Corporation
- b. Federal Deposit Insurance Corporation
- c. Internal Revenue Service
- d. Office of the Comptroller of the Currency

Guidance: level 1

:: Accounting source documents ::

A _____ or account statement is a summary of financial transactions which have occurred over a given period on a bank account held by a person or business with a financial institution.

Exam Probability: **Low**

36. *Answer choices:*

(see index for correct answer)

- a. Purchase order
- b. Bank statement
- c. Parcel audit
- d. Remittance advice

Guidance: level 1

:: ::

An _____ is the production of goods or related services within an economy. The major source of revenue of a group or company is the indicator of its relevant _____. When a large group has multiple sources of revenue generation, it is considered to be working in different industries. Manufacturing _____ became a key sector of production and labour in European and North American countries during the Industrial Revolution, upsetting previous mercantile and feudal economies. This came through many successive rapid advances in technology, such as the production of steel and coal.

Exam Probability: **Medium**

37. *Answer choices:*

(see index for correct answer)

- a. cultural
- b. Industry
- c. similarity-attraction theory
- d. deep-level diversity

Guidance: level 1

:: ::

_____ is a political and social philosophy promoting traditional social institutions in the context of culture and civilization. The central tenets of _____ include tradition, human imperfection, organic society, hierarchy, authority, and property rights. Conservatives seek to preserve a range of institutions such as religion, parliamentary government, and property rights, with the aim of emphasizing social stability and continuity. The more traditional elements—reactionaries—oppose modernism and seek a return to "the way things were".

Exam Probability: **Low**

38. *Answer choices:*

(see index for correct answer)

- a. Sarbanes-Oxley act of 2002
- b. hierarchical perspective
- c. surface-level diversity
- d. Conservatism

Guidance: level 1

:: Government bonds ::

A _____, commonly known as a Muni Bond, is a bond issued by a local government or territory, or one of their agencies. It is generally used to finance public projects such as roads, schools, airports and seaports, and infrastructure-related repairs. The term _____ is commonly used in the United States, which has the largest market of such trade-able securities in the world. As of 2011, the _____ market was valued at $3.7 trillion. Potential issuers of _____ s include states, cities, counties, redevelopment agencies, special-purpose districts, school districts, public utility districts, publicly owned airports and seaports, and other governmental entities at or below the state level having more than a de minimis amount of one of the three sovereign powers: the power of taxation, the power of eminent domain or the police power.

Exam Probability: **High**

39. *Answer choices:*
(see index for correct answer)

- a. Bond vigilante
- b. Municipal bond
- c. Risk-free bond
- d. Direct operations

Guidance: level 1

:: Business law ::

_____ is where a person's financial liability is limited to a fixed sum, most commonly the value of a person's investment in a company or partnership. If a company with _____ is sued, then the claimants are suing the company, not its owners or investors. A shareholder in a limited company is not personally liable for any of the debts of the company, other than for the amount already invested in the company and for any unpaid amount on the shares in the company, if any. The same is true for the members of a _____ partnership and the limited partners in a limited partnership. By contrast, sole proprietors and partners in general partnerships are each liable for all the debts of the business.

Exam Probability: **Low**

40. *Answer choices:*

(see index for correct answer)

- a. Economic torts
- b. Limited liability limited partnership
- c. Duty of fair representation
- d. Limited liability

Guidance: level 1

:: Market research ::

_____, an acronym for Information through Disguised Experimentation is an annual market research fair conducted by the students of IIM-Lucknow. Students create games and use various other simulated environments to capture consumers' subconscious thoughts. This innovative method of market research removes the sensitization effect that might bias peoples answers to questions. This ensures that the most truthful answers are captured to research questions. The games are designed in such a way that the observers can elicit all the required information just by observing and noting down the behaviour and the responses of the participants.

Exam Probability: **High**

41. *Answer choices:*

(see index for correct answer)

- a. Mall-intercept personal interview
- b. INDEX
- c. Respondent error
- d. IDDEA

Guidance: level 1

:: Mereology ::

_____ , in the abstract, is what belongs to or with something, whether as an attribute or as a component of said thing. In the context of this article, it is one or more components , whether physical or incorporeal, of a person's estate; or so belonging to, as in being owned by, a person or jointly a group of people or a legal entity like a corporation or even a society. Depending on the nature of the _____ , an owner of _____ has the right to consume, alter, share, redefine, rent, mortgage, pawn, sell, exchange, transfer, give away or destroy it, or to exclude others from doing these things, as well as to perhaps abandon it; whereas regardless of the nature of the _____ , the owner thereof has the right to properly use it , or at the very least exclusively keep it.

Exam Probability: **Medium**

42. *Answer choices:*

(see index for correct answer)

- a. Meronomy
- b. Gunk
- c. Mereological nihilism
- d. Property

Guidance: level 1

:: Banking ::

A _____ is a financial institution that accepts deposits from the public and creates credit. Lending activities can be performed either directly or indirectly through capital markets. Due to their importance in the financial stability of a country, _____ s are highly regulated in most countries. Most nations have institutionalized a system known as fractional reserve _____ ing under which _____ s hold liquid assets equal to only a portion of their current liabilities. In addition to other regulations intended to ensure liquidity, _____ s are generally subject to minimum capital requirements based on an international set of capital standards, known as the Basel Accords.

Exam Probability: **High**

43. *Answer choices:*

(see index for correct answer)

- a. Branch manager
- b. Prescreen
- c. Wholesale banking
- d. Bank

Guidance: level 1

:: Generally Accepted Accounting Principles ::

_____ is the accounting classification of an account. It is part of double-entry book-keeping technique.

Exam Probability: **High**

44. *Answer choices:*
(see index for correct answer)

- a. Reserve
- b. Normal balance
- c. Operating statement
- d. Chinese accounting standards

Guidance: level 1

:: ::

_____ is a marketing communication that employs an openly sponsored, non-personal message to promote or sell a product, service or idea. Sponsors of _____ are typically businesses wishing to promote their products or services. _____ is differentiated from public relations in that an advertiser pays for and has control over the message. It differs from personal selling in that the message is non-personal, i.e., not directed to a particular individual. _____ is communicated through various mass media, including traditional media such as newspapers, magazines, television, radio, outdoor _____ or direct mail; and new media such as search results, blogs, social media, websites or text messages. The actual presentation of the message in a medium is referred to as an advertisement, or "ad" or advert for short.

Exam Probability: **Low**

45. *Answer choices:*
(see index for correct answer)

- a. information systems assessment

- b. hierarchical perspective
- c. similarity-attraction theory
- d. Advertising

Guidance: level 1

:: ::

A _____ is an organization, usually a group of people or a company, authorized to act as a single entity and recognized as such in law. Early incorporated entities were established by charter. Most jurisdictions now allow the creation of new _____ s through registration.

Exam Probability: **Medium**

46. *Answer choices:*
(see index for correct answer)

- a. corporate values
- b. process perspective
- c. imperative
- d. personal values

Guidance: level 1

:: Financial economics ::

A _____ is defined to include property of any kind held by an assessee, whether connected with their business or profession or not connected with their business or profession. It includes all kinds of property, movable or immovable, tangible or intangible, fixed or circulating. Thus, land and building, plant and machinery, motorcar, furniture, jewellery, route permits, goodwill, tenancy rights, patents, trademarks, shares, debentures, securities, units, mutual funds, zero-coupon bonds etc. are _____ s.

Exam Probability: **Low**

47. *Answer choices:*
(see index for correct answer)

- a. Constant proportion portfolio insurance
- b. Capital asset
- c. Financial Markets and Portfolio Management
- d. Quasilinear utility

Guidance: level 1

:: ::

In the field of analysis of algorithms in computer science, the _____ is a method of amortized analysis based on accounting. The _____ often gives a more intuitive account of the amortized cost of an operation than either aggregate analysis or the potential method. Note, however, that this does not guarantee such analysis will be immediately obvious; often, choosing the correct parameters for the _____ requires as much knowledge of the problem and the complexity bounds one is attempting to prove as the other two methods.

Exam Probability: **High**

48. *Answer choices:*
(see index for correct answer)

- a. interpersonal communication
- b. information systems assessment
- c. Accounting method
- d. open system

Guidance: level 1

:: Elementary geometry ::

The _____ is the front of an animal's head that features three of the head's sense organs, the eyes, nose, and mouth, and through which animals express many of their emotions. The _____ is crucial for human identity, and damage such as scarring or developmental deformities affects the psyche adversely.

Exam Probability: **Low**

49. *Answer choices:*
(see index for correct answer)

- a. Crossed ladders problem
- b. Face
- c. Angular diameter
- d. Semicircle

Guidance: level 1

:: Money ::

Cash and _____ s are the most liquid current assets found on a business's balance sheet. _____ s are short-term commitments "with temporarily idle cash and easily convertible into a known cash amount". An investment normally counts to be a _____ when it has a short maturity period of 90 days or less, and can be included in the cash and _____ s balance from the date of acquisition when it carries an insignificant risk of changes in the asset value; with more than 90 days maturity, the asset is not considered as cash and _____ s. Equity investments mostly are excluded from _____ s, unless they are essentially _____ s, for instance, if the preferred shares acquired within a short maturity period and with specified recovery date.

Exam Probability: **Medium**

50. *Answer choices:*
(see index for correct answer)

- a. Standard of deferred payment
- b. Allowance
- c. Cash equivalent
- d. Nominal money

Guidance: level 1

:: Financial markets ::

The _____ is the part of the capital market that deals with the issuance and sale of equity-backed securities to investors directly by the issuer. Investor buy securities that were never traded before. _____ s create long term instruments through which corporate entities raise funds from the capital market. It is also known as the New Issue Market.

Exam Probability: **Medium**

51. *Answer choices:*
(see index for correct answer)

- a. Global Industry Classification Standard
- b. Global Financial Centres Index
- c. Primary market
- d. Price-weighted

Guidance: level 1

:: Bonds (finance) ::

A _____ is a type of bond that allows the issuer of the bond to retain the privilege of redeeming the bond at some point before the bond reaches its date of maturity. In other words, on the call date, the issuer has the right, but not the obligation, to buy back the bonds from the bond holders at a defined call price. Technically speaking, the bonds are not really bought and held by the issuer but are instead cancelled immediately.

Exam Probability: **Low**

52. *Answer choices:*

(see index for correct answer)

- a. Callable bond
- b. Auction rate security
- c. Revolver bond
- d. Alternative risk transfer

Guidance: level 1

:: Economics terminology ::

A corporation's share capital or _____ is the portion of a corporation's equity that has been obtained by the issue of shares in the corporation to a shareholder, usually for cash. "Share capital" may also denote the number and types of shares that compose a corporation's share structure.

Exam Probability: **High**

53. *Answer choices:*

(see index for correct answer)

- a. Capital stock
- b. spillover effect
- c. economic profit
- d. Normal profit

Guidance: level 1

:: Business law ::

A _____ is a group of people who jointly supervise the activities of an organization, which can be either a for-profit business, nonprofit organization, or a government agency. Such a board's powers, duties, and responsibilities are determined by government regulations and the organization's own constitution and bylaws. These authorities may specify the number of members of the board, how they are to be chosen, and how often they are to meet.

Exam Probability: **High**

54. *Answer choices:*
(see index for correct answer)

- a. Double ticketing
- b. Subordination
- c. Joint venture
- d. Undervalue transaction

Guidance: level 1

:: Actuarial science ::

_____ is the addition of interest to the principal sum of a loan or deposit, or in other words, interest on interest. It is the result of reinvesting interest, rather than paying it out, so that interest in the next period is then earned on the principal sum plus previously accumulated interest. _____ is standard in finance and economics.

Exam Probability: **Low**

55. *Answer choices:*
(see index for correct answer)

- a. Compound annual growth rate
- b. Actuarial exam
- c. Compound interest
- d. SWAG

Guidance: level 1

:: Commerce ::

A _____, is a document acknowledging that a person has received money or property in payment following a sale or other transfer of goods or provision of a service. All _____ s must have the date of purchase on them. If the recipient of the payment is legally required to collect sales tax or VAT from the customer, the amount would be added to the _____ and the collection would be deemed to have been on behalf of the relevant tax authority. In many countries, a retailer is required to include the sales tax or VAT in the displayed price of goods sold, from which the tax amount would be calculated at point of sale and remitted to the tax authorities in due course. Similarly, amounts may be deducted from amounts payable, as in the case of wage withholding taxes. On the other hand, tips or other gratuities given by a customer, for example in a restaurant, would not form part of the payment amount or appear on the _____ .

Exam Probability: **Medium**

56. *Answer choices:*

(see index for correct answer)

- a. Retail loss prevention
- b. Receipt
- c. Fixed price
- d. DataCash

Guidance: level 1

:: ::

In financial markets, a share is a unit used as mutual funds, limited partnerships, and real estate investment trusts. The owner of _____ in the corporation/company is a shareholder of the corporation. A share is an indivisible unit of capital, expressing the ownership relationship between the company and the shareholder. The denominated value of a share is its face value, and the total of the face value of issued _____ represent the capital of a company, which may not reflect the market value of those _____ .

Exam Probability: **Medium**

57. *Answer choices:*

(see index for correct answer)

- a. personal values
- b. hierarchical
- c. Shares
- d. empathy

Guidance: level 1

:: Management accounting ::

_____ is the process of recording, classifying, analyzing, summarizing, and allocating costs associated with a process, after that developing various courses of action to control the costs. Its goal is to advise the management on how to optimize business practices and processes based on cost efficiency and capability. _____ provides the detailed cost information that management needs to control current operations and plan for the future.

Exam Probability: **Medium**

58. *Answer choices:*
(see index for correct answer)

- a. Revenue center
- b. Institute of Management Accountants
- c. Owner earnings
- d. Cost accounting

Guidance: level 1

:: Accounting terminology ::

_____ are liabilities that reflect expenses that have not yet been paid or logged under accounts payable during an accounting period; in other words, a company's obligation to pay for goods and services that have been provided for which invoices have not yet been received. Examples would include accrued wages payable, accrued sales tax payable, and accrued rent payable.

Exam Probability: **Low**

59. *Answer choices:*
(see index for correct answer)

- a. Basis of accounting
- b. Accrued liabilities
- c. Fair value accounting
- d. Cash flow management

Guidance: level 1

Human resource management

Human resource (HR) management is the strategic approach to the effective management of organization workers so that they help the business gain a competitive advantage. It is designed to maximize employee performance in service of an employer's strategic objectives. HR is primarily concerned with the management of people within organizations, focusing on policies and on systems. HR departments are responsible for overseeing employee-benefits design, employee recruitment, training and development, performance appraisal, and rewarding (e.g., managing pay and benefit systems). HR also concerns itself with organizational change and industrial relations, that is, the balancing of organizational practices with requirements arising from collective bargaining and from governmental laws.

:: Business ethics ::

A _____ is a person who exposes any kind of information or activity that is deemed illegal, unethical, or not correct within an organization that is either private or public. The information of alleged wrongdoing can be classified in many ways: violation of company policy/rules, law, regulation, or threat to public interest/national security, as well as fraud, and corruption. Those who become _____ s can choose to bring information or allegations to surface either internally or externally. Internally, a _____ can bring his/her accusations to the attention of other people within the accused organization such as an immediate supervisor. Externally, a _____ can bring allegations to light by contacting a third party outside of an accused organization such as the media, government, law enforcement, or those who are concerned. _____ s, however, take the risk of facing stiff reprisal and retaliation from those who are accused or alleged of wrongdoing.

Exam Probability: **Medium**

1. *Answer choices:*

(see index for correct answer)

- a. Marketing ethics
- b. Business and Professional Ethics Journal

- c. Whistleblower
- d. Nishkam Karma

Guidance: level 1

:: Labor ::

_____ refers to the process of grouping activities into departments. Division of labour creates specialists who need coordination. This coordination is facilitated by grouping specialists together in departments.

Exam Probability: **Medium**

2. *Answer choices:*
(see index for correct answer)

- a. Departmentalization
- b. Green ban
- c. Labour festival
- d. Cincinnati Time Store

Guidance: level 1

:: Training ::

A _____ is commonly known as an individual taking part in a _____ program or a graduate program within a company after having graduated from university or college.

Exam Probability: **Medium**

3. *Answer choices:*
(see index for correct answer)

- a. Personal trainer
- b. Trainee
- c. ActivePresenter
- d. Enforcement

Guidance: level 1

:: International trade ::

_____ or globalisation is the process of interaction and integration among people, companies, and governments worldwide. As a complex and multifaceted phenomenon, _____ is considered by some as a form of capitalist expansion which entails the integration of local and national economies into a global, unregulated market economy. _____ has grown due to advances in transportation and communication technology. With the increased global interactions comes the growth of international trade, ideas, and culture. _____ is primarily an economic process of interaction and integration that's associated with social and cultural aspects. However, conflicts and diplomacy are also large parts of the history of _____ , and modern _____ .

Exam Probability: **Low**

4. *Answer choices:*

(see index for correct answer)

- a. Globalization
- b. Bilateral trade
- c. Development theory
- d. Linder hypothesis

Guidance: level 1

:: ::

On December 31, 2016, Xerox separated its business process service operations into a new publicly traded company, Conduent. Xerox focuses on its document technology and document outsourcing business, and continues to trade on the NYSE. On January 31, 2018, Xerox announced that it would sell a controlling stake to Fujifilm, which has maintained a joint venture in the Asia-Pacific region known as Fuji Xerox.

Exam Probability: **Medium**

5. *Answer choices:*

(see index for correct answer)

- a. Xerox Corporation
- b. co-culture
- c. process perspective
- d. levels of analysis

Guidance: level 1

:: Free market ::

Piece work is any type of employment in which a worker is paid a fixed _____ for each unit produced or action performed regardless of time.

Exam Probability: **Medium**

6. *Answer choices:*
(see index for correct answer)

- a. Regulated market
- b. Free market

Guidance: level 1

:: Human resource management ::

_____ is a method of job analysis that was developed by the Employment and Training Administration of the United States Department of Labor. FJA produces standardized occupational information specific to the performance of the work and the performer.

Exam Probability: **Low**

7. *Answer choices:*
(see index for correct answer)

- a. war for talent
- b. Functional job analysis
- c. Expense management
- d. Disciplinary probation

Guidance: level 1

:: Hazard analysis ::

A _____ is an agent which has the potential to cause harm to a vulnerable target. The terms "_____" and "risk" are often used interchangeably. However, in terms of risk assessment, they are two very distinct terms. A _____ is any agent that can cause harm or damage to humans, property, or the environment. Risk is defined as the probability that exposure to a _____ will lead to a negative consequence, or more simply, a _____ poses no risk if there is no exposure to that _____.

Exam Probability: **Low**

8. *Answer choices:*
(see index for correct answer)

- a. Swiss cheese model
- b. Hazard identification
- c. Risk assessment
- d. Hazardous Materials Identification System

Guidance: level 1

:: Developmental psychology ::

_____ behavior refers to behavior that enables a person to get along in his or her environment with greatest success and least conflict with others. This is a term used in the areas of psychology and special education. _____ behavior relates to every day skills or tasks that the average person is able to complete, similar to the term life skills.

Exam Probability: **Low**

9. *Answer choices:*
(see index for correct answer)

- a. Cognitive development
- b. Adaptive

Guidance: level 1

:: Human resource management ::

A _____ is a form of payment from an employer to an employee, which may be specified in an employment contract. It is contrasted with piece wages, where each job, hour or other unit is paid separately, rather than on a periodic basis. From the point of view of running a business, _____ can also be viewed as the cost of acquiring and retaining human resources for running operations, and is then termed personnel expense or _____ expense. In accounting, salaries are recorded in payroll accounts.

Exam Probability: **Low**

10. *Answer choices:*
(see index for correct answer)

- a. Adecco Group North America
- b. Organizational orientations
- c. Salary
- d. IDS HR in Practice

Guidance: level 1

:: ::

_____ is a form of government characterized by strong central power and limited political freedoms. Individual freedoms are subordinate to the state and there is no constitutional accountability and rule of law under an authoritarian regime. Authoritarian regimes can be autocratic with power concentrated in one person or it can be more spread out between multiple officials and government institutions. Juan Linz's influential 1964 description of _____ characterized authoritarian political systems by four qualities.

Exam Probability: **Low**

11. *Answer choices:*
(see index for correct answer)

- a. similarity-attraction theory
- b. levels of analysis
- c. Authoritarianism
- d. Character

Guidance: level 1

:: Labor rights ::

A _____ is a wrong or hardship suffered, real or supposed, which forms legitimate grounds of complaint. In the past, the word meant the infliction or cause of hardship.

Exam Probability: **High**

12. *Answer choices:*

(see index for correct answer)

- a. Kate Mullany House
- b. Right to work
- c. China Labour Bulletin
- d. Labor rights

Guidance: level 1

:: Labour relations ::

A bargaining _____ occurs when the two sides negotiating an agreement are unable to reach an agreement and become deadlocked. An _____ is almost invariably mutually harmful, either as a result of direct action which may be taken such as a strike in employment negotiation or sanctions/military action in international relations, or simply due to the resulting delay in negotiating a mutually beneficial agreement. The word _____ may also refer to any situation in which no progress can be made. _____ s provide opportunities for problem solving to provide an insight that leads to progress.

Exam Probability: **High**

13. *Answer choices:*

(see index for correct answer)

- a. Impasse
- b. Global union federation
- c. European Trade Union Confederation
- d. Passfield Memorandum

Guidance: level 1

:: Business law ::

An _____ is a natural person, business, or corporation that provides goods or services to another entity under terms specified in a contract or within a verbal agreement. Unlike an employee, an _____ does not work regularly for an employer but works as and when required, during which time they may be subject to law of agency. _____ s are usually paid on a freelance basis. Contractors often work through a limited company or franchise, which they themselves own, or may work through an umbrella company.

Exam Probability: **High**

14. *Answer choices:*

(see index for correct answer)

- a. Joint venture
- b. Business license
- c. Valuation using the Market Penetration Model
- d. General assignment

Guidance: level 1

:: Labour relations ::

_____ is the practice of hiring more workers than are needed to perform a given job, or to adopt work procedures which appear pointless, complex and time-consuming merely to employ additional workers. The term "make-work" is sometimes used as a synonym for _____ .

Exam Probability: **Medium**

15. *Answer choices:*

(see index for correct answer)

- a. Inflatable rat
- b. Big labor
- c. Featherbedding
- d. Scranton Declaration

Guidance: level 1

:: Persuasion techniques ::

_____ is a psychological technique in which an individual attempts to influence another person by becoming more likeable to their target. This term was coined by social psychologist Edward E. Jones, who further defined _____ as "a class of strategic behaviors illicitly designed to influence a particular other person concerning the attractiveness of one's personal qualities." _____ research has identified some specific tactics of employing _____ .

Exam Probability: **Low**

16. *Answer choices:*

(see index for correct answer)

- a. Door-in-the-face technique
- b. Superficial charm
- c. Crocodile tears
- d. Ingratiation

Guidance: level 1

:: Occupations ::

An _____ is a person who has a position of authority in a hierarchical organization. The term derives from the late Latin from officiarius, meaning "official".

Exam Probability: **Medium**

17. *Answer choices:*

(see index for correct answer)

- a. Party princess
- b. Clerk of the course
- c. Copyist
- d. International Association of Black Actuaries

Guidance: level 1

:: Management ::

In business, a _____ is the attribute that allows an organization to outperform its competitors. A _____ may include access to natural resources, such as high-grade ores or a low-cost power source, highly skilled labor, geographic location, high entry barriers, and access to new technology.

Exam Probability: **Medium**

18. *Answer choices:*
(see index for correct answer)

- a. Failure demand
- b. Porter five forces analysis
- c. Competitive advantage
- d. Fall guy

Guidance: level 1

:: Human resource management ::

_____ is athletic training in sports other than the athlete's usual sport. The goal is improving overall performance. It takes advantage of the particular effectiveness of one training method to negate the shortcomings of another.

Exam Probability: **Low**

19. *Answer choices:*
(see index for correct answer)

- a. Adaptive performance
- b. Competency-based job description
- c. Cross-training
- d. Labour is not a commodity

Guidance: level 1

:: ::

A _____ is a technical analysis of a biological specimen, for example urine, hair, blood, breath, sweat, and/or oral fluid/saliva—to determine the presence or absence of specified parent drugs or their metabolites. Major applications of _____ ing include detection of the presence of performance enhancing steroids in sport, employers and parole/probation officers screening for drugs prohibited by law and police officers testing for the presence and concentration of alcohol in the blood commonly referred to as BAC . BAC tests are typically administered via a breathalyzer while urinalysis is used for the vast majority of _____ ing in sports and the workplace. Numerous other methods with varying degrees of accuracy, sensitivity , and detection periods exist.

Exam Probability: **High**

20. *Answer choices:*

(see index for correct answer)

- a. Drug test
- b. hierarchical perspective
- c. levels of analysis
- d. similarity-attraction theory

Guidance: level 1

:: ::

An _____ is a process where candidates are examined to determine their suitability for specific types of employment, especially management or military command. The candidates' personality and aptitudes are determined by techniques including interviews, group exercises, presentations, examinations and psychometric testing.

Exam Probability: **Medium**

21. *Answer choices:*

(see index for correct answer)

- a. imperative
- b. hierarchical
- c. Assessment center
- d. functional perspective

Guidance: level 1

:: Recruitment ::

_____ , also known as Recruitment communications and Recruitment agency, includes all communications used by an organization to attract talent to work within it. Recruitment advertisements may be the first impression of a company for many job seekers. In turn, the strength of employer branding in job postings can directly impact interest in job openings.

Exam Probability: **High**

22. *Answer choices:*
(see index for correct answer)

- a. Recession-proof job
- b. Common Recruitment Examination
- c. Public employment service
- d. Employment discrimination against persons with criminal records in the United States

Guidance: level 1

:: Job interview ::

An _____ is a survey conducted with an individual who is separating from an organization or relationship. Most commonly, this occurs between an employee and an organization, a student and an educational institution, or a member and an association. An organization can use the information gained from an _____ to assess what should be improved, changed, or remain intact. More so, an organization can use the results from _____ s to reduce employee, student, or member turnover and increase productivity and engagement, thus reducing the high costs associated with turnover. Some examples of the value of conducting _____ s include shortening the recruiting and hiring process, reducing absenteeism, improving innovation, sustaining performance, and reducing possible litigation if issues mentioned in the _____ are addressed. It is important for each organization to customize its own _____ in order to maintain the highest levels of survey validity and reliability.

Exam Probability: **Medium**

23. *Answer choices:*
(see index for correct answer)

- a. Situation, Task, Action, Result

- b. Microsoft interview
- c. Informational interview
- d. Mock interview

Guidance: level 1

:: Socialism ::

In sociology, _____ is the process of internalizing the norms and ideologies of society. _____ encompasses both learning and teaching and is thus "the means by which social and cultural continuity are attained".

Exam Probability: **High**

24. *Answer choices:*
(see index for correct answer)

- a. Socialization
- b. Radical Society
- c. State socialism
- d. Lassallism

Guidance: level 1

:: ::

_____ is the formal act of giving up or quitting one's office or position. A _____ can occur when a person holding a position gained by election or appointment steps down, but leaving a position upon the expiration of a term, or choosing not to seek an additional term, is not considered _____.

Exam Probability: **Medium**

25. *Answer choices:*
(see index for correct answer)

- a. Resignation
- b. empathy
- c. interpersonal communication
- d. hierarchical perspective

Guidance: level 1

:: Business planning ::

_____ is an organization's process of defining its strategy, or direction, and making decisions on allocating its resources to pursue this strategy. It may also extend to control mechanisms for guiding the implementation of the strategy. _____ became prominent in corporations during the 1960s and remains an important aspect of strategic management. It is executed by strategic planners or strategists, who involve many parties and research sources in their analysis of the organization and its relationship to the environment in which it competes.

Exam Probability: **High**

26. *Answer choices:*
(see index for correct answer)

- a. operational planning
- b. Strategic planning
- c. Gap analysis
- d. Business war games

Guidance: level 1

:: Survey methodology ::

_____ is often used to assess thoughts, opinions, and feelings. Surveys can be specific and limited, or they can have more global, widespread goals. Psychologists and sociologists often use surveys to analyze behavior, while it is also used to meet the more pragmatic needs of the media, such as, in evaluating political candidates, public health officials, professional organizations, and advertising and marketing directors. A survey consists of a predetermined set of questions that is given to a sample. With a representative sample, that is, one that is representative of the larger population of interest, one can describe the attitudes of the population from which the sample was drawn. Further, one can compare the attitudes of different populations as well as look for changes in attitudes over time. A good sample selection is key as it allows one to generalize the findings from the sample to the population, which is the whole purpose of _____ .

Exam Probability: **High**

27. *Answer choices:*
(see index for correct answer)

- a. Self-report study
- b. World Association for Public Opinion Research
- c. Survey research
- d. American Association for Public Opinion Research

Guidance: level 1

:: ::

_____ is the stock of habits, knowledge, social and personality attributes embodied in the ability to perform labor so as to produce economic value.

Exam Probability: **Low**

28. *Answer choices:*
(see index for correct answer)

- a. open system
- b. corporate values
- c. empathy
- d. Human capital

Guidance: level 1

:: Employee relations ::

The _____ can be used to bring together employment and job-related information which employees need to know. It typically has three types of content.

Exam Probability: **High**

29. *Answer choices:*
(see index for correct answer)

- a. Employee engagement
- b. Industry Federation of the State of Rio de Janeiro
- c. Employee stock
- d. Fringe benefit

Guidance: level 1

:: ::

_____ is a belief that hard work and diligence have a moral benefit and an inherent ability, virtue or value to strengthen character and individual abilities. It is a set of values centered on importance of work and manifested by determination or desire to work hard. Social ingrainment of this value is considered to enhance character through hard work that is respective to an individual's field of work.

Exam Probability: **High**

30. *Answer choices:*

(see index for correct answer)

- a. similarity-attraction theory
- b. Work ethic
- c. cultural
- d. co-culture

Guidance: level 1

:: Trade union legislation ::

The _____ of 1935 is a foundational statute of United States labor law which guarantees the right of private sector employees to organize into trade unions, engage in collective bargaining, and take collective action such as strikes. The act was written by Senator Robert F. Wagner, passed by the 74th United States Congress, and signed into law by President Franklin D. Roosevelt.

Exam Probability: **High**

31. *Answer choices:*

(see index for correct answer)

- a. National Labor Relations Act
- b. Labor Management Relations Act
- c. Employment Act 1980
- d. Employee Free Choice Act

Guidance: level 1

:: Business ethics ::

_____ is a persistent pattern of mistreatment from others in the workplace that causes either physical or emotional harm. It can include such tactics as verbal, nonverbal, psychological, physical abuse and humiliation. This type of workplace aggression is particularly difficult because, unlike the typical school bully, workplace bullies often operate within the established rules and policies of their organization and their society. In the majority of cases, bullying in the workplace is reported as having been by someone who has authority over their victim. However, bullies can also be peers, and occasionally subordinates. Research has also investigated the impact of the larger organizational context on bullying as well as the group-level processes that impact on the incidence and maintenance of bullying behaviour. Bullying can be covert or overt. It may be missed by superiors; it may be known by many throughout the organization. Negative effects are not limited to the targeted individuals, and may lead to a decline in employee morale and a change in organizational culture. It can also take place as overbearing supervision, constant criticism, and blocking promotions.

Exam Probability: **Medium**

32. *Answer choices:*
(see index for correct answer)

- a. Unfree labour
- b. Workplace bullying
- c. Repugnant market
- d. Surface Transportation Assistance Act

Guidance: level 1

:: Project management ::

_____ is a name for various theories of human motivation built on Douglas McGregor's Theory X and Theory Y. Theories X, Y and various versions of Z have been used in human resource management, organizational behavior, organizational communication and organizational development.

Exam Probability: **High**

33. *Answer choices:*
(see index for correct answer)

- a. Multidisciplinary approach
- b. Theory Z

- c. Site survey
- d. Transport Initiatives Edinburgh

Guidance: level 1

:: Problem solving ::

In other words, _____ is a situation where a group of people meet to generate new ideas and solutions around a specific domain of interest by removing inhibitions. People are able to think more freely and they suggest as many spontaneous new ideas as possible. All the ideas are noted down and those ideas are not criticized and after _____ session the ideas are evaluated. The term was popularized by Alex Faickney Osborn in the 1953 book Applied Imagination.

Exam Probability: **High**

34. *Answer choices:*
(see index for correct answer)

- a. Rhetorical reason
- b. Convergent thinking
- c. How to Solve It
- d. Thinking outside the box

Guidance: level 1

:: Social psychology ::

_____ is a type of nonverbal communication in which physical behaviors, as opposed to words, are used to express or convey information. Such behavior includes facial expressions, body posture, gestures, eye movement, touch and the use of space. _____ exists in both animals and humans, but this article focuses on interpretations of human _____. It is also known as kinesics.

Exam Probability: **Low**

35. *Answer choices:*
(see index for correct answer)

- a. indoctrination
- b. Body language
- c. co-optation

- d. Production blocking

Guidance: level 1

:: Workplace ::

_____ is a systematic determination of a subject's merit, worth and significance, using criteria governed by a set of standards. It can assist an organization, program, design, project or any other intervention or initiative to assess any aim, realisable concept/proposal, or any alternative, to help in decision-making; or to ascertain the degree of achievement or value in regard to the aim and objectives and results of any such action that has been completed. The primary purpose of _____, in addition to gaining insight into prior or existing initiatives, is to enable reflection and assist in the identification of future change.

Exam Probability: **Low**

36. *Answer choices:*
(see index for correct answer)

- a. Workplace friendship
- b. Performance appraisal
- c. Evaluation
- d. Queen bee syndrome

Guidance: level 1

:: Employment compensation ::

In government contracting, a _____ is defined as the hourly wage, usual benefits and overtime, paid to the majority of workers, laborers, and mechanics within a particular area. This is usually the union wage.

Exam Probability: **Medium**

37. *Answer choices:*
(see index for correct answer)

- a. Compensation of employees
- b. Prevailing wage
- c. Flexible spending account
- d. Federal Wage System

Guidance: level 1

:: Corporate governance ::

An _____ is generally a person responsible for running an organization, although the exact nature of the role varies depending on the organization. In many militaries, an _____ , or "XO," is the second-in-command, reporting to the commanding officer. The XO is typically responsible for the management of day-to-day activities, freeing the commander to concentrate on strategy and planning the unit's next move.

Exam Probability: **Medium**

38. *Answer choices:*

(see index for correct answer)

- a. Directors and officers liability insurance
- b. Corporate security
- c. Executive officer
- d. Development director

Guidance: level 1

:: Trade unions in the United States ::

The _____ is an American labor union representing over 670,000 employees of the federal government, about 5,000 employees of the District of Columbia, and a few hundred private sector employees, mostly in and around federal facilities. AFGE is the largest union for civilian, non-postal federal employees and the largest union for District of Columbia employees who report directly to the mayor. It is affiliated with the AFL-CIO.

Exam Probability: **Low**

39. *Answer choices:*

(see index for correct answer)

- a. Coalition of Black Trade Unionists
- b. Coalition of Graduate Employee Unions
- c. American Federation of Government Employees
- d. American Federation of School Administrators

Guidance: level 1

:: Television terminology ::

Distance education or long-_____ is the education of students who may not always be physically present at a school. Traditionally, this usually involved correspondence courses wherein the student corresponded with the school via post. Today it involves online education. Courses that are conducted are either hybrid, blended or 100% _____ . Massive open online courses , offering large-scale interactive participation and open access through the World Wide Web or other network technologies, are recent developments in distance education. A number of other terms are used roughly synonymously with distance education.

Exam Probability: **Low**

40. *Answer choices:*

(see index for correct answer)

- a. nonprofit
- b. multiplexing
- c. Satellite television
- d. Distance learning

Guidance: level 1

:: Trade unions in the United States ::

_____ is a labor union in the United States and Canada with roughly 300,000 active members. The union's members work predominantly in the hotel, food service, laundry, warehouse, and casino gaming industries. The union was formed in 2004 by the merger of Union of Needletrades, Industrial, and Textile Employees and Hotel Employees and Restaurant Employees Union .

Exam Probability: **Low**

41. *Answer choices:*

(see index for correct answer)

- a. Washington State Nurses Association
- b. Professional Air Traffic Controllers Organization
- c. Oregon Education Association
- d. UNITE HERE

Guidance: level 1

:: Social psychology ::

In social psychology, _____ is the phenomenon of a person exerting less effort to achieve a goal when he or she works in a group than when working alone. This is seen as one of the main reasons groups are sometimes less productive than the combined performance of their members working as individuals, but should be distinguished from the accidental coordination problems that groups sometimes experience.

Exam Probability: **High**

42. *Answer choices:*
(see index for correct answer)

- a. Psychographic
- b. post-feminism
- c. Social loafing
- d. acculturation

Guidance: level 1

:: ::

The _____ or labour force is the labour pool in employment. It is generally used to describe those working for a single company or industry, but can also apply to a geographic region like a city, state, or country. Within a company, its value can be labelled as its " _____ in Place". The _____ of a country includes both the employed and the unemployed. The labour force participation rate, LFPR, is the ratio between the labour force and the overall size of their cohort. The term generally excludes the employers or management, and can imply those involved in manual labour. It may also mean all those who are available for work.

Exam Probability: **Medium**

43. *Answer choices:*
(see index for correct answer)

- a. Workforce
- b. Sarbanes-Oxley act of 2002
- c. personal values
- d. hierarchical

Guidance: level 1

:: Occupational safety and health organizations ::

The _____ is the United States federal agency responsible for conducting research and making recommendations for the prevention of work-related injury and illness. NIOSH is part of the Centers for Disease Control and Prevention within the U.S. Department of Health and Human Services.

Exam Probability: **Low**

44. *Answer choices:*

(see index for correct answer)

- a. Oregon Occupational Safety and Health Division
- b. Health and Safety Authority
- c. British Occupational Hygiene Society
- d. National Institute for Occupational Safety and Health

Guidance: level 1

:: Grounds for termination of employment ::

_____ is a habitual pattern of absence from a duty or obligation without good reason. Generally, _____ is unplanned absences. _____ has been viewed as an indicator of poor individual performance, as well as a breach of an implicit contract between employee and employer. It is seen as a management problem, and framed in economic or quasi-economic terms. More recent scholarship seeks to understand _____ as an indicator of psychological, medical, or social adjustment to work.

Exam Probability: **Medium**

45. *Answer choices:*

(see index for correct answer)

- a. Department of Defense Whistleblower Program
- b. Sleeping while on duty
- c. Defense Intelligence Community Whistleblower Protection
- d. Huffman v. Office of Personnel Management

Guidance: level 1

:: Design of experiments ::

In the design of experiments, treatments are applied to experimental units in the treatment group. In comparative experiments, members of the complementary group, the _____, receive either no treatment or a standard treatment.

Exam Probability: **Low**

46. *Answer choices:*
(see index for correct answer)

- a. Vaccine trial
- b. Difference in differences
- c. Fisher information
- d. Control group

Guidance: level 1

:: Human resource management ::

_____ is a continual process used to align the needs and priorities of the organization with those of its workforce to ensure it can meet its legislative, regulatory, service and production requirements and organizational objectives. _____ enables evidence based workforce development strategies.

Exam Probability: **Medium**

47. *Answer choices:*
(see index for correct answer)

- a. Employee silence
- b. Workforce planning
- c. Human relations movement
- d. Open plan

Guidance: level 1

:: Human resource management ::

_____ is the application of information technology for both networking and supporting at least two individual or collective actors in their shared performing of HR activities.

Exam Probability: **Low**

48. *Answer choices:*

(see index for correct answer)

- a. Organizational behavior and human resources
- b. E-HRM
- c. Workforce management
- d. Employee retention

Guidance: level 1

:: Business ethics ::

_____ is a pejorative term for a workplace that has very poor, socially unacceptable working conditions. The work may be difficult, dangerous, climatically challenged or underpaid. Workers in _____ s may work long hours with low pay, regardless of laws mandating overtime pay or a minimum wage; child labor laws may also be violated. The Fair Labor Association's "2006 Annual Public Report" inspected factories for FLA compliance in 18 countries including Bangladesh, El Salvador, Colombia, Guatemala, Malaysia, Thailand, Tunisia, Turkey, China, India, Vietnam, Honduras, Indonesia, Brazil, Mexico, and the US. The U.S. Department of Labor's "2015 Findings on the Worst Forms of Child Labor" found that "18 countries did not meet the International Labour Organization's recommendation for an adequate number of inspectors."

Exam Probability: **Low**

49. *Answer choices:*

(see index for correct answer)

- a. Business and Professional Ethics Journal
- b. Integrity management
- c. Precarity
- d. Financial privacy

Guidance: level 1

:: United States federal labor legislation ::

The _____ of 1967 is a US labor law that forbids employment discrimination against anyone at least 40 years of age in the United States. In 1967, the bill was signed into law by President Lyndon B. Johnson. The ADEA prevents age discrimination and provides equal employment opportunity under conditions that were not explicitly covered in Title VII of the Civil Rights Act of 1964. It also applies to the standards for pensions and benefits provided by employers, and requires that information concerning the needs of older workers be provided to the general public.

Exam Probability: **High**

50. *Answer choices:*
(see index for correct answer)

- a. Age Discrimination in Employment Act
- b. Workforce Investment Act of 1998
- c. Federal Emergency Relief Administration
- d. Landrum-Griffin Act

Guidance: level 1

:: ::

A trade union is an association of workers forming a legal unit or legal personhood, usually called a "bargaining unit", which acts as bargaining agent and legal representative for a unit of employees in all matters of law or right arising from or in the administration of a collective agreement. Labour unions typically fund the formal organisation, head office, and legal team functions of the labour union through regular fees or union dues. The delegate staff of the labour union representation in the workforce are made up of workplace volunteers who are appointed by members in democratic elections.

Exam Probability: **Medium**

51. *Answer choices:*
(see index for correct answer)

- a. empathy
- b. cultural
- c. personal values
- d. levels of analysis

Guidance: level 1

:: ::

In organizational behavior and industrial/organizational psychology, proactivity or _____ behavior by individuals refers to anticipatory, change-oriented and self-initiated behavior in situations. _____ behavior involves acting in advance of a future situation, rather than just reacting. It means taking control and making things happen rather than just adjusting to a situation or waiting for something to happen. _____ employees generally do not need to be asked to act, nor do they require detailed instructions.

Exam Probability: **Low**

52. *Answer choices:*

(see index for correct answer)

- a. empathy
- b. Sarbanes-Oxley act of 2002
- c. cultural
- d. Proactive

Guidance: level 1

:: Validity (statistics) ::

In psychometrics, _____ is the extent to which a score on a scale or test predicts scores on some criterion measure.

Exam Probability: **Medium**

53. *Answer choices:*

(see index for correct answer)

- a. Predictive validity
- b. Verification and validation
- c. Ecological validity
- d. Incremental validity

Guidance: level 1

:: Termination of employment ::

The _____ of 1988 is a US labor law which protects employees, their families, and communities by requiring most employers with 100 or more employees to provide 60 calendar-day advance notification of plant closings and mass layoffs of employees, as defined in the Act. In 2001, there were about 2,000 mass layoffs and plant closures which were subject to WARN advance notice requirements and which affected about 660,000 employees.

Exam Probability: **Medium**

54. *Answer choices:*
(see index for correct answer)

- a. Worker Adjustment and Retraining Notification Act
- b. Letter of resignation
- c. Notice period
- d. Enforced retirement

Guidance: level 1

:: Management ::

_____ is a technique used by some employers to rotate their employees' assigned jobs throughout their employment. Employers practice this technique for a number of reasons. It was designed to promote flexibility of employees and to keep employees interested into staying with the company/organization which employs them. There is also research that shows how _____s help relieve the stress of employees who work in a job that requires manual labor.

Exam Probability: **Medium**

55. *Answer choices:*
(see index for correct answer)

- a. Target culture
- b. Work breakdown structure
- c. Tacit knowledge
- d. Job rotation

Guidance: level 1

:: Psychometrics ::

A _____ is a set of categories designed to elicit information about a quantitative or a qualitative attribute. In the social sciences, particularly psychology, common examples are the Likert response scale and 1-10 _____ s in which a person selects the number which is considered to reflect the perceived quality of a product.

Exam Probability: **High**

56. *Answer choices:*

(see index for correct answer)

- a. Rating scale
- b. Anchor test
- c. Situational judgement test
- d. Pairwise comparison

Guidance: level 1

:: Validity (statistics) ::

In psychometrics, criterion or concrete validity is the extent to which a measure is related to an outcome. _____ is often divided into concurrent and predictive validity. Concurrent validity refers to a comparison between the measure in question and an outcome assessed at the same time. In Standards for Educational & Psychological Tests, it states, "concurrent validity reflects only the status quo at a particular time." Predictive validity, on the other hand, compares the measure in question with an outcome assessed at a later time. Although concurrent and predictive validity are similar, it is cautioned to keep the terms and findings separated. "Concurrent validity should not be used as a substitute for predictive validity without an appropriate supporting rationale."

Exam Probability: **Medium**

57. *Answer choices:*

(see index for correct answer)

- a. Construct validity
- b. Verification and validation
- c. Face validity
- d. Criterion validity

Guidance: level 1

:: United Kingdom labour law ::

The _____ was a series of programs, public work projects, financial reforms, and regulations enacted by President Franklin D. Roosevelt in the United States between 1933 and 1936. It responded to needs for relief, reform, and recovery from the Great Depression. Major federal programs included the Civilian Conservation Corps , the Civil Works Administration , the Farm Security Administration , the National Industrial Recovery Act of 1933 and the Social Security Administration . They provided support for farmers, the unemployed, youth and the elderly. The _____ included new constraints and safeguards on the banking industry and efforts to re-inflate the economy after prices had fallen sharply. _____ programs included both laws passed by Congress as well as presidential executive orders during the first term of the presidency of Franklin D. Roosevelt.

Exam Probability: **High**

58. *Answer choices:*

(see index for correct answer)

- a. Labour Exchanges Act 1909
- b. Paternity and Adoption Leave Regulations 2002
- c. Employment Rights Act 1996
- d. Common employment

Guidance: level 1

:: Occupational safety and health ::

A safety data sheet , _____ , or product safety data sheet is a document that lists information relating to occupational safety and health for the use of various substances and products. SDSs are a widely used system for cataloging information on chemicals, chemical compounds, and chemical mixtures. SDS information may include instructions for the safe use and potential hazards associated with a particular material or product, along with spill-handling procedures. SDS formats can vary from source to source within a country depending on national requirements.

Exam Probability: **Low**

59. *Answer choices:*

(see index for correct answer)

- a. Balsam of Peru
- b. Occupational hygiene
- c. Alice Hamilton
- d. Robert A. Kehoe

Guidance: level 1

Information systems

Information systems (IS) are formal, sociotechnical, organizational systems designed to collect, process, store, and distribute information. In a sociotechnical perspective Information Systems are composed by four components: technology, process, people and organizational structure.

:: Data management ::

_____ represents the business objects that contain the most valuable, agreed upon information shared across an organization. It can cover relatively static reference data, transactional, unstructured, analytical, hierarchical and metadata. It is the primary focus of the information technology discipline of _____ management.

Exam Probability: **Medium**

1. *Answer choices:*
(see index for correct answer)

- a. ADO.NET
- b. Parchive
- c. Master data
- d. Data warehouse

Guidance: level 1

:: Data management ::

_____, or IG, is the management of information at an organization. _____ balances the use and security of information. _____ helps with legal compliance, operational transparency, and reducing expenditures associated with legal discovery. An organization can establish a consistent and logical framework for employees to handle data through their _____ policies and procedures. These policies guide proper behavior regarding how organizations and their employees handle electronically stored information .

Exam Probability: **High**

2. *Answer choices:*
(see index for correct answer)

- a. ISO/IEC JTC 1/SC 32
- b. Asset Description Metadata Schema
- c. Information governance
- d. Geospatial metadata

Guidance: level 1

:: Business models ::

_____, or The Computer Utility, is a service provisioning model in which a service provider makes computing resources and infrastructure management available to the customer as needed, and charges them for specific usage rather than a flat rate. Like other types of on-demand computing , the utility model seeks to maximize the efficient use of resources and/or minimize associated costs. Utility is the packaging of system resources, such as computation, storage and services, as a metered service. This model has the advantage of a low or no initial cost to acquire computer resources; instead, resources are essentially rented.

Exam Probability: **Medium**

3. *Answer choices:*
(see index for correct answer)

- a. Utility computing
- b. Interactive contract manufacturing
- c. Dependent growth business model
- d. European Cooperative Society

Guidance: level 1

:: Data analysis ::

_____, also referred to as text data mining, roughly equivalent to text analytics, is the process of deriving high-quality information from text. High-quality information is typically derived through the devising of patterns and trends through means such as statistical pattern learning. _____ usually involves the process of structuring the input text, deriving patterns within the structured data, and finally evaluation and interpretation of the output. 'High quality' in _____ usually refers to some combination of relevance, novelty, and interest. Typical _____ tasks include text categorization, text clustering, concept/entity extraction, production of granular taxonomies, sentiment analysis, document summarization, and entity relation modeling .

Exam Probability: **Medium**

4. *Answer choices:*
(see index for correct answer)

- a. Text mining
- b. Limited dependent variable
- c. Overdispersion
- d. Neighbourhood components analysis

Guidance: level 1

:: ::

_____ is a free email service developed by Google. Users can access _____ on the web and using third-party programs that synchronize email content through POP or IMAP protocols. _____ started as a limited beta release on April 1, 2004 and ended its testing phase on July 7, 2009.

Exam Probability: **Low**

5. *Answer choices:*
(see index for correct answer)

- a. hierarchical perspective
- b. cultural
- c. functional perspective
- d. Gmail

Guidance: level 1

:: Information technology management ::

The term _____ is used to refer to periods when a system is unavailable. _____ or outage duration refers to a period of time that a system fails to provide or perform its primary function. Reliability, availability, recovery, and unavailability are related concepts. The unavailability is the proportion of a time-span that a system is unavailable or offline. This is usually a result of the system failing to function because of an unplanned event, or because of routine maintenance .

Exam Probability: **Low**

6. *Answer choices:*
(see index for correct answer)

- a. Service Measurement Index
- b. Data warehouse appliance
- c. Downtime
- d. Skills Framework for the Information Age

Guidance: level 1

:: Industrial design ::

Across the many fields concerned with _____ , including information science, computer science, human-computer interaction, communication, and industrial design, there is little agreement over the meaning of the term " _____ ", although all are related to interaction with computers and other machines with a user interface.

Exam Probability: **Medium**

7. *Answer choices:*
(see index for correct answer)

- a. Oxide jacking
- b. Skeuomorph
- c. Interactivity
- d. 3D printing

Guidance: level 1

:: ::

_____ is the fundamental facilities and systems serving a country, city, or other area, including the services and facilities necessary for its economy to function. _____ is composed of public and private physical improvements such as roads, bridges, tunnels, water supply, sewers, electrical grids, and telecommunications . In general, it has also been defined as "the physical components of interrelated systems providing commodities and services essential to enable, sustain, or enhance societal living conditions".

Exam Probability: **Low**

8. *Answer choices:*

(see index for correct answer)

- a. Infrastructure
- b. deep-level diversity
- c. surface-level diversity
- d. similarity-attraction theory

Guidance: level 1

:: E-commerce ::

_____ is a method of e-commerce where shoppers' friends become involved in the shopping experience. _____ attempts to use technology to mimic the social interactions found in physical malls and stores. With the rise of mobile devices, _____ is now extending beyond the online world and into the offline world of shopping.

Exam Probability: **Medium**

9. *Answer choices:*

(see index for correct answer)

- a. Social shopping
- b. ProStores
- c. WePay
- d. Loquo

Guidance: level 1

:: Management ::

_____ is the discipline of strategically planning for, and managing, all interactions with third party organizations that supply goods and/or services to an organization in order to maximize the value of those interactions. In practice, SRM entails creating closer, more collaborative relationships with key suppliers in order to uncover and realize new value and reduce risk of failure.

Exam Probability: **Low**

10. *Answer choices:*

(see index for correct answer)

- a. Social risk management
- b. Managerial economics
- c. Six phases of a big project
- d. Supplier relationship management

Guidance: level 1

:: Data transmission ::

In telecommunication a _____ is the means of connecting one location to another for the purpose of transmitting and receiving digital information. It can also refer to a set of electronics assemblies, consisting of a transmitter and a receiver and the interconnecting data telecommunication circuit. These are governed by a link protocol enabling digital data to be transferred from a data source to a data sink.

Exam Probability: **Medium**

11. *Answer choices:*

(see index for correct answer)

- a. Channel Division Multiple Access
- b. Control operation
- c. Data link
- d. Track warrant

Guidance: level 1

:: Ergonomics ::

_____ is the design of products, devices, services, or environments for people with disabilities. The concept of accessible design and practice of accessible development ensures both "direct access" and "indirect access" meaning compatibility with a person's assistive technology.

Exam Probability: **Medium**

12. *Answer choices:*
(see index for correct answer)

- a. Accessibility
- b. Saddle chair
- c. Redshift
- d. Alain Wisner

Guidance: level 1

:: Computing output devices ::

An _____ is any piece of computer hardware equipment which converts information into human-readable form.

Exam Probability: **Low**

13. *Answer choices:*
(see index for correct answer)

- a. LongPen
- b. Indexed color
- c. Output device
- d. GammaFax

Guidance: level 1

:: Finance ::

_____ is a financial estimate intended to help buyers and owners determine the direct and indirect costs of a product or system. It is a management accounting concept that can be used in full cost accounting or even ecological economics where it includes social costs.

Exam Probability: **High**

14. *Answer choices:*

(see index for correct answer)

- a. Wrap account
- b. Pet banks
- c. Total cost of ownership
- d. Property income

Guidance: level 1

:: ::

The _____ , commonly known as the Web, is an information system where documents and other web resources are identified by Uniform Resource Locators, which may be interlinked by hypertext, and are accessible over the Internet.
The resources of the WWW may be accessed by users by a software application called a web browser.

Exam Probability: **High**

15. *Answer choices:*

(see index for correct answer)

- a. imperative
- b. deep-level diversity
- c. World Wide Web
- d. hierarchical

Guidance: level 1

:: Content management systems ::

_____ is the textual, visual, or aural content that is encountered as part of the user experience on websites. It may include—among other things—text, images, sounds, videos, and animations.

Exam Probability: **High**

16. *Answer choices:*

(see index for correct answer)

- a. IDSlot
- b. Infotollgate
- c. Enprovia
- d. Web content

Guidance: level 1

:: Big data ::

_____ is the discovery, interpretation, and communication of meaningful patterns in data; and the process of applying those patterns towards effective decision making. In other words, _____ can be understood as the connective tissue between data and effective decision making, within an organization. Especially valuable in areas rich with recorded information, _____ relies on the simultaneous application of statistics, computer programming and operations research to quantify performance.

Exam Probability: **Low**

17. *Answer choices:*
(see index for correct answer)

- a. Datameer
- b. Virtuoso Universal Server
- c. Medio
- d. Sogamo

Guidance: level 1

:: Information technology ::

_____ is the reorientation of product and service designs to focus on the end user as an individual consumer, in contrast with an earlier era of only organization-oriented offerings . Technologies whose first commercialization was at the inter-organization level thus have potential for later _____ . The emergence of the individual consumer as the primary driver of product and service design is most commonly associated with the IT industry, as large business and government organizations dominated the early decades of computer usage and development. Thus the microcomputer revolution, in which electronic computing moved from exclusively enterprise and government use to include personal computing, is a cardinal example of _____ . But many technology-based products, such as calculators and mobile phones, have also had their origins in business markets, and only over time did they become dominated by high-volume consumer usage, as these products commoditized and prices fell. An example of enterprise software that became consumer software is optical character recognition software, which originated with banks and postal systems but eventually became personal productivity software.

Exam Probability: **High**

18. *Answer choices:*
(see index for correct answer)

- a. Local Government ICT Network
- b. Consumerization
- c. Technological convergence
- d. Levi, Ray %26 Shoup

Guidance: level 1

:: User interfaces ::

The _____ , in the industrial design field of human–computer interaction, is the space where interactions between humans and machines occur. The goal of this interaction is to allow effective operation and control of the machine from the human end, whilst the machine simultaneously feeds back information that aids the operators` decision-making process. Examples of this broad concept of _____ s include the interactive aspects of computer operating systems, hand tools, heavy machinery operator controls, and process controls. The design considerations applicable when creating _____ s are related to or involve such disciplines as ergonomics and psychology.

Exam Probability: **Medium**

19. *Answer choices:*
(see index for correct answer)

- a. Archy
- b. Ludic interface
- c. Display device
- d. Dasher

Guidance: level 1

:: Computer data ::

In computer science, _____ is the ability to access an arbitrary element of a sequence in equal time or any datum from a population of addressable elements roughly as easily and efficiently as any other, no matter how many elements may be in the set. It is typically contrasted to sequential access.

Exam Probability: **Medium**

20. *Answer choices:*
(see index for correct answer)

- a. Seed loading
- b. Hex editor
- c. Random access
- d. Termcap

Guidance: level 1

:: ::

A _____ is a knowledge base website on which users collaboratively modify content and structure directly from the web browser. In a typical _____, text is written using a simplified markup language and often edited with the help of a rich-text editor.

Exam Probability: **Low**

21. *Answer choices:*
(see index for correct answer)

- a. corporate values
- b. open system

- c. hierarchical perspective
- d. co-culture

Guidance: level 1

:: Market structure and pricing ::

_____ is a term denoting that a product includes permission to use its source code, design documents, or content. It most commonly refers to the open-source model, in which open-source software or other products are released under an open-source license as part of the open-source-software movement. Use of the term originated with software, but has expanded beyond the software sector to cover other open content and forms of open collaboration.

Exam Probability: **Medium**

22. *Answer choices:*
(see index for correct answer)

- a. Market structure
- b. Installed base
- c. industry concentration
- d. Open-source economics

Guidance: level 1

:: Reputation management ::

A _____ is an astronomical object consisting of a luminous spheroid of plasma held together by its own gravity. The nearest _____ to Earth is the Sun. Many other _____ s are visible to the naked eye from Earth during the night, appearing as a multitude of fixed luminous points in the sky due to their immense distance from Earth. Historically, the most prominent _____ s were grouped into constellations and asterisms, the brightest of which gained proper names. Astronomers have assembled _____ catalogues that identify the known _____ s and provide standardized stellar designations. However, most of the estimated 300 sextillion _____ s in the Universe are invisible to the naked eye from Earth, including all _____ s outside our galaxy, the Milky Way.

Exam Probability: **Medium**

23. *Answer choices:*

(see index for correct answer)

- a. Moderation system
- b. personal brand
- c. Distrust
- d. Star

Guidance: level 1

:: Online companies ::

_____ is a business directory service and crowd-sourced review forum, and a public company of the same name that is headquartered in San Francisco, California. The company develops, hosts and markets the _____.com website and the _____ mobile app, which publish crowd-sourced reviews about businesses. It also operates an online reservation service called _____ Reservations.

Exam Probability: **Low**

24. *Answer choices:*
(see index for correct answer)

- a. The Californian Ideology
- b. Ananova
- c. Mashape
- d. Kitbag

Guidance: level 1

:: Information systems ::

_____ is a process used in the life cycle area of the dynamic systems development method to collect business requirements while developing new information systems for a company. "The JAD process also includes approaches for enhancing user participation, expediting development, and improving the quality of specifications." It consists of a workshop where "knowledge workers and IT specialists meet, sometimes for several days, to define and review the business requirements for the system." The attendees include high level management officials who will ensure the product provides the needed reports and information at the end. This acts as "a management process which allows Corporate Information Services departments to work more effectively with users in a shorter time frame".

Exam Probability: **Low**

25. *Answer choices:*
(see index for correct answer)

- a. Expert system
- b. Joint application design
- c. LabLynx, Inc.
- d. Virtual USA

Guidance: level 1

:: Internet marketing ::

_____ is the measurement, collection, analysis and reporting of web data for purposes of understanding and optimizing web usage. However, _____ is not just a process for measuring web traffic but can be used as a tool for business and market research, and to assess and improve the effectiveness of a website. _____ applications can also help companies measure the results of traditional print or broadcast advertising campaigns. It helps one to estimate how traffic to a website changes after the launch of a new advertising campaign. _____ provides information about the number of visitors to a website and the number of page views. It helps gauge traffic and popularity trends which is useful for market research.

Exam Probability: **Low**

26. *Answer choices:*
(see index for correct answer)

- a. Keyword Services Platform
- b. Email remarketing
- c. Quality Score
- d. Avinash Kaushik

Guidance: level 1

:: ::

A _____ or data centre is a building, dedicated space within a building, or a group of buildings used to house computer systems and associated components, such as telecommunications and storage systems.

Exam Probability: **High**

27. *Answer choices:*

(see index for correct answer)

- a. empathy
- b. Data center
- c. levels of analysis
- d. interpersonal communication

Guidance: level 1

:: Credit cards ::

A _____ is a payment card issued to users to enable the cardholder to pay a merchant for goods and services based on the cardholder's promise to the card issuer to pay them for the amounts plus the other agreed charges. The card issuer creates a revolving account and grants a line of credit to the cardholder, from which the cardholder can borrow money for payment to a merchant or as a cash advance.

Exam Probability: **High**

28. *Answer choices:*

(see index for correct answer)

- a. CardLab
- b. Credit card
- c. Diners Club International
- d. Palladium Card

Guidance: level 1

:: Intelligence (information gathering) ::

_____ comprises the strategies and technologies used by enterprises for the data analysis of business information. BI technologies provide historical, current and predictive views of business operations. Common functions of _____ technologies include reporting, online analytical processing, analytics, data mining, process mining, complex event processing, business performance management, benchmarking, text mining, predictive analytics and prescriptive analytics. BI technologies can handle large amounts of structured and sometimes unstructured data to help identify, develop and otherwise create new strategic business opportunities. They aim to allow for the easy interpretation of these big data. Identifying new opportunities and implementing an effective strategy based on insights can provide businesses with a competitive market advantage and long-term stability.

Exam Probability: **Low**

29. *Answer choices:*
(see index for correct answer)

- a. Intelligence requirement
- b. Social media intelligence
- c. Technical intelligence
- d. Signals intelligence

Guidance: level 1

:: ::

The _____ is the global system of interconnected computer networks that use the _____ protocol suite to link devices worldwide. It is a network of networks that consists of private, public, academic, business, and government networks of local to global scope, linked by a broad array of electronic, wireless, and optical networking technologies. The _____ carries a vast range of information resources and services, such as the inter-linked hypertext documents and applications of the World Wide Web , electronic mail, telephony, and file sharing.

Exam Probability: **Low**

30. *Answer choices:*
(see index for correct answer)

- a. open system
- b. cultural

- c. similarity-attraction theory
- d. Internet

Guidance: level 1

:: Computer access control ::

_____ is the act of confirming the truth of an attribute of a single piece of data claimed true by an entity. In contrast with identification, which refers to the act of stating or otherwise indicating a claim purportedly attesting to a person or thing's identity, _____ is the process of actually confirming that identity. It might involve confirming the identity of a person by validating their identity documents, verifying the authenticity of a website with a digital certificate, determining the age of an artifact by carbon dating, or ensuring that a product is what its packaging and labeling claim to be. In other words, _____ often involves verifying the validity of at least one form of identification.

Exam Probability: **Medium**

31. *Answer choices:*
(see index for correct answer)

- a. Access Control Matrix
- b. Risk-based authentication
- c. OneLogin
- d. Numina Application Framework

Guidance: level 1

:: Data collection ::

_____ is the application of data mining techniques to discover patterns from the World Wide Web. As the name proposes, this is information gathered by mining the web. It makes utilization of automated apparatuses to reveal and extricate data from servers and web2 reports, and it permits organizations to get to both organized and unstructured information from browser activities, server logs, website and link structure, page content and different sources.

Exam Probability: **Medium**

32. *Answer choices:*
(see index for correct answer)

- a. Guardian
- b. Web mining
- c. Question
- d. Datalogix

Guidance: level 1

:: Database theory ::

A _____ is a digital database based on the relational model of data, as proposed by E. F. Codd in 1970. A software system used to maintain _____ s is a _____ management system. Virtually all _____ systems use SQL for querying and maintaining the database.

Exam Probability: **Medium**

33. *Answer choices:*

(see index for correct answer)

- a. Full table scan
- b. Canonical cover
- c. Relational database
- d. Conjunctive query

Guidance: level 1

:: E-commerce ::

The phrase _____ was originally coined in 1997 by Kevin Duffey at the launch of the Global _____ Forum, to mean "the delivery of electronic commerce capabilities directly into the consumer's hand, anywhere, via wireless technology." Many choose to think of _____ as meaning "a retail outlet in your customer's pocket."

Exam Probability: **High**

34. *Answer choices:*

(see index for correct answer)

- a. Switchwise
- b. Segundamano
- c. Online auction tools
- d. Mobile commerce

Guidance: level 1

:: Information science ::

The United States National Forum on _____ defines _____ as "... the hyper ability to know when there is a need for information, to be able to identify, locate, evaluate, and effectively use that information for the issue or problem at hand." The American Library Association defines " _____ " as a set of abilities requiring individuals to "recognize when information is needed and have the ability to locate, evaluate, and use effectively the needed information. Other definitions incorporate aspects of "skepticism, judgement, free thinking, questioning, and understanding..." or incorporate competencies that an informed citizen of an information society ought to possess to participate intelligently and actively in that society.

Exam Probability: **Low**

35. *Answer choices:*
(see index for correct answer)

- a. General formal ontology
- b. Library and Information Science Abstracts
- c. Information literacy
- d. Transliteracy

Guidance: level 1

:: Supply chain management terms ::

In business and finance, _____ is a system of organizations, people, activities, information, and resources involved in moving a product or service from supplier to customer. _____ activities involve the transformation of natural resources, raw materials, and components into a finished product that is delivered to the end customer. In sophisticated _____ systems, used products may re-enter the _____ at any point where residual value is recyclable. _____ s link value chains.

Exam Probability: **High**

36. *Answer choices:*
(see index for correct answer)

- a. Supply-chain management
- b. Will call
- c. Overstock
- d. Supply chain

Guidance: level 1

:: Information systems ::

_____ , Chief Digital Information Officer or Information Technology Director, is a job title commonly given to the most senior executive in an enterprise who works for the traditional information technology and computer systems that support enterprise goals.

Exam Probability: **Medium**

37. *Answer choices:*
(see index for correct answer)

- a. Sticky information
- b. Chief information officer
- c. Hospital information system
- d. Disparate system

Guidance: level 1

:: Data ::

In computer main memory, auxiliary storage and computer buses, _____ is the existence of data that is additional to the actual data and permits correction of errors in stored or transmitted data. The additional data can simply be a complete copy of the actual data, or only select pieces of data that allow detection of errors and reconstruction of lost or damaged data up to a certain level.

Exam Probability: **Medium**

38. *Answer choices:*
(see index for correct answer)

- a. One Source Networks
- b. Data redundancy
- c. Empress Embedded Database
- d. S-LINK

Guidance: level 1

:: Google services ::

_____ is a word processor included as part of a free, web-based software office suite offered by Google within its Google Drive service. This service also includes Google Sheets and Google Slides, a spreadsheet and presentation program respectively. _____ is available as a web application, mobile app for Android, iOS, Windows, BlackBerry, and as a desktop application on Google's ChromeOS. The app is compatible with Microsoft Office file formats.The application allows users to create and edit files online while collaborating with other users in real-time. Edits are tracked by user with a revision history presenting changes. An editor's position is highlighted with an editor-specific color and cursor. A permissions system regulates what users can do. Updates have introduced features using machine learning, including "Explore", offering search results based on the contents of a document, and "Action items", allowing users to assign tasks to other users.

Exam Probability: **Low**

39. *Answer choices:*
(see index for correct answer)

- a. Google Apps Marketplace
- b. Google Docs
- c. Google Grants
- d. Living stories

Guidance: level 1

:: Data management ::

In computing, a _____ , also known as an enterprise _____ , is a system used for reporting and data analysis, and is considered a core component of business intelligence. DWs are central repositories of integrated data from one or more disparate sources. They store current and historical data in one single place that are used for creating analytical reports for workers throughout the enterprise.

Exam Probability: **Medium**

40. *Answer choices:*
(see index for correct answer)

- a. ROOT
- b. Match report
- c. Content re-appropriation

- d. Data profiling

Guidance: level 1

:: Information retrieval ::

_____ is the practice of making content from multiple enterprise-type sources, such as databases and intranets, searchable to a defined audience.

Exam Probability: **Low**

41. *Answer choices:*
(see index for correct answer)

- a. Cosine similarity
- b. Enterprise search
- c. Collaborative search engine
- d. Globrix

Guidance: level 1

:: Global Positioning System ::

The _____, originally Navstar GPS, is a satellite-based radionavigation system owned by the United States government and operated by the United States Air Force. It is a global navigation satellite system that provides geolocation and time information to a GPS receiver anywhere on or near the Earth where there is an unobstructed line of sight to four or more GPS satellites. Obstacles such as mountains and buildings block the relatively weak GPS signals.

Exam Probability: **Medium**

42. *Answer choices:*
(see index for correct answer)

- a. Global Positioning System
- b. Defense Advanced GPS Receiver
- c. Undulation of the geoid
- d. Fleet telematics system

Guidance: level 1

:: Information technology organisations ::

The Internet Corporation for Assigned Names and Numbers is a nonprofit organization responsible for coordinating the maintenance and procedures of several databases related to the namespaces and numerical spaces of the Internet, ensuring the network's stable and secure operation. _____ performs the actual technical maintenance work of the Central Internet Address pools and DNS root zone registries pursuant to the Internet Assigned Numbers Authority function contract. The contract regarding the IANA stewardship functions between _____ and the National Telecommunications and Information Administration of the United States Department of Commerce ended on October 1, 2016, formally transitioning the functions to the global multistakeholder community.

Exam Probability: **High**

43. *Answer choices:*

(see index for correct answer)

- a. ICANN
- b. Institute of IT Training
- c. National Internet Exchange of India
- d. Information and Communications Technology Council

Guidance: level 1

:: Domain name system ::

_____, Inc. is an American company based in Reston, Virginia, United States that operates a diverse array of network infrastructure, including two of the Internet's thirteen root nameservers, the authoritative registry for the .com, .net, and .name generic top-level domains and the .cc and .tv country-code top-level domains, and the back-end systems for the .jobs, .gov, and .edu top-level domains. _____ also offers a range of security services, including managed DNS, distributed denial-of-service attack mitigation and cyber-threat reporting.

Exam Probability: **High**

44. *Answer choices:*

(see index for correct answer)

- a. Dynamic DNS
- b. Wildcard DNS record
- c. Internationalized country code top-level domain

- d. Verisign

Guidance: level 1

:: Commerce ::

_____, Inc. is an American media-services provider headquartered in Los Gatos, California, founded in 1997 by Reed Hastings and Marc Randolph in Scotts Valley, California. The company's primary business is its subscription-based streaming OTT service which offers online streaming of a library of films and television programs, including those produced in-house. As of April 2019, _____ had over 148 million paid subscriptions worldwide, including 60 million in the United States, and over 154 million subscriptions total including free trials. It is available almost worldwide except in mainland China as well as Syria, North Korea, and Crimea . The company also has offices in the Netherlands, Brazil, India, Japan, and South Korea. _____ is a member of the Motion Picture Association of America .

Exam Probability: **Low**

45. *Answer choices:*
(see index for correct answer)

- a. Non-commercial
- b. Commodity market
- c. Church sale
- d. Perfect tender rule

Guidance: level 1

:: ::

The _____ of 1996 was enacted by the 104th United States Congress and signed by President Bill Clinton in 1996. It was created primarily to modernize the flow of healthcare information, stipulate how Personally Identifiable Information maintained by the healthcare and healthcare insurance industries should be protected from fraud and theft, and address limitations on healthcare insurance coverage.

Exam Probability: **Medium**

46. *Answer choices:*
(see index for correct answer)

- a. Health Insurance Portability and Accountability Act
- b. process perspective
- c. personal values
- d. hierarchical

Guidance: level 1

:: Network management ::

_____ is the process of administering and managing computer networks. Services provided by this discipline include fault analysis, performance management, provisioning of networks and maintaining the quality of service. Software that enables network administrators to perform their functions is called _____ software.

Exam Probability: **Medium**

47. *Answer choices:*
(see index for correct answer)

- a. Fault management
- b. Object identifier
- c. NetCrunch
- d. Bipartite network projection

Guidance: level 1

:: ::

_____ are electronic transfer of money from one bank account to another, either within a single financial institution or across multiple institutions, via computer-based systems, without the direct intervention of bank staff.

Exam Probability: **High**

48. *Answer choices:*
(see index for correct answer)

- a. hierarchical perspective
- b. Sarbanes-Oxley act of 2002
- c. Electronic funds transfer
- d. interpersonal communication

Guidance: level 1

:: ::

A _____ is an organized collection of data, generally stored and accessed electronically from a computer system. Where _____ s are more complex they are often developed using formal design and modeling techniques.

Exam Probability: **Medium**

49. *Answer choices:*
(see index for correct answer)

- a. Database
- b. information systems assessment
- c. levels of analysis
- d. hierarchical perspective

Guidance: level 1

:: ::

_____ is software designed to provide a platform for other software. Examples of _____ include operating systems like macOS, Ubuntu and Microsoft Windows, computational science software, game engines, industrial automation, and software as a service applications.

Exam Probability: **Low**

50. *Answer choices:*
(see index for correct answer)

- a. System software
- b. levels of analysis
- c. interpersonal communication
- d. co-culture

Guidance: level 1

:: Management ::

A _____ defines or constrains some aspect of business and always resolves to either true or false. _____ s are intended to assert business structure or to control or influence the behavior of the business. _____ s describe the operations, definitions and constraints that apply to an organization. _____ s can apply to people, processes, corporate behavior and computing systems in an organization, and are put in place to help the organization achieve its goals.

Exam Probability: **Low**

51. *Answer choices:*
(see index for correct answer)

- a. Business rule
- b. Job rotation
- c. Power structure
- d. Failure demand

Guidance: level 1

:: Data management ::

Given organizations' increasing dependency on information technology to run their operations, Business continuity planning covers the entire organization, and Disaster recovery focuses on IT.

Exam Probability: **High**

52. *Answer choices:*
(see index for correct answer)

- a. Disaster recovery plan
- b. Linked data
- c. Conference on Innovative Data Systems Research
- d. Metadata controller

Guidance: level 1

:: Behavioral and social facets of systemic risk ::

_____ is the difficulty in understanding an issue and effectively making decisions when one has too much information about that issue. Generally, the term is associated with the excessive quantity of daily information.
_____ most likely originated from information theory, which are studies in the storage, preservation, communication, compression, and extraction of information. The term, _____ , was first used in Bertram Gross' 1964 book, The Managing of Organizations, and it was further popularized by Alvin Toffler in his bestselling 1970 book Future Shock. Speier et al. stated.

Exam Probability: **Low**

53. *Answer choices:*
(see index for correct answer)

- a. Tulip mania
- b. Connectionism
- c. Information overload
- d. Meme

Guidance: level 1

:: Big data ::

_____ refers to the skills, technologies, practices for continuous iterative exploration and investigation of past business performance to gain insight and drive business planning. _____ focuses on developing new insights and understanding of business performance based on data and statistical methods. In contrast, business intelligence traditionally focuses on using a consistent set of metrics to both measure past performance and guide business planning, which is also based on data and statistical methods.

Exam Probability: **Low**

54. *Answer choices:*
(see index for correct answer)

- a. Business analytics
- b. Attivio
- c. Greenplum
- d. Datameer

Guidance: level 1

:: Information technology management ::

_____ concerns a cycle of organizational activity: the acquisition of information from one or more sources, the custodianship and the distribution of that information to those who need it, and its ultimate disposition through archiving or deletion.

Exam Probability: **Low**

55. *Answer choices:*
(see index for correct answer)

- a. Run Book Automation
- b. IT cost transparency
- c. Prolifics
- d. Information management

Guidance: level 1

:: ::

A _____ is a telecommunications network that extends over a large geographical distance for the primary purpose of computer networking. _____ s are often established with leased telecommunication circuits.

Exam Probability: **Low**

56. *Answer choices:*
(see index for correct answer)

- a. imperative
- b. Character
- c. Wide Area Network
- d. personal values

Guidance: level 1

:: Product testing ::

_____ is a characteristic of a product or system, whose interfaces are completely understood, to work with other products or systems, at present or in the future, in either implementation or access, without any restrictions.

Exam Probability: **Low**

57. *Answer choices:*

(see index for correct answer)

- a. Conformance testing
- b. Market testing
- c. Rocket engine test facility
- d. Interoperability

Guidance: level 1

:: Information systems ::

_____ is the process of creating, sharing, using and managing the knowledge and information of an organisation. It refers to a multidisciplinary approach to achieving organisational objectives by making the best use of knowledge.

Exam Probability: **Low**

58. *Answer choices:*

(see index for correct answer)

- a. Association for Information Systems
- b. Social Study of Information Systems
- c. Digital marketing system
- d. Knowledge management

Guidance: level 1

:: ::

A _____ is a discussion or informational website published on the World Wide Web consisting of discrete, often informal diary-style text entries. Posts are typically displayed in reverse chronological order, so that the most recent post appears first, at the top of the web page. Until 2009, _____ s were usually the work of a single individual, occasionally of a small group, and often covered a single subject or topic. In the 2010s, "multi-author _____ s" emerged, featuring the writing of multiple authors and sometimes professionally edited. MABs from newspapers, other media outlets, universities, think tanks, advocacy groups, and similar institutions account for an increasing quantity of _____ traffic. The rise of Twitter and other "micro _____ ging" systems helps integrate MABs and single-author _____ s into the news media. _____ can also be used as a verb, meaning to maintain or add content to a _____ .

Exam Probability: **Low**

59. *Answer choices:*

(see index for correct answer)

- a. process perspective
- b. open system
- c. Blog
- d. imperative

Guidance: level 1

Marketing

Marketing is the study and management of exchange relationships. Marketing is the business process of creating relationships with and satisfying customers. With its focus on the customer, marketing is one of the premier components of business management.

Marketing is defined by the American Marketing Association as "the activity, set of institutions, and processes for creating, communicating, delivering, and exchanging offerings that have value for customers, clients, partners, and society at large."

:: Stock market ::

The _____ of a corporation is all of the shares into which ownership of the corporation is divided. In American English, the shares are commonly known as "_____ s". A single share of the _____ represents fractional ownership of the corporation in proportion to the total number of shares. This typically entitles the _____ holder to that fraction of the company's earnings, proceeds from liquidation of assets, or voting power, often dividing these up in proportion to the amount of money each _____ holder has invested. Not all _____ is necessarily equal, as certain classes of _____ may be issued for example without voting rights, with enhanced voting rights, or with a certain priority to receive profits or liquidation proceeds before or after other classes of shareholders.

Exam Probability: **Low**

1. *Answer choices:*
(see index for correct answer)

- a. Intermarket analysis
- b. Direct participation program
- c. Profit warning
- d. Concentrated stock

Guidance: level 1

:: Television commercials ::

_____ is a characteristic that distinguishes physical entities that have biological processes, such as signaling and self-sustaining processes, from those that do not, either because such functions have ceased , or because they never had such functions and are classified as inanimate. Various forms of _____ exist, such as plants, animals, fungi, protists, archaea, and bacteria. The criteria can at times be ambiguous and may or may not define viruses, viroids, or potential synthetic _____ as "living". Biology is the science concerned with the study of _____ .

Exam Probability: **Low**

2. *Answer choices:*
(see index for correct answer)

- a. Life
- b. BK Dinner Baskets
- c. Universal Business Adapter
- d. Bo Knows

Guidance: level 1

:: Direct selling ::

_____ consists of two main business models: single-level marketing, in which a direct seller makes money by buying products from a parent organization and selling them directly to customers, and multi-level marketing , in which the direct seller may earn money from both direct sales to customers and by sponsoring new direct sellers and potentially earning a commission from their efforts.

Exam Probability: **Low**

3. *Answer choices:*
(see index for correct answer)

- a. Direct Selling News
- b. CVSL
- c. The Longaberger Company
- d. Direct selling

Guidance: level 1

:: Retailing ::

A _____ is a retail establishment offering a wide range of consumer goods in different product categories known as "departments". In modern major cities, the _____ made a dramatic appearance in the middle of the 19th century, and permanently reshaped shopping habits, and the definition of service and luxury. Similar developments were under way in London, in Paris and in New York.

Exam Probability: **High**

4. *Answer choices:*

(see index for correct answer)

- a. Second-hand shop
- b. Retail Systems Research
- c. Video game store
- d. People counter

Guidance: level 1

:: Income ::

In business and accounting, net income is an entity's income minus cost of goods sold, expenses and taxes for an accounting period. It is computed as the residual of all revenues and gains over all expenses and losses for the period, and has also been defined as the net increase in shareholders' equity that results from a company's operations. In the context of the presentation of financial statements, the IFRS Foundation defines net income as synonymous with profit and loss. The difference between revenue and the cost of making a product or providing a service, before deducting overheads, payroll, taxation, and interest payments. This is different from operating income.

Exam Probability: **Medium**

5. *Answer choices:*

(see index for correct answer)

- a. Total personal income
- b. Pay grade
- c. Bottom line

- d. Private income

Guidance: level 1

:: Marketing analytics ::

_____ is a long-term, forward-looking approach to planning with the fundamental goal of achieving a sustainable competitive advantage. Strategic planning involves an analysis of the company's strategic initial situation prior to the formulation, evaluation and selection of market-oriented competitive position that contributes to the company's goals and marketing objectives.

Exam Probability: **High**

6. *Answer choices:*

(see index for correct answer)

- a. Marketing resource management
- b. marketing dashboard
- c. Sumall
- d. Marketing strategy

Guidance: level 1

:: Business terms ::

A _____ is a short statement of why an organization exists, what its overall goal is, identifying the goal of its operations: what kind of product or service it provides, its primary customers or market, and its geographical region of operation. It may include a short statement of such fundamental matters as the organization's values or philosophies, a business's main competitive advantages, or a desired future state—the "vision".

Exam Probability: **High**

7. *Answer choices:*

(see index for correct answer)

- a. organizational capital
- b. customer base
- c. organic growth
- d. Mission statement

Guidance: level 1

:: Marketing ::

_____ is "commercial competition characterized by the repeated cutting of prices below those of competitors". One competitor will lower its price, then others will lower their prices to match. If one of them reduces their price again, a new round of reductions starts. In the short term, _____s are good for buyers, who can take advantage of lower prices. Often they are not good for the companies involved because the lower prices reduce profit margins and can threaten their survival.

Exam Probability: **Low**

8. *Answer choices:*
(see index for correct answer)

- a. Price war
- b. Immersion marketing
- c. Customer insight
- d. Object Value

Guidance: level 1

:: Marketing ::

_____ is the process of using surveys to evaluate consumer acceptance of a new product idea prior to the introduction of a product to the market. It is important not to confuse _____ with advertising testing, brand testing and packaging testing; as is sometimes done. _____ focuses on the basic product idea, without the embellishments and puffery inherent in advertising.

Exam Probability: **Medium**

9. *Answer choices:*
(see index for correct answer)

- a. Cyberdoc
- b. Marketing brochure
- c. Concept testing
- d. Market sector

Guidance: level 1

:: Competition regulators ::

The _____ is an independent agency of the United States government, established in 1914 by the _____ Act. Its principal mission is the promotion of consumer protection and the elimination and prevention of anticompetitive business practices, such as coercive monopoly. It is headquartered in the _____ Building in Washington, D.C.

Exam Probability: **Medium**

10. *Answer choices:*

(see index for correct answer)

- a. Federal Trade Commission
- b. Federal Antimonopoly Service
- c. National Board for Prices and Incomes
- d. Competition and Markets Authority

Guidance: level 1

:: Market research ::

_____ is an organized effort to gather information about target markets or customers. It is a very important component of business strategy. The term is commonly interchanged with marketing research; however, expert practitioners may wish to draw a distinction, in that marketing research is concerned specifically about marketing processes, while _____ is concerned specifically with markets.

Exam Probability: **Low**

11. *Answer choices:*

(see index for correct answer)

- a. Cambashi
- b. Market research
- c. Monroe Mendelsohn Research
- d. IDDEA

Guidance: level 1

:: Survey methodology ::

A _____ is the procedure of systematically acquiring and recording information about the members of a given population. The term is used mostly in connection with national population and housing _____ es; other common _____ es include agriculture, business, and traffic _____ es. The United Nations defines the essential features of population and housing _____ es as "individual enumeration, universality within a defined territory, simultaneity and defined periodicity", and recommends that population _____ es be taken at least every 10 years. United Nations recommendations also cover _____ topics to be collected, official definitions, classifications and other useful information to co-ordinate international practice.

Exam Probability: **High**

12. *Answer choices:*

(see index for correct answer)

- a. Computer-assisted survey information collection
- b. Inverse probability weighting
- c. National Health Interview Survey
- d. Political forecasting

Guidance: level 1

:: Investment ::

In finance, the benefit from an _____ is called a return. The return may consist of a gain realised from the sale of property or an _____ , unrealised capital appreciation , or _____ income such as dividends, interest, rental income etc., or a combination of capital gain and income. The return may also include currency gains or losses due to changes in foreign currency exchange rates.

Exam Probability: **Medium**

13. *Answer choices:*

(see index for correct answer)

- a. Individual Pension Plan
- b. Investment
- c. Psychology of previous investment
- d. APMEX

Guidance: level 1

:: ::

A _____ consists of one people who live in the same dwelling and share meals. It may also consist of a single family or another group of people. A dwelling is considered to contain multiple _____ s if meals or living spaces are not shared. The _____ is the basic unit of analysis in many social, microeconomic and government models, and is important to economics and inheritance.

Exam Probability: **High**

14. *Answer choices:*
(see index for correct answer)

- a. information systems assessment
- b. Household
- c. hierarchical perspective
- d. Sarbanes-Oxley act of 2002

Guidance: level 1

:: Materials ::

A _____, also known as a feedstock, unprocessed material, or primary commodity, is a basic material that is used to produce goods, finished products, energy, or intermediate materials which are feedstock for future finished products. As feedstock, the term connotes these materials are bottleneck assets and are highly important with regard to producing other products. An example of this is crude oil, which is a _____ and a feedstock used in the production of industrial chemicals, fuels, plastics, and pharmaceutical goods; lumber is a _____ used to produce a variety of products including all types of furniture. The term "_____" denotes materials in minimally processed or unprocessed in states; e.g., raw latex, crude oil, cotton, coal, raw biomass, iron ore, air, logs, or water i.e. "...any product of agriculture, forestry, fishing and any other mineral that is in its natural form or which has undergone the transformation required to prepare it for internationally marketing in substantial volumes."

Exam Probability: **Low**

15. *Answer choices:*
(see index for correct answer)

- a. Raw material
- b. Ion Gel
- c. Layered double hydroxides
- d. Aerospace materials

Guidance: level 1

:: Credit cards ::

The _____ Company, also known as Amex, is an American multinational financial services corporation headquartered in Three World Financial Center in New York City. The company was founded in 1850 and is one of the 30 components of the Dow Jones Industrial Average. The company is best known for its charge card, credit card, and traveler's cheque businesses.

Exam Probability: **High**

16. *Answer choices:*
(see index for correct answer)

- a. American Express
- b. Centurion Card
- c. Bankcard
- d. CardLab

Guidance: level 1

:: Data collection ::

A _____ is an utterance which typically functions as a request for information. _____ s can thus be understood as a kind of illocutionary act in the field of pragmatics or as special kinds of propositions in frameworks of formal semantics such as alternative semantics or inquisitive semantics. The information requested is expected to be provided in the form of an answer. _____ s are often conflated with interrogatives, which are the grammatical forms typically used to achieve them. Rhetorical _____ s, for example, are interrogative in form but may not be considered true _____ s as they are not expected to be answered. Conversely, non-interrogative grammatical structures may be considered _____ s as in the case of the imperative sentence "tell me your name".

Exam Probability: **Medium**

17. *Answer choices:*

(see index for correct answer)

- a. Surveylab
- b. Synthetic Environment for Analysis and Simulations
- c. IPUMS
- d. Question

Guidance: level 1

:: Advertising ::

A _____ is a document used by creative professionals and agencies to develop creative deliverables: visual design, copy, advertising, web sites, etc. The document is usually developed by the requestor and approved by the creative team of designers, writers, and project managers. In some cases, the project's _____ may need creative director approval before work will commence.

Exam Probability: **Low**

18. *Answer choices:*

(see index for correct answer)

- a. Retargeter
- b. Tradio
- c. Creative brief
- d. SocioBranding

Guidance: level 1

:: Consumer theory ::

A _____ is a technical term in psychology, economics and philosophy usually used in relation to choosing between alternatives. For example, someone prefers A over B if they would rather choose A than B.

Exam Probability: **High**

19. *Answer choices:*

(see index for correct answer)

- a. Business contract hire
- b. Elasticity of substitution
- c. Preference
- d. Hicksian demand function

Guidance: level 1

:: ::

_____ LLC is an American multinational technology company that specializes in Internet-related services and products, which include online advertising technologies, search engine, cloud computing, software, and hardware. It is considered one of the Big Four technology companies, alongside Amazon, Apple and Facebook.

Exam Probability: **Medium**

20. *Answer choices:*
(see index for correct answer)

- a. interpersonal communication
- b. information systems assessment
- c. Google
- d. co-culture

Guidance: level 1

:: Management ::

In economics and marketing, _____ is the process of distinguishing a product or service from others, to make it more attractive to a particular target market. This involves differentiating it from competitors' products as well as a firm's own products. The concept was proposed by Edward Chamberlin in his 1933 The Theory of Monopolistic Competition.

Exam Probability: **Low**

21. *Answer choices:*
(see index for correct answer)

- a. Third-generation balanced scorecard
- b. Organizational space
- c. Product differentiation
- d. Data Item Descriptions

Guidance: level 1

:: Marketing ::

_____ or stock is the goods and materials that a business holds for the ultimate goal of resale.

Exam Probability: **High**

22. *Answer choices:*

(see index for correct answer)

- a. Business-to-employee
- b. Interruption marketing
- c. Inventory
- d. Inventory control

Guidance: level 1

:: Logistics ::

_____ is generally the detailed organization and implementation of a complex operation. In a general business sense, _____ is the management of the flow of things between the point of origin and the point of consumption in order to meet requirements of customers or corporations. The resources managed in _____ may include tangible goods such as materials, equipment, and supplies, as well as food and other consumable items. The _____ of physical items usually involves the integration of information flow, materials handling, production, packaging, inventory, transportation, warehousing, and often security.

Exam Probability: **High**

23. *Answer choices:*

(see index for correct answer)

- a. Tracking number
- b. Logistics
- c. Dispatch
- d. Loading dock

Guidance: level 1

:: ::

Bloomberg Businessweek is an American weekly business magazine published since 2009 by Bloomberg L.P. Businessweek, founded in 1929, aimed to provide information and interpretation about events in the business world. The magazine is headquartered in New York City. Megan Murphy served as editor from November 2016; she stepped down from the role in January 2018 and Joel Weber was appointed in her place. The magazine is published 47 times a year.

Exam Probability: **Medium**

24. *Answer choices:*

(see index for correct answer)

- a. open system
- b. surface-level diversity
- c. Character
- d. personal values

Guidance: level 1

:: Commerce ::

A _____ is a company or individual that purchases goods or services with the intention of selling them rather than consuming or using them. This is usually done for profit. One example can be found in the industry of telecommunications, where companies buy excess amounts of transmission capacity or call time from other carriers and resell it to smaller carriers.

Exam Probability: **High**

25. *Answer choices:*

(see index for correct answer)

- a. Requisition
- b. Real prices and ideal prices
- c. Reseller
- d. White Elephant Sale

Guidance: level 1

:: ::

An _____, often referred to as a creative agency or an ad agency, is a business dedicated to creating, planning, and handling advertising and sometimes other forms of promotion and marketing for its clients. An ad agency is generally independent from the client; it may be an internal department or agency that provides an outside point of view to the effort of selling the client's products or services, or an outside firm. An agency can also handle overall marketing and branding strategies promotions for its clients, which may include sales as well.

Exam Probability: **Low**

26. *Answer choices:*
(see index for correct answer)

- a. similarity-attraction theory
- b. Advertising agency
- c. surface-level diversity
- d. Character

Guidance: level 1

:: Marketing ::

A _____ is a group of customers within a business's serviceable available market at which a business aims its marketing efforts and resources. A _____ is a subset of the total market for a product or service. The _____ typically consists of consumers who exhibit similar characteristics and are considered most likely to buy a business's market offerings or are likely to be the most profitable segments for the business to service.

Exam Probability: **Medium**

27. *Answer choices:*
(see index for correct answer)

- a. Gift suite
- b. Gladvertising
- c. Target market
- d. LIDA

Guidance: level 1

:: Monopoly (economics) ::

The _____ of 1890 was a United States antitrust law that regulates competition among enterprises, which was passed by Congress under the presidency of Benjamin Harrison.

Exam Probability: **Medium**

28. *Answer choices:*

(see index for correct answer)

- a. Herfindahl index
- b. Intellectual property
- c. Private finance initiative
- d. Practice of law

Guidance: level 1

:: Marketing ::

_____ is the percentage of a market accounted for by a specific entity. In a survey of nearly 200 senior marketing managers, 67% responded that they found the revenue- "dollar _____ " metric very useful, while 61% found "unit _____ " very useful.

Exam Probability: **Medium**

29. *Answer choices:*

(see index for correct answer)

- a. Market share
- b. Marketing supply chain
- c. reverse marketing
- d. Servicescape

Guidance: level 1

:: Data management ::

In computing, a _____, also known as an enterprise _____, is a system used for reporting and data analysis, and is considered a core component of business intelligence. DWs are central repositories of integrated data from one or more disparate sources. They store current and historical data in one single place that are used for creating analytical reports for workers throughout the enterprise.

Exam Probability: **Medium**

30. *Answer choices:*

(see index for correct answer)

- a. ISO 8000
- b. Data custodian
- c. Meta-data management
- d. Content inventory

Guidance: level 1

:: ::

_____ is a marketing communication that employs an openly sponsored, non-personal message to promote or sell a product, service or idea. Sponsors of _____ are typically businesses wishing to promote their products or services. _____ is differentiated from public relations in that an advertiser pays for and has control over the message. It differs from personal selling in that the message is non-personal, i.e., not directed to a particular individual. _____ is communicated through various mass media, including traditional media such as newspapers, magazines, television, radio, outdoor _____ or direct mail; and new media such as search results, blogs, social media, websites or text messages. The actual presentation of the message in a medium is referred to as an advertisement, or "ad" or advert for short.

Exam Probability: **High**

31. *Answer choices:*

(see index for correct answer)

- a. deep-level diversity
- b. Advertising
- c. information systems assessment
- d. open system

Guidance: level 1

:: ::

In production, research, retail, and accounting, a _____ is the value of money that has been used up to produce something or deliver a service, and hence is not available for use anymore. In business, the _____ may be one of acquisition, in which case the amount of money expended to acquire it is counted as _____ . In this case, money is the input that is gone in order to acquire the thing. This acquisition _____ may be the sum of the _____ of production as incurred by the original producer, and further _____ s of transaction as incurred by the acquirer over and above the price paid to the producer. Usually, the price also includes a mark-up for profit over the _____ of production.

Exam Probability: **Medium**

32. *Answer choices:*
(see index for correct answer)

- a. Cost
- b. personal values
- c. process perspective
- d. open system

Guidance: level 1

:: Consumer theory ::

_____ is the quantity of a good that consumers are willing and able to purchase at various prices during a given period of time.

Exam Probability: **Low**

33. *Answer choices:*
(see index for correct answer)

- a. Price elasticity of demand
- b. End-of-life
- c. Cross elasticity of demand
- d. Slutsky equation

Guidance: level 1

:: Behaviorism ::

In behavioral psychology, _____ is a consequence applied that will strengthen an organism's future behavior whenever that behavior is preceded by a specific antecedent stimulus. This strengthening effect may be measured as a higher frequency of behavior, longer duration, greater magnitude, or shorter latency. There are two types of _____, known as positive _____ and negative _____; positive is where by a reward is offered on expression of the wanted behaviour and negative is taking away an undesirable element in the persons environment whenever the desired behaviour is achieved.

Exam Probability: **Medium**

34. *Answer choices:*

(see index for correct answer)

- a. Reinforcement
- b. Systematic desensitization
- c. social facilitation
- d. Matching Law

Guidance: level 1

:: ::

_____ is the act of conveying meanings from one entity or group to another through the use of mutually understood signs, symbols, and semiotic rules.

Exam Probability: **Low**

35. *Answer choices:*

(see index for correct answer)

- a. Communication
- b. deep-level diversity
- c. surface-level diversity
- d. Sarbanes-Oxley act of 2002

Guidance: level 1

:: ::

_____ is the provision of service to customers before, during and after a purchase. The perception of success of such interactions is dependent on employees "who can adjust themselves to the personality of the guest". _____ concerns the priority an organization assigns to _____ relative to components such as product innovation and pricing. In this sense, an organization that values good _____ may spend more money in training employees than the average organization or may proactively interview customers for feedback.

Exam Probability: **High**

36. *Answer choices:*
(see index for correct answer)

- a. Customer service
- b. personal values
- c. co-culture
- d. open system

Guidance: level 1

:: Commodities ::

In economics, a _____ is an economic good or service that has full or substantial fungibility: that is, the market treats instances of the good as equivalent or nearly so with no regard to who produced them. Most commodities are raw materials, basic resources, agricultural, or mining products, such as iron ore, sugar, or grains like rice and wheat. Commodities can also be mass-produced unspecialized products such as chemicals and computer memory.

Exam Probability: **Low**

37. *Answer choices:*
(see index for correct answer)

- a. Commodity pathway diversion
- b. Commoditization
- c. Commodity money
- d. Commodity

Guidance: level 1

:: Evaluation methods ::

In natural and social sciences, and sometimes in other fields, _____ is the systematic empirical investigation of observable phenomena via statistical, mathematical, or computational techniques. The objective of _____ is to develop and employ mathematical models, theories, and hypotheses pertaining to phenomena. The process of measurement is central to _____ because it provides the fundamental connection between empirical observation and mathematical expression of quantitative relationships.

Exam Probability: **Low**

38. *Answer choices:*
(see index for correct answer)

- a. Participant observation
- b. Event correlation
- c. Fixtureless in-circuit test
- d. Quantitative research

Guidance: level 1

:: ::

_____ is the process of gathering and measuring information on targeted variables in an established system, which then enables one to answer relevant questions and evaluate outcomes. _____ is a component of research in all fields of study including physical and social sciences, humanities, and business. While methods vary by discipline, the emphasis on ensuring accurate and honest collection remains the same. The goal for all _____ is to capture quality evidence that allows analysis to lead to the formulation of convincing and credible answers to the questions that have been posed.

Exam Probability: **Low**

39. *Answer choices:*
(see index for correct answer)

- a. Character
- b. functional perspective
- c. Data collection
- d. hierarchical perspective

Guidance: level 1

:: ::

A _____ is a graphic mark, emblem, or symbol used to aid and promote public identification and recognition. It may be of an abstract or figurative design or include the text of the name it represents as in a wordmark.

Exam Probability: **High**

40. *Answer choices:*
(see index for correct answer)

- a. personal values
- b. process perspective
- c. Logo
- d. functional perspective

Guidance: level 1

:: ::

_____ refers to a diverse array of media technologies that reach a large audience via mass communication. The technologies through which this communication takes place include a variety of outlets.

Exam Probability: **High**

41. *Answer choices:*
(see index for correct answer)

- a. deep-level diversity
- b. Mass media
- c. imperative
- d. empathy

Guidance: level 1

:: Promotion and marketing communications ::

_____ is one of the elements of the promotional mix. . _____ uses both media and non-media marketing communications for a pre-determined, limited time to increase consumer demand, stimulate market demand or improve product availability. Examples include contests, coupons, freebies, loss leaders, point of purchase displays, premiums, prizes, product samples, and rebates.

Exam Probability: **High**

42. *Answer choices:*
(see index for correct answer)

- a. Aisle411
- b. Radio advertisement
- c. Sales force automation
- d. Sales promotion

Guidance: level 1

:: Progressive Era in the United States ::

The Clayton Antitrust Act of 1914, was a part of United States antitrust law with the goal of adding further substance to the U.S. antitrust law regime; the _____ sought to prevent anticompetitive practices in their incipiency. That regime started with the Sherman Antitrust Act of 1890, the first Federal law outlawing practices considered harmful to consumers. The _____ specified particular prohibited conduct, the three-level enforcement scheme, the exemptions, and the remedial measures.

Exam Probability: **Medium**

43. *Answer choices:*
(see index for correct answer)

- a. Mann Act
- b. Clayton Antitrust Act
- c. pragmatism

Guidance: level 1

:: Brand management ::

_____ is defined as positive feelings towards a brand and dedication to purchase the same product or service repeatedly now and in the future from the same brand, regardless of a competitor's actions or changes in the environment. It can also be demonstrated with other behaviors such as positive word-of-mouth advocacy. _____ is where an individual buys products from the same manufacturer repeatedly rather than from other suppliers. Businesses whose financial and ethical values, for example ESG responsibilities, rest in large part on their _____ are said to use the loyalty business model.

Exam Probability: **High**

44. *Answer choices:*

(see index for correct answer)

- a. Napa Declaration on Place
- b. Brand loyalty
- c. Brand culture
- d. Brand strength analysis

Guidance: level 1

:: Supply chain management terms ::

In business and finance, _____ is a system of organizations, people, activities, information, and resources involved in moving a product or service from supplier to customer. _____ activities involve the transformation of natural resources, raw materials, and components into a finished product that is delivered to the end customer. In sophisticated _____ systems, used products may re-enter the _____ at any point where residual value is recyclable. _____ s link value chains.

Exam Probability: **High**

45. *Answer choices:*

(see index for correct answer)

- a. Supply-chain management
- b. Will call
- c. Supply chain
- d. Last mile

Guidance: level 1

:: Brokered programming ::

An _____ is a form of television commercial, which generally includes a toll-free telephone number or website. Most often used as a form of direct response television , long-form _____ s are typically 28:30 or 58:30 minutes in length. _____ s are also known as paid programming . This phenomenon started in the United States, where _____ s were typically shown overnight , outside peak prime time hours for commercial broadcasters. Some television stations chose to air _____ s as an alternative to the former practice of signing off. Some channels air _____ s 24 hours. Some stations also choose to air _____ s during the daytime hours mostly on weekends to fill in for unscheduled network or syndicated programming. By 2009, most _____ spending in the U.S. occurred during the early morning, daytime and evening hours, or in the afternoon. Stations in most countries around the world have instituted similar media structures. The _____ industry is worth over $200 billion.

Exam Probability: **High**

46. *Answer choices:*
(see index for correct answer)

- a. Toonzai
- b. Infomercial
- c. One Magnificent Morning
- d. Leased access

Guidance: level 1

:: ::

In regulatory jurisdictions that provide for it , _____ is a group of laws and organizations designed to ensure the rights of consumers as well as fair trade, competition and accurate information in the marketplace. The laws are designed to prevent the businesses that engage in fraud or specified unfair practices from gaining an advantage over competitors. They may also provides additional protection for those most vulnerable in society. _____ laws are a form of government regulation that aim to protect the rights of consumers. For example, a government may require businesses to disclose detailed information about products—particularly in areas where safety or public health is an issue, such as food.

Exam Probability: **Medium**

47. *Answer choices:*
(see index for correct answer)

- a. hierarchical perspective
- b. interpersonal communication
- c. corporate values
- d. Consumer Protection

Guidance: level 1

:: Management ::

A _____ is a promise of value to be delivered, communicated, and acknowledged. It is also a belief from the customer about how value will be delivered, experienced and acquired.

Exam Probability: **Medium**

48. *Answer choices:*
(see index for correct answer)

- a. Resource management
- b. Coworking
- c. Intopia
- d. Value proposition

Guidance: level 1

:: ::

_____, also referred to as orthostasis, is a human position in which the body is held in an upright position and supported only by the feet.

Exam Probability: **High**

49. *Answer choices:*
(see index for correct answer)

- a. Character
- b. hierarchical
- c. Standing
- d. levels of analysis

Guidance: level 1

:: Retailing ::

A _____ is a self-service shop offering a wide variety of food, beverages and household products, organized into sections and shelves. It is larger and has a wider selection than earlier grocery stores, but is smaller and more limited in the range of merchandise than a hypermarket or big-box market.

Exam Probability: **High**

50. *Answer choices:*
(see index for correct answer)

- a. Sales per unit area
- b. Supermarket
- c. Shopping mall
- d. Shopfitting

Guidance: level 1

:: Business law ::

A _____ is an arrangement where parties, known as partners, agree to cooperate to advance their mutual interests. The partners in a _____ may be individuals, businesses, interest-based organizations, schools, governments or combinations. Organizations may partner to increase the likelihood of each achieving their mission and to amplify their reach. A _____ may result in issuing and holding equity or may be only governed by a contract.

Exam Probability: **Low**

51. *Answer choices:*
(see index for correct answer)

- a. Subordination
- b. United Kingdom commercial law
- c. Unfair business practices
- d. Negotiable instrument

Guidance: level 1

:: ::

_____, known in Europe as research and technological development, refers to innovative activities undertaken by corporations or governments in developing new services or products, or improving existing services or products. _____ constitutes the first stage of development of a potential new service or the production process.

Exam Probability: **High**

52. *Answer choices:*

(see index for correct answer)

- a. empathy
- b. hierarchical
- c. imperative
- d. Research and development

Guidance: level 1

:: Monopoly (economics) ::

A _____ is a form of intellectual property that gives its owner the legal right to exclude others from making, using, selling, and importing an invention for a limited period of years, in exchange for publishing an enabling public disclosure of the invention. In most countries _____ rights fall under civil law and the _____ holder needs to sue someone infringing the _____ in order to enforce his or her rights. In some industries _____ s are an essential form of competitive advantage; in others they are irrelevant.

Exam Probability: **Medium**

53. *Answer choices:*

(see index for correct answer)

- a. State monopoly capitalism
- b. Complementary monopoly
- c. Patent
- d. Concentration ratio

Guidance: level 1

:: Management ::

A _____ describes the rationale of how an organization creates, delivers, and captures value, in economic, social, cultural or other contexts. The process of _____ construction and modification is also called _____ innovation and forms a part of business strategy.

Exam Probability: **Medium**

54. *Answer choices:*

(see index for correct answer)

- a. Business model
- b. Project management simulation
- c. Supplier relationship management
- d. Formula for change

Guidance: level 1

:: ::

A _____ service is an online platform which people use to build social networks or social relationship with other people who share similar personal or career interests, activities, backgrounds or real-life connections.

Exam Probability: **Medium**

55. *Answer choices:*

(see index for correct answer)

- a. imperative
- b. cultural
- c. co-culture
- d. similarity-attraction theory

Guidance: level 1

:: ::

In financial markets, a share is a unit used as mutual funds, limited partnerships, and real estate investment trusts. The owner of _____ in the corporation/company is a shareholder of the corporation. A share is an indivisible unit of capital, expressing the ownership relationship between the company and the shareholder. The denominated value of a share is its face value, and the total of the face value of issued _____ represent the capital of a company, which may not reflect the market value of those _____ .

Exam Probability: **Low**

56. *Answer choices:*
(see index for correct answer)

- a. functional perspective
- b. information systems assessment
- c. hierarchical
- d. Character

Guidance: level 1

:: Marketing ::

_____ s are structured marketing strategies designed by merchants to encourage customers to continue to shop at or use the services of businesses associated with each program. These programs exist covering most types of commerce, each one having varying features and rewards-schemes.

Exam Probability: **Low**

57. *Answer choices:*
(see index for correct answer)

- a. Loyalty program
- b. City marketing
- c. Personalized marketing
- d. MARC USA

Guidance: level 1

:: Marketing ::

_____ is research conducted for a problem that has not been studied more clearly, intended to establish priorities, develop operational definitions and improve the final research design. _____ helps determine the best research design, data-collection method and selection of subjects. It should draw definitive conclusions only with extreme caution. Given its fundamental nature, _____ often relies on techniques such as.

Exam Probability: **Medium**

58. *Answer choices:*
(see index for correct answer)

- a. Multicultural marketing
- b. Cult brand
- c. Exploratory research
- d. The International Customer Service Institute

Guidance: level 1

:: Reputation management ::

A _____ is an astronomical object consisting of a luminous spheroid of plasma held together by its own gravity. The nearest _____ to Earth is the Sun. Many other _____ s are visible to the naked eye from Earth during the night, appearing as a multitude of fixed luminous points in the sky due to their immense distance from Earth. Historically, the most prominent _____ s were grouped into constellations and asterisms, the brightest of which gained proper names. Astronomers have assembled _____ catalogues that identify the known _____ s and provide standardized stellar designations. However, most of the estimated 300 sextillion _____ s in the Universe are invisible to the naked eye from Earth, including all _____ s outside our galaxy, the Milky Way.

Exam Probability: **Medium**

59. *Answer choices:*
(see index for correct answer)

- a. Advogato
- b. ClaimID
- c. Slashdot
- d. Star

Guidance: level 1

Manufacturing

Manufacturing is the production of merchandise for use or sale using labor and machines, tools, chemical and biological processing, or formulation. The term may refer to a range of human activity, from handicraft to high tech, but is most commonly applied to industrial design, in which raw materials are transformed into finished goods on a large scale. Such finished goods may be sold to other manufacturers for the production of other, more complex products, such as aircraft, household appliances, furniture, sports equipment or automobiles, or sold to wholesalers, who in turn sell them to retailers, who then sell them to end users and consumers.

:: Consortia ::

A _____ is an association of two or more individuals, companies, organizations or governments with the objective of participating in a common activity or pooling their resources for achieving a common goal.

Exam Probability: **Medium**

1. *Answer choices:*
(see index for correct answer)

- a. Bonyad
- b. Consortium
- c. Open Grid Forum
- d. Indiana Space Grant Consortium

Guidance: level 1

:: Project management ::

A _____ is one of a series of numbered markers placed along a road or boundary at intervals of one mile or occasionally, parts of a mile. They are typically located at the side of the road or in a median or central reservation. They are alternatively known as mile markers, mileposts or mile posts . Mileage is the distance along the road from a fixed commencement point. Commonly the term " _____ " may also refer to markers placed at other distances, such as every kilometre.

Exam Probability: **Low**

2. *Answer choices:*

(see index for correct answer)

- a. Resource
- b. Case competition
- c. Rapid Results
- d. ISO 21500

Guidance: level 1

:: Quality management ::

_____ is a not-for-profit membership foundation in Brussels, established in 1989 to increase the competitiveness of the European economy. The initial impetus for forming _____ was a response to the work of W. Edwards Deming and the development of the concepts of Total Quality Management.

Exam Probability: **Low**

3. *Answer choices:*

(see index for correct answer)

- a. E-TQM College
- b. Dana Ulery
- c. Common Assessment Framework
- d. EFQM

Guidance: level 1

:: Asset ::

In financial accounting, an _____ is any resource owned by the business. Anything tangible or intangible that can be owned or controlled to produce value and that is held by a company to produce positive economic value is an _____ . Simply stated, _____ s represent value of ownership that can be converted into cash . The balance sheet of a firm records the monetary value of the _____ s owned by that firm. It covers money and other valuables belonging to an individual or to a business.

Exam Probability: **Low**

4. *Answer choices:*
(see index for correct answer)

- a. Current asset
- b. Fixed asset

Guidance: level 1

:: Management ::

In economics and marketing, _____ is the process of distinguishing a product or service from others, to make it more attractive to a particular target market. This involves differentiating it from competitors' products as well as a firm's own products. The concept was proposed by Edward Chamberlin in his 1933 The Theory of Monopolistic Competition.

Exam Probability: **High**

5. *Answer choices:*
(see index for correct answer)

- a. Line of business
- b. Meeting
- c. Product differentiation
- d. Managing stage boundaries

Guidance: level 1

:: Marketing ::

_____ or stock is the goods and materials that a business holds for the ultimate goal of resale.

Exam Probability: **Low**

6. *Answer choices:*
(see index for correct answer)

- a. Demand generation
- b. Interruption marketing
- c. Inventory
- d. Promotional mix

Guidance: level 1

:: Lean manufacturing ::

_____ is a scheduling system for lean manufacturing and just-in-time manufacturing. Taiichi Ohno, an industrial engineer at Toyota, developed _____ to improve manufacturing efficiency. _____ is one method to achieve JIT. The system takes its name from the cards that track production within a factory. For many in the automotive sector, _____ is known as the "Toyota nameplate system" and as such the term is not used by some other automakers.

Exam Probability: **Medium**

7. *Answer choices:*
(see index for correct answer)

- a. Lean CFP driven
- b. Supply chain responsiveness matrix
- c. Kanban
- d. Muri

Guidance: level 1

:: ::

_____ refers to the confirmation of certain characteristics of an object, person, or organization. This confirmation is often, but not always, provided by some form of external review, education, assessment, or audit. Accreditation is a specific organization's process of _____. According to the National Council on Measurement in Education, a _____ test is a credentialing test used to determine whether individuals are knowledgeable enough in a given occupational area to be labeled "competent to practice" in that area.

Exam Probability: **Medium**

8. *Answer choices:*
(see index for correct answer)

- a. interpersonal communication
- b. imperative
- c. Certification
- d. co-culture

Guidance: level 1

:: Debt ::

_____ is the trust which allows one party to provide money or resources to another party wherein the second party does not reimburse the first party immediately, but promises either to repay or return those resources at a later date. In other words, _____ is a method of making reciprocity formal, legally enforceable, and extensible to a large group of unrelated people.

Exam Probability: **Low**

9. *Answer choices:*
(see index for correct answer)

- a. Phantom debt
- b. Credit
- c. Sum certain
- d. Financial assistance

Guidance: level 1

:: Sensitivity analysis ::

_____ is the study of how the uncertainty in the output of a mathematical model or system can be divided and allocated to different sources of uncertainty in its inputs. A related practice is uncertainty analysis, which has a greater focus on uncertainty quantification and propagation of uncertainty; ideally, uncertainty and _____ should be run in tandem.

Exam Probability: **Medium**

10. *Answer choices:*
(see index for correct answer)

- a. Elementary effects method
- b. Sensitivity analysis
- c. Variance-based sensitivity analysis
- d. Fourier amplitude sensitivity testing

Guidance: level 1

:: Management ::

Business _____ is a discipline in operations management in which people use various methods to discover, model, analyze, measure, improve, optimize, and automate business processes. BPM focuses on improving corporate performance by managing business processes. Any combination of methods used to manage a company's business processes is BPM. Processes can be structured and repeatable or unstructured and variable. Though not required, enabling technologies are often used with BPM.

Exam Probability: **High**

11. *Answer choices:*
(see index for correct answer)

- a. Intopia
- b. Management entrenchment
- c. Process management
- d. Pareto analysis

Guidance: level 1

:: E-commerce ::

_____ is the business-to-business or business-to-consumer or business-to-government purchase and sale of supplies, work, and services through the Internet as well as other information and networking systems, such as electronic data interchange and enterprise resource planning.

Exam Probability: **Medium**

12. *Answer choices:*
(see index for correct answer)

- a. United Nations Convention on the Use of Electronic Communications in International Contracts
- b. Network Security Services
- c. E-commerce payment system
- d. E-procurement

Guidance: level 1

:: ::

A _____ or till is a mechanical or electronic device for registering and calculating transactions at a point of sale. It is usually attached to a drawer for storing cash and other valuables. A modern _____ is usually attached to a printer that can print out receipts for record-keeping purposes.

Exam Probability: **Medium**

13. *Answer choices:*
(see index for correct answer)

- a. Cash register
- b. interpersonal communication
- c. corporate values
- d. deep-level diversity

Guidance: level 1

:: Business planning ::

_____ is a critical component to the successful delivery of any project, programme or activity. A stakeholder is any individual, group or organization that can affect, be affected by, or perceive itself to be affected by a programme.

Exam Probability: **High**

14. *Answer choices:*

(see index for correct answer)

- a. Exit planning
- b. Business war games
- c. Strategic planning
- d. operational planning

Guidance: level 1

:: ::

The _____ is a project plan of how the production budget will be spent over a given timescale, for every phase of a business project.

Exam Probability: **Medium**

15. *Answer choices:*

(see index for correct answer)

- a. Production schedule
- b. surface-level diversity
- c. process perspective
- d. similarity-attraction theory

Guidance: level 1

:: Industrial organization ::

In economics, specifically general equilibrium theory, a perfect market is defined by several idealizing conditions, collectively called _____. In theoretical models where conditions of _____ hold, it has been theoretically demonstrated that a market will reach an equilibrium in which the quantity supplied for every product or service, including labor, equals the quantity demanded at the current price. This equilibrium would be a Pareto optimum.

Exam Probability: **High**

16. *Answer choices:*

(see index for correct answer)

- a. Hold-up problem
- b. Countervailing power

- c. Switching cost
- d. Perfect competition

Guidance: level 1

:: Production and manufacturing ::

_____ is a concept in purchasing and project management for securing the quality and timely delivery of goods and components.

Exam Probability: **High**

17. *Answer choices:*
(see index for correct answer)

- a. SafetyBUS p
- b. Alarm management
- c. Material requirements planning
- d. Expediting

Guidance: level 1

:: Data management ::

_____ refers to a data-driven improvement cycle used for improving, optimizing and stabilizing business processes and designs. The _____ improvement cycle is the core tool used to drive Six Sigma projects. However, _____ is not exclusive to Six Sigma and can be used as the framework for other improvement applications.

Exam Probability: **High**

18. *Answer choices:*
(see index for correct answer)

- a. SQL/PSM
- b. DMAIC
- c. Tagsistant
- d. Head/tail Breaks

Guidance: level 1

:: Elementary mathematics ::

In mathematics, a _____ is an enumerated collection of objects in which repetitions are allowed. Like a set, it contains members. The number of elements is called the length of the _____. Unlike a set, the same elements can appear multiple times at different positions in a _____, and order matters. Formally, a _____ can be defined as a function whose domain is either the set of the natural numbers or the set of the first n natural numbers. The position of an element in a _____ is its rank or index; it is the natural number from which the element is the image. It depends on the context or a specific convention, if the first element has index 0 or 1.

When a symbol has been chosen for denoting a _____, the nth element of the _____ is denoted by this symbol with n as subscript; for example, the nth element of the Fibonacci _____ is generally denoted Fn.

Exam Probability: **Low**

19. *Answer choices:*
(see index for correct answer)

- a. Rational number
- b. Distance
- c. Elementary mathematics
- d. Sequence

Guidance: level 1

:: Evaluation ::

_____ is a way of preventing mistakes and defects in manufactured products and avoiding problems when delivering products or services to customers; which ISO 9000 defines as "part of quality management focused on providing confidence that quality requirements will be fulfilled". This defect prevention in _____ differs subtly from defect detection and rejection in quality control and has been referred to as a shift left since it focuses on quality earlier in the process.

Exam Probability: **High**

20. *Answer choices:*
(see index for correct answer)

- a. Cryptographic Module Testing Laboratory
- b. Common Criteria Testing Laboratory
- c. Integrity

- d. Quality assurance

Guidance: level 1

:: Building materials ::

_____ is an alloy of iron and carbon, and sometimes other elements. Because of its high tensile strength and low cost, it is a major component used in buildings, infrastructure, tools, ships, automobiles, machines, appliances, and weapons.

Exam Probability: **Low**

21. *Answer choices:*
(see index for correct answer)

- a. Jesmonite
- b. Steel
- c. Welded wire mesh
- d. Fiber cement siding

Guidance: level 1

:: Management ::

In inventory management, _____ is the order quantity that minimizes the total holding costs and ordering costs. It is one of the oldest classical production scheduling models. The model was developed by Ford W. Harris in 1913, but R. H. Wilson, a consultant who applied it extensively, and K. Andler are given credit for their in-depth analysis.

Exam Probability: **Medium**

22. *Answer choices:*
(see index for correct answer)

- a. Process-based management
- b. Managerial Psychology
- c. Security management
- d. Economic order quantity

Guidance: level 1

:: Production and manufacturing ::

An _____ is a manufacturing process in which parts are added as the semi-finished assembly moves from workstation to workstation where the parts are added in sequence until the final assembly is produced. By mechanically moving the parts to the assembly work and moving the semi-finished assembly from work station to work station, a finished product can be assembled faster and with less labor than by having workers carry parts to a stationary piece for assembly.

Exam Probability: **High**

23. *Answer choices:*

(see index for correct answer)

- a. DeviceNet
- b. Product layout
- c. SynqNet
- d. Enterprise control

Guidance: level 1

:: Lean manufacturing ::

_____ is the Sino-Japanese word for "improvement". In business, _____ refers to activities that continuously improve all functions and involve all employees from the CEO to the assembly line workers. It also applies to processes, such as purchasing and logistics, that cross organizational boundaries into the supply chain. It has been applied in healthcare, psychotherapy, life-coaching, government, and banking.

Exam Probability: **Medium**

24. *Answer choices:*

(see index for correct answer)

- a. Overall equipment effectiveness
- b. Mura
- c. Kaizen
- d. Autonomation

Guidance: level 1

:: E-commerce ::

_____ is the activity of buying or selling of products on online services or over the Internet. Electronic commerce draws on technologies such as mobile commerce, electronic funds transfer, supply chain management, Internet marketing, online transaction processing, electronic data interchange , inventory management systems, and automated data collection systems.

Exam Probability: **Medium**

25. *Answer choices:*
(see index for correct answer)

- a. SIE
- b. The Cluetrain Manifesto
- c. Billing and Settlement Plan
- d. PagSeguro

Guidance: level 1

:: Materials ::

A _____ , also known as a feedstock, unprocessed material, or primary commodity, is a basic material that is used to produce goods, finished products, energy, or intermediate materials which are feedstock for future finished products. As feedstock, the term connotes these materials are bottleneck assets and are highly important with regard to producing other products. An example of this is crude oil, which is a _____ and a feedstock used in the production of industrial chemicals, fuels, plastics, and pharmaceutical goods; lumber is a _____ used to produce a variety of products including all types of furniture. The term " _____ " denotes materials in minimally processed or unprocessed in states; e.g., raw latex, crude oil, cotton, coal, raw biomass, iron ore, air, logs, or water i.e. "...any product of agriculture, forestry, fishing and any other mineral that is in its natural form or which has undergone the transformation required to prepare it for internationally marketing in substantial volumes."

Exam Probability: **Medium**

26. *Answer choices:*
(see index for correct answer)

- a. Three-dimensional quartz phenolic
- b. Exotic material
- c. Materials for use in vacuum

- d. Raw material

Guidance: level 1

:: Risk analysis ::

Supply-chain risk management is "the implementation of strategies to manage both everyday and exceptional risks along the supply chain based on continuous risk assessment with the objective of reducing vulnerability and ensuring continuity".

Exam Probability: **Low**

27. *Answer choices:*
(see index for correct answer)

- a. European Risk Observatory
- b. Supply chain risk management
- c. Sneak circuit analysis
- d. Litigation risk analysis

Guidance: level 1

:: Project management ::

In economics, _____ is the assignment of available resources to various uses. In the context of an entire economy, resources can be allocated by various means, such as markets or central planning.

Exam Probability: **Medium**

28. *Answer choices:*
(see index for correct answer)

- a. Elemental cost planning
- b. Project manufacturing
- c. Critical path drag
- d. Terms of reference

Guidance: level 1

:: Project management ::

A _____ is a type of bar chart that illustrates a project schedule, named after its inventor, Henry Gantt, who designed such a chart around the years 1910–1915. Modern _____ s also show the dependency relationships between activities and current schedule status.

Exam Probability: **Low**

29. *Answer choices:*
_(see index for correct answer)

- a. Project manufacturing
- b. Initiative
- c. Stages of project finance
- d. Life-cycle cost analysis

Guidance: level 1

:: ::

In sales, commerce and economics, a _____ is the recipient of a good, service, product or an idea - obtained from a seller, vendor, or supplier via a financial transaction or exchange for money or some other valuable consideration.

Exam Probability: **Medium**

30. *Answer choices:*
_(see index for correct answer)

- a. deep-level diversity
- b. process perspective
- c. Customer
- d. functional perspective

Guidance: level 1

:: Production and manufacturing ::

_____ is the process of determining the production capacity needed by an organization to meet changing demands for its products. In the context of _____, design capacity is the maximum amount of work that an organization is capable of completing in a given period. Effective capacity is the maximum amount of work that an organization is capable of completing in a given period due to constraints such as quality problems, delays, material handling, etc.

Exam Probability: **Low**

31. *Answer choices:*

(see index for correct answer)

- a. Follow-the-sun
- b. Capacity planning
- c. Pre-shipment inspection
- d. Variable rate feeder

Guidance: level 1

:: ::

An _____ is, most an organized examination or formal evaluation exercise. In engineering activities _____ involves the measurements, tests, and gauges applied to certain characteristics in regard to an object or activity. The results are usually compared to specified requirements and standards for determining whether the item or activity is in line with these targets, often with a Standard _____ Procedure in place to ensure consistent checking. _____ s are usually non-destructive.

Exam Probability: **Low**

32. *Answer choices:*

(see index for correct answer)

- a. Inspection
- b. open system
- c. interpersonal communication
- d. imperative

Guidance: level 1

:: Project management ::

_____s can take many forms depending on the type of project being implemented and the nature of the organization. The _____ details the project deliverables and describes the major objectives. The objectives should include measurable success criteria for the project.

Exam Probability: **High**

33. *Answer choices:*

(see index for correct answer)

- a. Basis of estimate
- b. Collaborative project management
- c. Project team
- d. Scope statement

Guidance: level 1

:: Gas technologies ::

A _____ is a device used to transfer heat between two or more fluids. _____s are used in both cooling and heating processes. The fluids may be separated by a solid wall to prevent mixing or they may be in direct contact. They are widely used in space heating, refrigeration, air conditioning, power stations, chemical plants, petrochemical plants, petroleum refineries, natural-gas processing, and sewage treatment. The classic example of a _____ is found in an internal combustion engine in which a circulating fluid known as engine coolant flows through radiator coils and air flows past the coils, which cools the coolant and heats the incoming air. Another example is the heat sink, which is a passive _____ that transfers the heat generated by an electronic or a mechanical device to a fluid medium, often air or a liquid coolant.

Exam Probability: **High**

34. *Answer choices:*

(see index for correct answer)

- a. Heat exchanger
- b. Intercooler
- c. Restrictive flow orifice
- d. HEGA

Guidance: level 1

_____ is the process of finding an estimate, or approximation, which is a value that is usable for some purpose even if input data may be incomplete, uncertain, or unstable. The value is nonetheless usable because it is derived from the best information available. Typically, _____ involves "using the value of a statistic derived from a sample to estimate the value of a corresponding population parameter". The sample provides information that can be projected, through various formal or informal processes, to determine a range most likely to describe the missing information. An estimate that turns out to be incorrect will be an overestimate if the estimate exceeded the actual result, and an underestimate if the estimate fell short of the actual result.

Exam Probability: **Medium**

35. *Answer choices:*
(see index for correct answer)

- a. co-culture
- b. deep-level diversity
- c. Estimation
- d. imperative

Guidance: level 1

:: Project management ::

_____ is the right to exercise power, which can be formalized by a state and exercised by way of judges, appointed executives of government, or the ecclesiastical or priestly appointed representatives of a God or other deities.

Exam Probability: **High**

36. *Answer choices:*
(see index for correct answer)

- a. Assumption-based planning
- b. Identifying and Managing Project Risk
- c. Authority
- d. Mandated lead arranger

Guidance: level 1

:: Information technology management ::

The term _____ is used to refer to periods when a system is unavailable. _____ or outage duration refers to a period of time that a system fails to provide or perform its primary function. Reliability, availability, recovery, and unavailability are related concepts. The unavailability is the proportion of a time-span that a system is unavailable or offline. This is usually a result of the system failing to function because of an unplanned event, or because of routine maintenance.

Exam Probability: **Medium**

37. *Answer choices:*
(see index for correct answer)

- a. ODMA
- b. Downtime
- c. IT service management
- d. ITIL security management

Guidance: level 1

:: Production and manufacturing ::

_____ is the production under license of technology developed elsewhere. It is an especially prominent commercial practice in developing nations, which often approach _____ as a starting point for indigenous industrial development.

Exam Probability: **Medium**

38. *Answer choices:*
(see index for correct answer)

- a. Production part approval process
- b. Advanced product quality planning
- c. Licensed production
- d. Continuous production

Guidance: level 1

:: Gas technologies ::

A _____ is a rotary mechanical device that extracts energy from a fluid flow and converts it into useful work. The work produced by a _____ can be used for generating electrical power when combined with a generator. A _____ is a turbomachine with at least one moving part called a rotor assembly, which is a shaft or drum with blades attached. Moving fluid acts on the blades so that they move and impart rotational energy to the rotor. Early _____ examples are windmills and waterwheels.

Exam Probability: **Medium**

39. *Answer choices:*
(see index for correct answer)

- a. Heat exchanger
- b. Turbine
- c. Demister
- d. Molecular sieve

Guidance: level 1

:: ::

_____ refers to a business or organization attempting to acquire goods or services to accomplish its goals. Although there are several organizations that attempt to set standards in the _____ process, processes can vary greatly between organizations. Typically the word "_____" is not used interchangeably with the word "procurement", since procurement typically includes expediting, supplier quality, and transportation and logistics in addition to _____ .

Exam Probability: **Low**

40. *Answer choices:*
(see index for correct answer)

- a. interpersonal communication
- b. co-culture
- c. Purchasing
- d. levels of analysis

Guidance: level 1

:: ::

_____ is the process of making predictions of the future based on past and present data and most commonly by analysis of trends. A commonplace example might be estimation of some variable of interest at some specified future date. Prediction is a similar, but more general term. Both might refer to formal statistical methods employing time series, cross-sectional or longitudinal data, or alternatively to less formal judgmental methods. Usage can differ between areas of application: for example, in hydrology the terms "forecast" and "_____" are sometimes reserved for estimates of values at certain specific future times, while the term "prediction" is used for more general estimates, such as the number of times floods will occur over a long period.

Exam Probability: **Medium**

41. *Answer choices:*
(see index for correct answer)

- a. hierarchical perspective
- b. functional perspective
- c. similarity-attraction theory
- d. personal values

Guidance: level 1

:: Metal forming ::

_____ is a type of motion that combines rotation and translation of that object with respect to a surface, such that, if ideal conditions exist, the two are in contact with each other without sliding.

Exam Probability: **Low**

42. *Answer choices:*
(see index for correct answer)

- a. Roller burnishing
- b. Embossing
- c. Electroforming
- d. Raising

Guidance: level 1

:: Metal heat treatments ::

_____ is a group of industrial and metalworking processes used to alter the physical, and sometimes chemical, properties of a material. The most common application is metallurgical. Heat treatments are also used in the manufacture of many other materials, such as glass. Heat treatment involves the use of heating or chilling, normally to extreme temperatures, to achieve a desired result such as hardening or softening of a material. Heat treatment techniques include annealing, case hardening, precipitation strengthening, tempering, carburizing, normalizing and quenching. It is noteworthy that while the term heat treatment applies only to processes where the heating and cooling are done for the specific purpose of altering properties intentionally, heating and cooling often occur incidentally during other manufacturing processes such as hot forming or welding.

Exam Probability: **High**

43. *Answer choices:*

(see index for correct answer)

- a. Quench polish quench
- b. Induction hardening
- c. Ferritic nitrocarburizing
- d. Martempering

Guidance: level 1

:: Water ::

_____ is a transparent, tasteless, odorless, and nearly colorless chemical substance, which is the main constituent of Earth's streams, lakes, and oceans, and the fluids of most living organisms. It is vital for all known forms of life, even though it provides no calories or organic nutrients. Its chemical formula is H2O, meaning that each of its molecules contains one oxygen and two hydrogen atoms, connected by covalent bonds. _____ is the name of the liquid state of H2O at standard ambient temperature and pressure. It forms precipitation in the form of rain and aerosols in the form of fog. Clouds are formed from suspended droplets of _____ and ice, its solid state. When finely divided, crystalline ice may precipitate in the form of snow. The gaseous state of _____ is steam or _____ vapor. _____ moves continually through the _____ cycle of evaporation, transpiration, condensation, precipitation, and runoff, usually reaching the sea.

Exam Probability: **Medium**

44. *Answer choices:*

(see index for correct answer)

- a. Water privatization
- b. Water
- c. Orange County Water District
- d. Brine rejection

Guidance: level 1

:: Process management ::

A _____ is a diagram commonly used in chemical and process engineering to indicate the general flow of plant processes and equipment. The PFD displays the relationship between major equipment of a plant facility and does not show minor details such as piping details and designations. Another commonly used term for a PFD is a flowsheet.

Exam Probability: **High**

45. *Answer choices:*

(see index for correct answer)

- a. Process lifecycle
- b. Throughput
- c. Process window
- d. Process flow diagram

Guidance: level 1

:: Alchemical processes ::

In chemistry, a _____ is a special type of homogeneous mixture composed of two or more substances. In such a mixture, a solute is a substance dissolved in another substance, known as a solvent. The mixing process of a _____ happens at a scale where the effects of chemical polarity are involved, resulting in interactions that are specific to solvation. The _____ assumes the phase of the solvent when the solvent is the larger fraction of the mixture, as is commonly the case. The concentration of a solute in a _____ is the mass of that solute expressed as a percentage of the mass of the whole _____. The term aqueous _____ is when one of the solvents is water.

Exam Probability: **Medium**

46. *Answer choices:*

(see index for correct answer)

- a. Digestion
- b. Putrefying bacteria
- c. Unity of opposites
- d. Solution

Guidance: level 1

:: ::

_____ is the production of products for use or sale using labour and machines, tools, chemical and biological processing, or formulation. The term may refer to a range of human activity, from handicraft to high tech, but is most commonly applied to industrial design, in which raw materials are transformed into finished goods on a large scale. Such finished goods may be sold to other manufacturers for the production of other, more complex products, such as aircraft, household appliances, furniture, sports equipment or automobiles, or sold to wholesalers, who in turn sell them to retailers, who then sell them to end users and consumers.

Exam Probability: **Medium**

47. *Answer choices:*

(see index for correct answer)

- a. Sarbanes-Oxley act of 2002
- b. Manufacturing
- c. open system
- d. similarity-attraction theory

Guidance: level 1

:: Process management ::

_____ is a statistics package developed at the Pennsylvania State University by researchers Barbara F. Ryan, Thomas A. Ryan, Jr., and Brian L. Joiner in 1972. It began as a light version of OMNITAB 80, a statistical analysis program by NIST. Statistical analysis software such as _____ automates calculations and the creation of graphs, allowing the user to focus more on the analysis of data and the interpretation of results. It is compatible with other _____ , Inc. software.

Exam Probability: **Medium**

48. *Answer choices:*

(see index for correct answer)

- a. Business process redesign
- b. Minitab
- c. Six Sigma for ROI
- d. Process optimization

Guidance: level 1

:: Production and manufacturing ::

_____ is a theory of management that analyzes and synthesizes workflows. Its main objective is improving economic efficiency, especially labor productivity. It was one of the earliest attempts to apply science to the engineering of processes and to management. _____ is sometimes known as Taylorism after its founder, Frederick Winslow Taylor.

Exam Probability: **Medium**

49. *Answer choices:*

(see index for correct answer)

- a. Scientific management
- b. Plant layout study
- c. Job shop
- d. Continuous production

Guidance: level 1

:: Promotion and marketing communications ::

The _____ of American Manufacturers, now ThomasNet, is an online platform for supplier discovery and product sourcing in the US and Canada. It was once known as the "big green books" and "Thomas Registry", and was a multi-volume directory of industrial product information covering 650,000 distributors, manufacturers and service companies within 67,000-plus industrial categories that is now published on ThomasNet.

Exam Probability: **High**

50. *Answer choices:*
(see index for correct answer)

- a. Keep Calm and Carry On
- b. Infoganda
- c. Air Miles
- d. Thomas Register

Guidance: level 1

:: Business process ::

A committee is a body of one or more persons that is subordinate to a deliberative assembly. Usually, the assembly sends matters into a committee as a way to explore them more fully than would be possible if the assembly itself were considering them. Committees may have different functions and their type of work differ depending on the type of the organization and its needs.

Exam Probability: **Low**

51. *Answer choices:*
(see index for correct answer)

- a. Steering committee
- b. Information technology outsourcing
- c. Desktop outsourcing
- d. Business communication

Guidance: level 1

:: Auditing ::

_____ is the process of systematic examination of a quality system carried out by an internal or external _____ or or an audit team. It is an important part of an organization's quality management system and is a key element in the ISO quality system standard, ISO 9001.

Exam Probability: **High**

52. *Answer choices:*
(see index for correct answer)

- a. SOFT audit
- b. Assurance services
- c. Continuous auditing
- d. Environmental audit

Guidance: level 1

:: Data management ::

_____ is an object-oriented program and library developed by CERN. It was originally designed for particle physics data analysis and contains several features specific to this field, but it is also used in other applications such as astronomy and data mining. The latest release is 6.16.00, as of 2018-11-14.

Exam Probability: **Medium**

53. *Answer choices:*
(see index for correct answer)

- a. Electronically stored information
- b. BBC Archives
- c. ROOT
- d. Data independence

Guidance: level 1

:: Production and manufacturing ::

_____ is a production planning, scheduling, and inventory control system used to manage manufacturing processes. Most MRP systems are software-based, but it is possible to conduct MRP by hand as well.

Exam Probability: **High**

54. *Answer choices:*

(see index for correct answer)

- a. Process layout
- b. Material requirements planning
- c. Production engineering
- d. Accelerated aging

Guidance: level 1

:: Management ::

A supply-chain network is an evolution of the basic supply chain. Due to rapid technological advancement, organisations with a basic supply chain can develop this chain into a more complex structure involving a higher level of interdependence and connectivity between more organisations, this constitutes a supply-chain network.

Exam Probability: **Low**

55. *Answer choices:*

(see index for correct answer)

- a. manager's right to manage
- b. Supply chain network
- c. Energy monitoring and targeting
- d. Energy management software

Guidance: level 1

:: Industrial processes ::

_____ is a technique involving the condensation of vapors and the return of this condensate to the system from which it originated. It is used in industrial and laboratory distillations. It is also used in chemistry to supply energy to reactions over a long period of time.

Exam Probability: **Medium**

56. *Answer choices:*

(see index for correct answer)

- a. Reflux
- b. Cryogenic oxygen plant

- c. Cathodic arc deposition
- d. Textile bleaching

Guidance: level 1

:: Production and manufacturing ::

_____ was a management-led program to eliminate defects in industrial production that enjoyed brief popularity in American industry from 1964 to the early 1970s. Quality expert Philip Crosby later incorporated it into his "Absolutes of Quality Management" and it enjoyed a renaissance in the American automobile industry—as a performance goal more than as a program—in the 1990s. Although applicable to any type of enterprise, it has been primarily adopted within supply chains wherever large volumes of components are being purchased.

Exam Probability: **High**

57. *Answer choices:*
(see index for correct answer)

- a. Zero Defects
- b. Wireless DNC
- c. Managed services
- d. Alarm fatigue

Guidance: level 1

:: Inventory ::

The _____ is the level of inventory which triggers an action to replenish that particular inventory stock. It is a minimum amount of an item which a firm holds in stock, such that, when stock falls to this amount, the item must be reordered. It is normally calculated as the forecast usage during the replenishment lead time plus safety stock. In the EOQ model, it was assumed that there is no time lag between ordering and procuring of materials. Therefore the _____ for replenishing the stocks occurs at that level when the inventory level drops to zero and because instant delivery by suppliers, the stock level bounce back.

Exam Probability: **Low**

58. *Answer choices:*
(see index for correct answer)

- a. New old stock
- b. Specific identification
- c. Reorder point
- d. Lower of cost or market

Guidance: level 1

:: Quality management ::

In quality management system, a _____ is a document developed by management to express the directive of the top management with respect to quality. _____ management is a strategic item.

Exam Probability: **Low**

59. *Answer choices:*
(see index for correct answer)

- a. Quality management
- b. Quality policy
- c. Management by wandering around
- d. Flemish Quality Management Center

Guidance: level 1

Commerce

Commerce relates to "the exchange of goods and services, especially on a large scale." It includes legal, economic, political, social, cultural and technological systems that operate in any country or internationally.

:: E-commerce ::

E-commerce is the activity of buying or selling of products on online services or over the Internet. _____ draws on technologies such as mobile commerce, electronic funds transfer, supply chain management, Internet marketing, online transaction processing, electronic data interchange, inventory management systems, and automated data collection systems.

Exam Probability: **Low**

1. *Answer choices:*
_(see index for correct answer)

- a. CXML
- b. Electronic commerce
- c. Loquo
- d. Loppi

Guidance: level 1

:: ::

_____ refers to the overall process of attracting, shortlisting, selecting and appointing suitable candidates for jobs within an organization. _____ can also refer to processes involved in choosing individuals for unpaid roles. Managers, human resource generalists and _____ specialists may be tasked with carrying out _____, but in some cases public-sector employment agencies, commercial _____ agencies, or specialist search consultancies are used to undertake parts of the process. Internet-based technologies which support all aspects of _____ have become widespread.

Exam Probability: **Low**

2. *Answer choices:*
(see index for correct answer)

- a. levels of analysis
- b. Recruitment
- c. Character
- d. cultural

Guidance: level 1

:: ::

Business Model Canvas is a strategic management and lean startup template for developing new or documenting existing business models. It is a visual chart with elements describing a firm's or product's value proposition, infrastructure, customers, and finances. It assists firms in aligning their activities by illustrating potential trade-offs.

Exam Probability: **High**

3. *Answer choices:*
(see index for correct answer)

- a. hierarchical perspective
- b. process perspective
- c. functional perspective
- d. levels of analysis

Guidance: level 1

:: Stock market ::

_____ is freedom from, or resilience against, potential harm caused by others. Beneficiaries of _____ may be of persons and social groups, objects and institutions, ecosystems or any other entity or phenomenon vulnerable to unwanted change by its environment.

Exam Probability: **High**

4. *Answer choices:*
(see index for correct answer)

- a. Reverse stock split
- b. FTSE Global Equity Index Series
- c. American depositary receipt
- d. Security

Guidance: level 1

:: Supply chain management ::

_____ is the removal of intermediaries in economics from a supply chain, or cutting out the middlemen in connection with a transaction or a series of transactions. Instead of going through traditional distribution channels, which had some type of intermediary, companies may now deal with customers directly, for example via the Internet. Hence, the use of factory direct and direct from the factory to mean the same thing.

Exam Probability: **High**

5. *Answer choices:*
(see index for correct answer)

- a. Customs-Trade Partnership Against Terrorism
- b. Disintermediation
- c. Dynamic discounting
- d. Netchain analysis

Guidance: level 1

:: ::

A _____ is a graphic mark, emblem, or symbol used to aid and promote public identification and recognition. It may be of an abstract or figurative design or include the text of the name it represents as in a wordmark.

Exam Probability: **Medium**

6. *Answer choices:*
(see index for correct answer)

- a. imperative
- b. Logo
- c. deep-level diversity
- d. corporate values

Guidance: level 1

:: Business law ::

A _____ is a contractual arrangement calling for the lessee to pay the lessor for use of an asset. Property, buildings and vehicles are common assets that are _____ d. Industrial or business equipment is also _____ d.

Exam Probability: **Medium**

7. *Answer choices:*
(see index for correct answer)

- a. Limited partnership
- b. Business license
- c. Principal
- d. Extraordinary resolution

Guidance: level 1

:: International trade ::

In finance, an _____ is the rate at which one currency will be exchanged for another. It is also regarded as the value of one country's currency in relation to another currency. For example, an interbank _____ of 114 Japanese yen to the United States dollar means that ¥114 will be exchanged for each US$1 or that US$1 will be exchanged for each ¥114. In this case it is said that the price of a dollar in relation to yen is ¥114, or equivalently that the price of a yen in relation to dollars is $1/114.

Exam Probability: **Medium**

8. *Answer choices:*
(see index for correct answer)

- a. Section 201
- b. Schedules of concessions
- c. Lee Byung-chul
- d. Maquiladora

Guidance: level 1

:: E-commerce ::

_____ is the business-to-business or business-to-consumer or business-to-government purchase and sale of supplies, work, and services through the Internet as well as other information and networking systems, such as electronic data interchange and enterprise resource planning.

Exam Probability: **Medium**

9. *Answer choices:*
(see index for correct answer)

- a. Auction software
- b. E-procurement
- c. Yakala.co
- d. RSA

Guidance: level 1

:: Mereology ::

_____, in the abstract, is what belongs to or with something, whether as an attribute or as a component of said thing. In the context of this article, it is one or more components, whether physical or incorporeal, of a person's estate; or so belonging to, as in being owned by, a person or jointly a group of people or a legal entity like a corporation or even a society. Depending on the nature of the _____, an owner of _____ has the right to consume, alter, share, redefine, rent, mortgage, pawn, sell, exchange, transfer, give away or destroy it, or to exclude others from doing these things, as well as to perhaps abandon it; whereas regardless of the nature of the _____, the owner thereof has the right to properly use it, or at the very least exclusively keep it.

Exam Probability: **Medium**

10. *Answer choices:*
(see index for correct answer)

- a. Mereological essentialism
- b. Simple
- c. Mereology
- d. Property

Guidance: level 1

:: Consortia ::

A _____ is an association of two or more individuals, companies, organizations or governments with the objective of participating in a common activity or pooling their resources for achieving a common goal.

Exam Probability: **High**

11. *Answer choices:*
(see index for correct answer)

- a. Builder homesite
- b. Kamco
- c. 4C Entity
- d. Consortium

Guidance: level 1

:: Industry ::

_____ describes various measures of the efficiency of production. Often, a _____ measure is expressed as the ratio of an aggregate output to a single input or an aggregate input used in a production process, i.e. output per unit of input. Most common example is the labour _____ measure, e.g., such as GDP per worker. There are many different definitions of _____ and the choice among them depends on the purpose of the _____ measurement and/or data availability. The key source of difference between various _____ measures is also usually related to how the outputs and the inputs are aggregated into scalars to obtain such a ratio-type measure of _____.

Exam Probability: **Low**

12. *Answer choices:*
(see index for correct answer)

- a. Sunset industry
- b. Industrialisation
- c. Productivity
- d. Metal expansion joint

Guidance: level 1

:: ::

_____ s is the linguistic and philosophical study of meaning, in language, programming languages, formal logics, and semiotics. It is concerned with the relationship between signifiers—like words, phrases, signs, and symbols—and what they stand for in reality, their denotation.

Exam Probability: **Low**

13. *Answer choices:*
(see index for correct answer)

- a. Character
- b. Semantic
- c. functional perspective
- d. imperative

Guidance: level 1

:: Market research ::

_____ is an organized effort to gather information about target markets or customers. It is a very important component of business strategy. The term is commonly interchanged with marketing research; however, expert practitioners may wish to draw a distinction, in that marketing research is concerned specifically about marketing processes, while _____ is concerned specifically with markets.

Exam Probability: **High**

14. *Answer choices:*

(see index for correct answer)

- a. PreTesting Company
- b. Market research
- c. DigitalMR
- d. Preference regression

Guidance: level 1

:: ::

Regulatory economics is the economics of regulation. It is the application of law by government or independent administrative agencies for various purposes, including remedying market failure, protecting the environment, centrally-planning an economy, enriching well-connected firms, or benefiting politicians.

Exam Probability: **High**

15. *Answer choices:*

(see index for correct answer)

- a. Economic regulation
- b. functional perspective
- c. personal values
- d. hierarchical perspective

Guidance: level 1

:: Retailing ::

A _____ or trolley, also known by a variety of other names, is a cart supplied by a shop, especially supermarkets, for use by customers inside the shop for transport of merchandise to the checkout counter during shopping. In many cases customers can then also use the cart to transport their purchased goods to their vehicles, but some carts are designed to prevent them from leaving the shop.

Exam Probability: **Medium**

16. *Answer choices:*

(see index for correct answer)

- a. Returning
- b. Tourist trap
- c. Vendor log
- d. Shopping cart

Guidance: level 1

:: Management ::

Logistics is generally the detailed organization and implementation of a complex operation. In a general business sense, logistics is the management of the flow of things between the point of origin and the point of consumption in order to meet requirements of customers or corporations. The resources managed in logistics may include tangible goods such as materials, equipment, and supplies, as well as food and other consumable items. The logistics of physical items usually involves the integration of information flow, materials handling, production, packaging, inventory, transportation, warehousing, and often security.

Exam Probability: **High**

17. *Answer choices:*

(see index for correct answer)

- a. Court of Assistants
- b. Logistics Management
- c. Enterprise planning system
- d. Operations research

Guidance: level 1

:: E-commerce ::

_____ , cybersecurity or information technology security is the protection of computer systems from theft or damage to their hardware, software or electronic data, as well as from disruption or misdirection of the services they provide.

Exam Probability: **Low**

18. *Answer choices:*
(see index for correct answer)

- a. Computer security
- b. SMS banking
- c. Network Security Services
- d. Loppi

Guidance: level 1

:: Commercial item transport and distribution ::

In commerce, supply-chain management , the management of the flow of goods and services, involves the movement and storage of raw materials, of work-in-process inventory, and of finished goods from point of origin to point of consumption. Interconnected or interlinked networks, channels and node businesses combine in the provision of products and services required by end customers in a supply chain. Supply-chain management has been defined as the "design, planning, execution, control, and monitoring of supply-chain activities with the objective of creating net value, building a competitive infrastructure, leveraging worldwide logistics, synchronizing supply with demand and measuring performance globally."SCM practice draws heavily from the areas of industrial engineering, systems engineering, operations management, logistics, procurement, information technology, and marketing and strives for an integrated approach. Marketing channels play an important role in supply-chain management. Current research in supply-chain management is concerned with topics related to sustainability and risk management, among others. Some suggest that the "people dimension" of SCM, ethical issues, internal integration, transparency/visibility, and human capital/talent management are topics that have, so far, been underrepresented on the research agenda.

Exam Probability: **Medium**

19. *Answer choices:*
(see index for correct answer)

- a. Skid unit
- b. Supply chain management
- c. Distribution deal
- d. Commercial Vehicle Inspection

Guidance: level 1

:: Dot-com bubble ::

_____ is an internet portal launched in 1995 that provides a variety of content including news and weather, a metasearch engine, a web-based email, instant messaging, stock quotes, and a customizable user homepage. It is currently operated by IAC Applications of IAC, and _____ Networks. In the U.S., the main _____ site has long been a personal start page called My _____. _____ also operates an e-mail service, although it is no longer open for new customers.

Exam Probability: **Low**

20. *Answer choices:*
(see index for correct answer)

- a. AllAdvantage
- b. DrinkExchange
- c. Fucked Company
- d. @Home Network

Guidance: level 1

:: ::

Walter Elias Disney was an American entrepreneur, animator, voice actor and film producer. A pioneer of the American animation industry, he introduced several developments in the production of cartoons. As a film producer, Disney holds the record for most Academy Awards earned by an individual, having won 22 Oscars from 59 nominations. He was presented with two Golden Globe Special Achievement Awards and an Emmy Award, among other honors. Several of his films are included in the National Film Registry by the Library of Congress.

Exam Probability: **Low**

21. *Answer choices:*
(see index for correct answer)

- a. deep-level diversity
- b. process perspective
- c. hierarchical perspective
- d. open system

Guidance: level 1

:: ::

_____ is getting a diploma or academic degree or the ceremony that is sometimes associated with it, in which students become graduates. The date of _____ is often called _____ day. The _____ ceremony itself is also called commencement, convocation or invocation.

Exam Probability: **High**

22. *Answer choices:*
(see index for correct answer)

- a. interpersonal communication
- b. similarity-attraction theory
- c. functional perspective
- d. imperative

Guidance: level 1

:: ::

_____, or auditory perception, is the ability to perceive sounds by detecting vibrations, changes in the pressure of the surrounding medium through time, through an organ such as the ear. The academic field concerned with _____ is auditory science.

Exam Probability: **High**

23. *Answer choices:*
(see index for correct answer)

- a. interpersonal communication
- b. co-culture
- c. functional perspective

- d. corporate values

Guidance: level 1

:: Information retrieval ::

_____ is a technique used by recommender systems. _____ has two senses, a narrow one and a more general one.

Exam Probability: **Low**

24. *Answer choices:*
(see index for correct answer)

- a. Expertise finding
- b. Collaborative filtering
- c. Index term
- d. Latent semantic mapping

Guidance: level 1

:: ::

_____ is a means of protection from financial loss. It is a form of risk management, primarily used to hedge against the risk of a contingent or uncertain loss

Exam Probability: **Medium**

25. *Answer choices:*
(see index for correct answer)

- a. functional perspective
- b. levels of analysis
- c. empathy
- d. Insurance

Guidance: level 1

:: Auctioneering ::

_____ are electronic auctions, which can be used by sellers to sell their items to many potential buyers. Sellers and buyers can be individuals, organizations etc.

Exam Probability: **High**

26. *Answer choices:*

(see index for correct answer)

- a. Vickrey auction
- b. Reppert School of Auctioneering
- c. National Auctioneers Association
- d. Forward auction

Guidance: level 1

:: Business law ::

A _____ is a group of people who jointly supervise the activities of an organization, which can be either a for-profit business, nonprofit organization, or a government agency. Such a board's powers, duties, and responsibilities are determined by government regulations and the organization's own constitution and bylaws. These authorities may specify the number of members of the board, how they are to be chosen, and how often they are to meet.

Exam Probability: **Medium**

27. *Answer choices:*

(see index for correct answer)

- a. Commercial law
- b. Board of directors
- c. Family and Medical Leave Act of 1993
- d. Business courts

Guidance: level 1

:: Industrial automation ::

_____ is the technology by which a process or procedure is performed with minimal human assistance. _____ or automatic control is the use of various control systems for operating equipment such as machinery, processes in factories, boilers and heat treating ovens, switching on telephone networks, steering and stabilization of ships, aircraft and other applications and vehicles with minimal or reduced human intervention.

Exam Probability: **Low**

28. *Answer choices:*
(see index for correct answer)

- a. Automation
- b. Stack light
- c. Collaborative process automation systems
- d. Sequential function chart

Guidance: level 1

:: ::

Advertising is a marketing communication that employs an openly sponsored, non-personal message to promote or sell a product, service or idea. Sponsors of advertising are typically businesses wishing to promote their products or services. Advertising is differentiated from public relations in that an advertiser pays for and has control over the message. It differs from personal selling in that the message is non-personal, i.e., not directed to a particular individual. Advertising is communicated through various mass media, including traditional media such as newspapers, magazines, television, radio, outdoor advertising or direct mail; and new media such as search results, blogs, social media, websites or text messages. The actual presentation of the message in a medium is referred to as an _____ , or "ad" or advert for short.

Exam Probability: **Medium**

29. *Answer choices:*
(see index for correct answer)

- a. personal values
- b. Advertisement
- c. process perspective
- d. Character

Guidance: level 1

:: Commodities ::

In economics, a _____ is an economic good or service that has full or substantial fungibility: that is, the market treats instances of the good as equivalent or nearly so with no regard to who produced them. Most commodities are raw materials, basic resources, agricultural, or mining products, such as iron ore, sugar, or grains like rice and wheat. Commodities can also be mass-produced unspecialized products such as chemicals and computer memory.

Exam Probability: **Low**

30. *Answer choices:*
(see index for correct answer)

- a. Commoditization
- b. IRely
- c. Commodity
- d. Sample grade

Guidance: level 1

:: Theories ::

A _____ union is a type of multinational political union where negotiated power is delegated to an authority by governments of member states.

Exam Probability: **Low**

31. *Answer choices:*
(see index for correct answer)

- a. Taylorism
- b. incrementalism

Guidance: level 1

:: ::

_____ is an emotion involving pleasure, , or anxiety in considering or awaiting an expected event.

Exam Probability: **Low**

32. *Answer choices:*
(see index for correct answer)

- a. personal values
- b. co-culture
- c. imperative
- d. Sarbanes-Oxley act of 2002

Guidance: level 1

:: E-commerce ::

Customer to customer markets provide an innovative way to allow customers to interact with each other. Traditional markets require business to customer relationships, in which a customer goes to the business in order to purchase a product or service. In customer to customer markets, the business facilitates an environment where customers can sell goods or services to each other. Other types of markets include business to business and business to customer.

Exam Probability: **High**

33. *Answer choices:*
(see index for correct answer)

- a. Click fraud
- b. Entrust
- c. Consumer-to-consumer
- d. Social shopping

Guidance: level 1

:: E-commerce ::

A _____ is a financial transaction involving a very small sum of money and usually one that occurs online. A number of _____ systems were proposed and developed in the mid-to-late 1990s, all of which were ultimately unsuccessful. A second generation of _____ systems emerged in the 2010s.

Exam Probability: **Medium**

34. *Answer choices:*
(see index for correct answer)

- a. SupaDupa
- b. Electronic sell-through
- c. Beamdog
- d. Micropayment

Guidance: level 1

:: Asset ::

In financial accounting, an _____ is any resource owned by the business. Anything tangible or intangible that can be owned or controlled to produce value and that is held by a company to produce positive economic value is an _____ . Simply stated, _____ s represent value of ownership that can be converted into cash . The balance sheet of a firm records the monetary value of the _____ s owned by that firm. It covers money and other valuables belonging to an individual or to a business.

Exam Probability: **Medium**

35. *Answer choices:*
(see index for correct answer)

- a. Current asset
- b. Asset

Guidance: level 1

:: Meetings ::

A _____ is a body of one or more persons that is subordinate to a deliberative assembly. Usually, the assembly sends matters into a _____ as a way to explore them more fully than would be possible if the assembly itself were considering them. _____ s may have different functions and their type of work differ depending on the type of the organization and its needs.

Exam Probability: **High**

36. *Answer choices:*
(see index for correct answer)

- a. Middle East Electricity
- b. Parley
- c. Committee

- d. European Architecture Students Assembly

Guidance: level 1

:: ::

In mathematics, computer science and operations research, mathematical optimization or mathematical programming is the selection of a best element from some set of available alternatives.

Exam Probability: **Medium**

37. *Answer choices:*
(see index for correct answer)

- a. interpersonal communication
- b. functional perspective
- c. levels of analysis
- d. Character

Guidance: level 1

:: ::

_____ is "property consisting of land and the buildings on it, along with its natural resources such as crops, minerals or water; immovable property of this nature; an interest vested in this an item of real property, buildings or housing in general. Also: the business of _____ ; the profession of buying, selling, or renting land, buildings, or housing." It is a legal term used in jurisdictions whose legal system is derived from English common law, such as India, England, Wales, Northern Ireland, United States, Canada, Pakistan, Australia, and New Zealand.

Exam Probability: **Low**

38. *Answer choices:*
(see index for correct answer)

- a. process perspective
- b. Real estate
- c. information systems assessment
- d. functional perspective

Guidance: level 1

:: International trade ::

An _____ is a good brought into a jurisdiction, especially across a national border, from an external source. The party bringing in the good is called an _____ er. An _____ in the receiving country is an export from the sending country. _____ ation and exportation are the defining financial transactions of international trade.

Exam Probability: **Medium**

39. *Answer choices:*
(see index for correct answer)

- a. International Association for Technology Trade
- b. Hong Kong Economic and Trade Office
- c. Foreign Sales Corporation
- d. Trading nation

Guidance: level 1

:: ::

_____ is a concept of English common law and is a necessity for simple contracts but not for special contracts. The concept has been adopted by other common law jurisdictions, including the US.

Exam Probability: **High**

40. *Answer choices:*
(see index for correct answer)

- a. empathy
- b. surface-level diversity
- c. cultural
- d. Consideration

Guidance: level 1

:: ::

_____ is a process whereby a person assumes the parenting of another, usually a child, from that person's biological or legal parent or parents. Legal _____ s permanently transfers all rights and responsibilities, along with filiation, from the biological parent or parents.

Exam Probability: **Medium**

41. *Answer choices:*
(see index for correct answer)

- a. Sarbanes-Oxley act of 2002
- b. Adoption
- c. cultural
- d. co-culture

Guidance: level 1

:: ::

Senior management, executive management, upper management, or a _____ is generally a team of individuals at the highest level of management of an organization who have the day-to-day tasks of managing that organization — sometimes a company or a corporation.

Exam Probability: **Medium**

42. *Answer choices:*
(see index for correct answer)

- a. similarity-attraction theory
- b. Management team
- c. cultural
- d. hierarchical perspective

Guidance: level 1

:: Customs duties ::

A _____ is a tax on imports or exports between sovereign states. It is a form of regulation of foreign trade and a policy that taxes foreign products to encourage or safeguard domestic industry. _____ s are the simplest and oldest instrument of trade policy. Traditionally, states have used them as a source of income. Now, they are among the most widely used instruments of protection, along with import and export quotas.

Exam Probability: **High**

43. *Answer choices:*

(see index for correct answer)

- a. Malaysian motor vehicle import duties
- b. Carnet de Passages
- c. Duty-free shop
- d. Canada Corn Act

Guidance: level 1

:: Business terms ::

_____ ning is an organization's process of defining its strategy, or direction, and making decisions on allocating its resources to pursue this strategy. It may also extend to control mechanisms for guiding the implementation of the strategy. _____ ning became prominent in corporations during the 1960s and remains an important aspect of strategic management. It is executed by _____ ners or strategists, who involve many parties and research sources in their analysis of the organization and its relationship to the environment in which it competes.

Exam Probability: **Low**

44. *Answer choices:*

(see index for correct answer)

- a. Owner Controlled Insurance Program
- b. Strategic plan
- c. centralization
- d. churn rate

Guidance: level 1

:: Industry ::

_____ , also known as flow production or continuous production, is the production of large amounts of standardized products, including and especially on assembly lines. Together with job production and batch production, it is one of the three main production methods.

Exam Probability: **High**

45. *Answer choices:*
(see index for correct answer)

- a. Prefabrication
- b. Mass production
- c. Chemical process
- d. Production line

Guidance: level 1

:: Payment systems ::

A _____ is any system used to settle financial transactions through the transfer of monetary value. This includes the institutions, instruments, people, rules, procedures, standards, and technologies that make it exchange possible. A common type of _____ is called an operational network that links bank accounts and provides for monetary exchange using bank deposits. Some _____ s also include credit mechanisms, which are essentially a different aspect of payment.

Exam Probability: **High**

46. *Answer choices:*
(see index for correct answer)

- a. Electronic Benefit Transfer
- b. Invoicera
- c. TIPANET
- d. Cheque truncation

Guidance: level 1

:: Payments ::

A _____ or government incentive is a form of financial aid or support extended to an economic sector generally with the aim of promoting economic and social policy. Although commonly extended from government, the term _____ can relate to any type of support – for example from NGOs or as implicit subsidies. Subsidies come in various forms including: direct and indirect.

Exam Probability: **High**

47. *Answer choices:*
(see index for correct answer)

- a. VersaPay
- b. Direct Payments
- c. Deficiency payments
- d. Incentive payments

Guidance: level 1

:: Supply chain management ::

A _____ is a type of auction in which the traditional roles of buyer and seller are reversed. Thus, there is one buyer and many potential sellers. In an ordinary auction, buyers compete to obtain goods or services by offering increasingly higher prices. In contrast, in a _____ , the sellers compete to obtain business from the buyer and prices will typically decrease as the sellers underbid each other.

Exam Probability: **Medium**

48. *Answer choices:*
(see index for correct answer)

- a. Reverse logistics
- b. Dealer Business System
- c. Reverse auction
- d. ClearOrbit

Guidance: level 1

:: Generally Accepted Accounting Principles ::

Expenditure is an outflow of money to another person or group to pay for an item or service, or for a category of costs. For a tenant, rent is an _____. For students or parents, tuition is an _____. Buying food, clothing, furniture or an automobile is often referred to as an _____. An _____ is a cost that is "paid" or "remitted", usually in exchange for something of value. Something that seems to cost a great deal is "expensive". Something that seems to cost little is "inexpensive". "_____s of the table" are _____s of dining, refreshments, a feast, etc.

Exam Probability: **Low**

49. *Answer choices:*
(see index for correct answer)

- a. Depreciation
- b. Cost principle
- c. Expense
- d. AICPA Statements of Position

Guidance: level 1

:: Investment ::

In finance, the benefit from an _____ is called a return. The return may consist of a gain realised from the sale of property or an _____, unrealised capital appreciation, or _____ income such as dividends, interest, rental income etc., or a combination of capital gain and income. The return may also include currency gains or losses due to changes in foreign currency exchange rates.

Exam Probability: **Medium**

50. *Answer choices:*
(see index for correct answer)

- a. Buy-write
- b. Investment
- c. Benchmark-driven investment strategy
- d. Binary option

Guidance: level 1

:: ::

In law, a _____ is a coming together of parties to a dispute, to present information in a tribunal, a formal setting with the authority to adjudicate claims or disputes. One form of tribunal is a court. The tribunal, which may occur before a judge, jury, or other designated trier of fact, aims to achieve a resolution to their dispute.

Exam Probability: **High**

51. *Answer choices:*

(see index for correct answer)

- a. personal values
- b. empathy
- c. Trial
- d. deep-level diversity

Guidance: level 1

:: Marketing ::

_____ —an information- and communication-based electronic exchange environment—is a relatively new concept in marketing. Since physical boundaries no longer interfere with buy/sell decisions, the world has grown into several industry specific _____ s which are integration of marketplaces through sophisticated computer and telecommunication technologies. The term _____ was introduced by Jeffrey Rayport and John Sviokla in 1994 in their article "Managing in the _____" that appeared in Harvard Business Review. In the article the authors distinguished between electronic and conventional markets. In a _____, information and/or physical goods are exchanged, and transactions take place through computers and networks. These networks consist of blogs, forum threads, and micro-blogging services like Twitter. Businesses and their customers are enabled to create conversations and two-way communications about products and services. These conversations may also happen outside the sphere of control of a given business, when a marketing campaign or customer-service issue captures the attention of web-savvy consumers.

Exam Probability: **Medium**

52. *Answer choices:*

(see index for correct answer)

- a. Green market
- b. Markup

- c. Marketspace
- d. Performance-based advertising

Guidance: level 1

:: Materials ::

A _____ , also known as a feedstock, unprocessed material, or primary commodity, is a basic material that is used to produce goods, finished products, energy, or intermediate materials which are feedstock for future finished products. As feedstock, the term connotes these materials are bottleneck assets and are highly important with regard to producing other products. An example of this is crude oil, which is a _____ and a feedstock used in the production of industrial chemicals, fuels, plastics, and pharmaceutical goods; lumber is a _____ used to produce a variety of products including all types of furniture. The term " _____ " denotes materials in minimally processed or unprocessed in states; e.g., raw latex, crude oil, cotton, coal, raw biomass, iron ore, air, logs, or water i.e. "...any product of agriculture, forestry, fishing and any other mineral that is in its natural form or which has undergone the transformation required to prepare it for internationally marketing in substantial volumes."

Exam Probability: **Medium**

53. *Answer choices:*
(see index for correct answer)

- a. Raw material
- b. Technora
- c. Ceramic materials
- d. Intumescent

Guidance: level 1

:: Marketing ::

_____ is the percentage of a market accounted for by a specific entity. In a survey of nearly 200 senior marketing managers, 67% responded that they found the revenue- "dollar _____ " metric very useful, while 61% found "unit _____ " very useful.

Exam Probability: **High**

54. *Answer choices:*
(see index for correct answer)

- a. Marketing decision support system
- b. Market share
- c. Matomy Media
- d. Online lead generation

Guidance: level 1

:: Dot-com bubble ::

_____, Inc., is a web search engine and web portal established in 1994, spun out of Carnegie Mellon University. _____ also encompasses a network of email, webhosting, social networking, and entertainment websites. The company is based in Waltham, Massachusetts, and is currently a subsidiary of Kakao.

Exam Probability: **Medium**

55. *Answer choices:*
(see index for correct answer)

- a. Cyberian Outpost
- b. GeoCities
- c. Lycos
- d. Internet time

Guidance: level 1

:: ::

A trade union is an association of workers forming a legal unit or legal personhood, usually called a "bargaining unit", which acts as bargaining agent and legal representative for a unit of employees in all matters of law or right arising from or in the administration of a collective agreement. Labour unions typically fund the formal organisation, head office, and legal team functions of the labour union through regular fees or union dues. The delegate staff of the labour union representation in the workforce are made up of workplace volunteers who are appointed by members in democratic elections.

Exam Probability: **Medium**

56. *Answer choices:*

(see index for correct answer)

- a. co-culture
- b. personal values
- c. empathy
- d. Labor union

Guidance: level 1

:: Commerce ::

_____ relates to "the exchange of goods and services, especially on a large scale". It includes legal, economic, political, social, cultural and technological systems that operate in a country or in international trade.

Exam Probability: **High**

57. *Answer choices:*
(see index for correct answer)

- a. Council of the Americas
- b. Export restriction
- c. Church sale
- d. Global Commerce Initiative

Guidance: level 1

:: Statutory law ::

_____ or statute law is written law set down by a body of legislature or by a singular legislator . This is as opposed to oral or customary law; or regulatory law promulgated by the executive or common law of the judiciary. Statutes may originate with national, state legislatures or local municipalities.

Exam Probability: **High**

58. *Answer choices:*
(see index for correct answer)

- a. Statutory law
- b. ratification
- c. incorporation by reference
- d. statute law

Guidance: level 1

:: Commerce ::

_____, Inc. is an American media-services provider headquartered in Los Gatos, California, founded in 1997 by Reed Hastings and Marc Randolph in Scotts Valley, California. The company's primary business is its subscription-based streaming OTT service which offers online streaming of a library of films and television programs, including those produced in-house. As of April 2019, _____ had over 148 million paid subscriptions worldwide, including 60 million in the United States, and over 154 million subscriptions total including free trials. It is available almost worldwide except in mainland China as well as Syria, North Korea, and Crimea. The company also has offices in the Netherlands, Brazil, India, Japan, and South Korea. _____ is a member of the Motion Picture Association of America.

Exam Probability: **Low**

59. *Answer choices:*
(see index for correct answer)

- a. Sales quote
- b. Netflix
- c. Bunker adjustment factor
- d. Return merchandise authorization

Guidance: level 1

Business ethics

Business ethics (also known as corporate ethics) is a form of applied ethics or professional ethics, that examines ethical principles and moral or ethical problems that can arise in a business environment. It applies to all aspects of business conduct and is relevant to the conduct of individuals and entire organizations. These ethics originate from individuals, organizational statements or from the legal system. These norms, values, ethical, and unethical practices are what is used to guide business. They help those businesses maintain a better connection with their stakeholders.

:: ::

_____ is a private Dominican liberal arts college in Madison, Wisconsin. The college occupies a 55 acres campus overlooking the shores of Lake Wingra.

Exam Probability: **Medium**

1. *Answer choices:*
(see index for correct answer)

- a. Edgewood College
- b. personal values
- c. surface-level diversity
- d. process perspective

Guidance: level 1

:: Electronic waste ::

_____ or e-waste describes discarded electrical or electronic devices. Used electronics which are destined for refurbishment, reuse, resale, salvage, recycling through material recovery, or disposal are also considered e-waste. Informal processing of e-waste in developing countries can lead to adverse human health effects and environmental pollution.

Exam Probability: **High**

2. *Answer choices:*
(see index for correct answer)

- a. Electronic waste
- b. World Reuse, Repair and Recycling Association
- c. Digger gold
- d. Computer liquidator

Guidance: level 1

:: Business ethics ::

_____ is a type of international private business self-regulation. While once it was possible to describe CSR as an internal organisational policy or a corporate ethic strategy, that time has passed as various international laws have been developed and various organisations have used their authority to push it beyond individual or even industry-wide initiatives. While it has been considered a form of corporate self-regulation for some time, over the last decade or so it has moved considerably from voluntary decisions at the level of individual organisations, to mandatory schemes at regional, national and even transnational levels.

Exam Probability: **High**

3. *Answer choices:*
(see index for correct answer)

- a. Product stewardship
- b. Corporate social responsibility
- c. Equator Principles
- d. Interfaith Center on Corporate Responsibility

Guidance: level 1

:: Minimum wage ::

The _____ are working people whose incomes fall below a given poverty line due to lack of work hours and/or low wages. Largely because they are earning such low wages, the _____ face numerous obstacles that make it difficult for many of them to find and keep a job, save up money, and maintain a sense of self-worth.

Exam Probability: **Low**

4. *Answer choices:*

(see index for correct answer)

- a. Minimum wage
- b. Minimum Wage Fairness Act
- c. Working poor
- d. National Anti-Sweating League

Guidance: level 1

:: ::

The _____, the Calvinist work ethic or the Puritan work ethic is a work ethic concept in theology, sociology, economics and history that emphasizes that hard work, discipline and frugality are a result of a person's subscription to the values espoused by the Protestant faith, particularly Calvinism. The phrase was initially coined in 1904–1905 by Max Weber in his book The Protestant Ethic and the Spirit of Capitalism.

Exam Probability: **Low**

5. *Answer choices:*

(see index for correct answer)

- a. information systems assessment
- b. imperative
- c. empathy
- d. Protestant work ethic

Guidance: level 1

:: Occupational safety and health ::

_____ is a chemical element with symbol Pb and atomic number 82. It is a heavy metal that is denser than most common materials. _____ is soft and malleable, and also has a relatively low melting point. When freshly cut, _____ is silvery with a hint of blue; it tarnishes to a dull gray color when exposed to air. _____ has the highest atomic number of any stable element and three of its isotopes are endpoints of major nuclear decay chains of heavier elements.

Exam Probability: **Medium**

6. *Answer choices:*
(see index for correct answer)

- a. Chromium
- b. Radiation dose reconstruction
- c. Lead
- d. Bernardino Ramazzini

Guidance: level 1

:: ::

Sustainability is the process of people maintaining change in a balanced environment, in which the exploitation of resources, the direction of investments, the orientation of technological development and institutional change are all in harmony and enhance both current and future potential to meet human needs and aspirations. For many in the field, sustainability is defined through the following interconnected domains or pillars: environment, economic and social, which according to Fritjof Capra is based on the principles of Systems Thinking. Sub-domains of _____ development have been considered also: cultural, technological and political. While _____ development may be the organizing principle for sustainability for some, for others, the two terms are paradoxical. _____ development is the development that meets the needs of the present without compromising the ability of future generations to meet their own needs. Brundtland Report for the World Commission on Environment and Development introduced the term of _____ development.

Exam Probability: **Medium**

7. *Answer choices:*
(see index for correct answer)

- a. personal values
- b. deep-level diversity
- c. corporate values
- d. Sustainable

Guidance: level 1

:: ::

The _____ is an agency of the United States Department of Labor. Congress established the agency under the Occupational Safety and Health Act, which President Richard M. Nixon signed into law on December 29, 1970. OSHA's mission is to "assure safe and healthy working conditions for working men and women by setting and enforcing standards and by providing training, outreach, education and assistance". The agency is also charged with enforcing a variety of whistleblower statutes and regulations. OSHA is currently headed by Acting Assistant Secretary of Labor Loren Sweatt. OSHA's workplace safety inspections have been shown to reduce injury rates and injury costs without adverse effects to employment, sales, credit ratings, or firm survival.

Exam Probability: **Low**

8. *Answer choices:*
(see index for correct answer)

- a. corporate values
- b. Occupational Safety and Health Administration
- c. levels of analysis
- d. co-culture

Guidance: level 1

:: Cultural appropriation ::

:::::: is a social and economic order that encourages the acquisition of goods and services in ever-increasing amounts. With the industrial revolution, but particularly in the 20th century, mass production led to an economic crisis: there was overproduction—the supply of goods would grow beyond consumer demand, and so manufacturers turned to planned obsolescence and advertising to manipulate consumer spending. In 1899, a book on _____ published by Thorstein Veblen, called The Theory of the Leisure Class, examined the widespread values and economic institutions emerging along with the widespread "leisure time" in the beginning of the 20th century. In it Veblen "views the activities and spending habits of this leisure class in terms of conspicuous and vicarious consumption and waste. Both are related to the display of status and not to functionality or usefulness."

Exam Probability: **Low**

9. *Answer choices:*

(see index for correct answer)

- a. Atlanta Braves
- b. Washington Redskins name controversy
- c. Consumerism
- d. Cool

Guidance: level 1

:: ::

_____ is a product prepared from the leaves of the _____ plant by curing them. The plant is part of the genus Nicotiana and of the Solanaceae family. While more than 70 species of _____ are known, the chief commercial crop is N. tabacum. The more potent variant N. rustica is also used around the world.

Exam Probability: **Medium**

10. *Answer choices:*

(see index for correct answer)

- a. Character
- b. Tobacco
- c. surface-level diversity
- d. imperative

Guidance: level 1

:: Industrial ecology ::

_____ is a strategy for reducing the amount of waste created and released into the environment, particularly by industrial facilities, agriculture, or consumers. Many large corporations view P2 as a method of improving the efficiency and profitability of production processes by technology advancements. Legislative bodies have enacted P2 measures, such as the _____ Act of 1990 and the Clean Air Act Amendments of 1990 by the United States Congress.

Exam Probability: **Medium**

11. *Answer choices:*
(see index for correct answer)

- a. Eco-efficiency
- b. Waste hierarchy
- c. Energy efficiency in Europe
- d. Material flow accounting

Guidance: level 1

:: Anti-Revisionism ::

_____, officially the German Democratic Republic, was a country that existed from 1949 to 1990, when the eastern portion of Germany was part of the Eastern Bloc during the Cold War. It described itself as a socialist "workers' and peasants' state", and the territory was administered and occupied by Soviet forces at the end of World War II — the Soviet Occupation Zone of the Potsdam Agreement, bounded on the east by the Oder–Neisse line. The Soviet zone surrounded West Berlin but did not include it; as a result, West Berlin remained outside the jurisdiction of the GDR.

Exam Probability: **Medium**

12. *Answer choices:*
(see index for correct answer)

- a. Ho Chi Minh Thought
- b. Anti-Party Group
- c. Anti-Revisionism
- d. Hoxhaism

Guidance: level 1

:: ::

Bernard Lawrence _____ is an American former market maker, investment advisor, financier, fraudster, and convicted felon, who is currently serving a federal prison sentence for offenses related to a massive Ponzi scheme. He is the former non-executive chairman of the NASDAQ stock market, the confessed operator of the largest Ponzi scheme in world history, and the largest financial fraud in U.S. history. Prosecutors estimated the fraud to be worth $64.8 billion based on the amounts in the accounts of _____ 's 4,800 clients as of November 30, 2008.

Exam Probability: **Low**

13. *Answer choices:*

(see index for correct answer)

- a. personal values
- b. Madoff
- c. levels of analysis
- d. interpersonal communication

Guidance: level 1

:: Real estate ::

_____ s serve several societal needs – primarily as shelter from weather, security, living space, privacy, to store belongings, and to comfortably live and work. A _____ as a shelter represents a physical division of the human habitat and the outside .

Exam Probability: **Medium**

14. *Answer choices:*

(see index for correct answer)

- a. Building
- b. Real estate contract
- c. Extraterrestrial real estate
- d. Corporate Real Estate

Guidance: level 1

:: Statutory law ::

_____ or statute law is written law set down by a body of legislature or by a singular legislator. This is as opposed to oral or customary law; or regulatory law promulgated by the executive or common law of the judiciary. Statutes may originate with national, state legislatures or local municipalities.

Exam Probability: **High**

15. *Answer choices:*

(see index for correct answer)

- a. statute law
- b. Statutory law
- c. Statute of repose
- d. incorporation by reference

Guidance: level 1

:: Reputation management ::

_____ or image of a social entity is an opinion about that entity, typically as a result of social evaluation on a set of criteria.

Exam Probability: **Medium**

16. *Answer choices:*

(see index for correct answer)

- a. ClaimID
- b. Star
- c. Lithium Technologies
- d. Reputation

Guidance: level 1

:: Corporate scandals ::

Exxon Mobil Corporation, doing business as _____, is an American multinational oil and gas corporation headquartered in Irving, Texas. It is the largest direct descendant of John D. Rockefeller's Standard Oil Company, and was formed on November 30, 1999 by the merger of Exxon and Mobil. _____'s primary brands are Exxon, Mobil, Esso, and _____ Chemical.

Exam Probability: **High**

17. *Answer choices:*

(see index for correct answer)

- a. ExxonMobil
- b. Avon Products
- c. Baptist Foundation of Arizona
- d. Barings Bank

Guidance: level 1

:: Human resource management ::

_____ encompasses values and behaviors that contribute to the unique social and psychological environment of a business. The _____ influences the way people interact, the context within which knowledge is created, the resistance they will have towards certain changes, and ultimately the way they share knowledge. _____ represents the collective values, beliefs and principles of organizational members and is a product of factors such as history, product, market, technology, strategy, type of employees, management style, and national culture; culture includes the organization's vision, values, norms, systems, symbols, language, assumptions, environment, location, beliefs and habits.

Exam Probability: **High**

18. *Answer choices:*

(see index for correct answer)

- a. Management development
- b. Induction programme
- c. Organizational culture
- d. Human resource policies

Guidance: level 1

:: Waste ::

_____ is any unwanted material in all forms that can cause harm. Many of today's household products such as televisions, computers and phones contain toxic chemicals that can pollute the air and contaminate soil and water. Disposing of such waste is a major public health issue.

Exam Probability: **Medium**

19. *Answer choices:*
(see index for correct answer)

- a. Industrial waste
- b. Biodegradable waste
- c. Used good
- d. Toxic waste

Guidance: level 1

:: Ethical banking ::

A _____ or community development finance institution - abbreviated in both cases to CDFI - is a financial institution that provides credit and financial services to underserved markets and populations, primarily in the USA but also in the UK. A CDFI may be a community development bank, a community development credit union, a community development loan fund, a community development venture capital fund, a microenterprise development loan fund, or a community development corporation.

Exam Probability: **High**

20. *Answer choices:*
(see index for correct answer)

- a. Cultura Sparebank
- b. Community development financial institution
- c. Triodos Bank
- d. Principles for Responsible Investment

Guidance: level 1

:: Decentralization ::

_____ or sub _____ mainly refers to the unrestricted growth in many urban areas of housing, commercial development, and roads over large expanses of land, with little concern for urban planning. In addition to describing a particular form of urbanization, the term also relates to the social and environmental consequences associated with this development. In Continental Europe the term "peri-urbanisation" is often used to denote similar dynamics and phenomena, although the term _____ is currently being used by the European Environment Agency. There is widespread disagreement about what constitutes sprawl and how to quantify it. For example, some commentators measure sprawl only with the average number of residential units per acre in a given area. But others associate it with decentralization, discontinuity, segregation of uses, and so forth.

Exam Probability: **High**

21. *Answer choices:*
(see index for correct answer)

- a. Ralph Borsodi
- b. Urban sprawl
- c. District Rural Development Agencies
- d. Water supply and sanitation in Benin

Guidance: level 1

:: ::

_____ ism is a form of government characterized by strong central power and limited political freedoms. Individual freedoms are subordinate to the state and there is no constitutional accountability and rule of law under an _____ regime. _____ regimes can be autocratic with power concentrated in one person or it can be more spread out between multiple officials and government institutions. Juan Linz's influential 1964 description of _____ ism characterized _____ political systems by four qualities.

Exam Probability: **Medium**

22. *Answer choices:*
(see index for correct answer)

- a. corporate values
- b. Authoritarian

- c. process perspective
- d. functional perspective

Guidance: level 1

:: Cognitive biases ::

In personality psychology, _____ is the degree to which people believe that they have control over the outcome of events in their lives, as opposed to external forces beyond their control. Understanding of the concept was developed by Julian B. Rotter in 1954, and has since become an aspect of personality studies. A person's "locus" is conceptualized as internal or external .

Exam Probability: **High**

23. *Answer choices:*

(see index for correct answer)

- a. Empathy gap
- b. Money illusion
- c. Locus of control
- d. Generation effect

Guidance: level 1

:: ::

Oriental Nicety, formerly _____ , Exxon Mediterranean, SeaRiver Mediterranean, S/R Mediterranean, Mediterranean, and Dong Fang Ocean, was an oil tanker that gained notoriety after running aground in Prince William Sound spilling hundreds of thousands of barrels of crude oil in Alaska. On March 24, 1989, while owned by the former Exxon Shipping Company, and captained by Joseph Hazelwood and First Mate James Kunkel bound for Long Beach, California, the vessel ran aground on the Bligh Reef resulting in the second largest oil spill in United States history. The size of the spill is estimated to have been 40,900 to 120,000 m3 , or 257,000 to 750,000 barrels. In 1989, the _____ oil spill was listed as the 54th largest spill in history.

Exam Probability: **Low**

24. *Answer choices:*

(see index for correct answer)

- a. Exxon Valdez
- b. process perspective
- c. similarity-attraction theory
- d. co-culture

Guidance: level 1

:: Progressive Era in the United States ::

The Clayton Antitrust Act of 1914, was a part of United States antitrust law with the goal of adding further substance to the U.S. antitrust law regime; the _____ sought to prevent anticompetitive practices in their incipiency. That regime started with the Sherman Antitrust Act of 1890, the first Federal law outlawing practices considered harmful to consumers. The _____ specified particular prohibited conduct, the three-level enforcement scheme, the exemptions, and the remedial measures.

Exam Probability: **High**

25. *Answer choices:*

(see index for correct answer)

- a. Clayton Antitrust Act
- b. pragmatism
- c. Mann Act

Guidance: level 1

:: Renewable energy ::

_____ is the conversion of energy from sunlight into electricity, either directly using photovoltaics, indirectly using concentrated _____, or a combination. Concentrated _____ systems use lenses or mirrors and tracking systems to focus a large area of sunlight into a small beam. Photovoltaic cells convert light into an electric current using the photovoltaic effect.

Exam Probability: **High**

26. *Answer choices:*

(see index for correct answer)

- a. Wildpoldsried
- b. Solar thermal energy

- c. Solar power
- d. Renewable energy debate

Guidance: level 1

:: Social enterprise ::

Corporate social responsibility is a type of international private business self-regulation. While once it was possible to describe CSR as an internal organisational policy or a corporate ethic strategy, that time has passed as various international laws have been developed and various organisations have used their authority to push it beyond individual or even industry-wide initiatives. While it has been considered a form of corporate self-regulation for some time, over the last decade or so it has moved considerably from voluntary decisions at the level of individual organisations, to mandatory schemes at regional, national and even transnational levels.

Exam Probability: **Medium**

27. *Answer choices:*
(see index for correct answer)

- a. Social venture
- b. Social enterprise

Guidance: level 1

:: Confidence tricks ::

A _____ is a business model that recruits members via a promise of payments or services for enrolling others into the scheme, rather than supplying investments or sale of products. As recruiting multiplies, recruiting becomes quickly impossible, and most members are unable to profit; as such, _____ s are unsustainable and often illegal.

Exam Probability: **Medium**

28. *Answer choices:*
(see index for correct answer)

- a. Mock auction
- b. Black money scam
- c. Flim-Flam!
- d. Pyramid scheme

Guidance: level 1

:: Financial regulatory authorities of the United States ::

The _____ is an agency of the United States government responsible for consumer protection in the financial sector. CFPB's jurisdiction includes banks, credit unions, securities firms, payday lenders, mortgage-servicing operations, foreclosure relief services, debt collectors and other financial companies operating in the United States.

Exam Probability: **High**

29. *Answer choices:*

(see index for correct answer)

- a. Municipal Securities Rulemaking Board
- b. Internal Revenue Service
- c. Federal Deposit Insurance Corporation
- d. Office of Thrift Supervision

Guidance: level 1

:: ::

_____ is a bundle of characteristics, including ways of thinking, feeling, and acting, which humans are said to have naturally. The term is often regarded as capturing what it is to be human, or the essence of humanity. The term is controversial because it is disputed whether or not such an essence exists. Arguments about _____ have been a mainstay of philosophy for centuries and the concept continues to provoke lively philosophical debate. The concept also continues to play a role in science, with neuroscientists, psychologists and social scientists sometimes claiming that their results have yielded insight into _____ . _____ is traditionally contrasted with characteristics that vary among humans, such as characteristics associated with specific cultures. Debates about _____ are related to, although not the same as, debates about the comparative importance of genes and environment in development.

Exam Probability: **High**

30. *Answer choices:*

(see index for correct answer)

- a. functional perspective
- b. hierarchical perspective
- c. surface-level diversity
- d. Human nature

Guidance: level 1

:: Majority–minority relations ::

It was established as axiomatic in anthropological research by Franz Boas in the first few decades of the 20th century and later popularized by his students. Boas first articulated the idea in 1887: "civilization is not something absolute, but ... is relative, and ... our ideas and conceptions are true only so far as our civilization goes". However, Boas did not coin the term.

Exam Probability: **Low**

31. *Answer choices:*
(see index for correct answer)

- a. Cultural relativism
- b. cultural dissonance
- c. Affirmative action

Guidance: level 1

:: Majority–minority relations ::

_____ , also known as reservation in India and Nepal, positive discrimination / action in the United Kingdom, and employment equity in Canada and South Africa, is the policy of promoting the education and employment of members of groups that are known to have previously suffered from discrimination. Historically and internationally, support for _____ has sought to achieve goals such as bridging inequalities in employment and pay, increasing access to education, promoting diversity, and redressing apparent past wrongs, harms, or hindrances.

Exam Probability: **High**

32. *Answer choices:*
(see index for correct answer)

- a. Affirmative action

- b. cultural dissonance
- c. cultural Relativism

Guidance: level 1

:: Advertising techniques ::

The _____ is a story from the Trojan War about the subterfuge that the Greeks used to enter the independent city of Troy and win the war. In the canonical version, after a fruitless 10-year siege, the Greeks constructed a huge wooden horse, and hid a select force of men inside including Odysseus. The Greeks pretended to sail away, and the Trojans pulled the horse into their city as a victory trophy. That night the Greek force crept out of the horse and opened the gates for the rest of the Greek army, which had sailed back under cover of night. The Greeks entered and destroyed the city of Troy, ending the war.

Exam Probability: **Medium**

33. *Answer choices:*
(see index for correct answer)

- a. Incomplete comparison
- b. Debranding
- c. Surrogate advertising
- d. Trojan horse

Guidance: level 1

:: Workplace ::

In business management, _____ is a management style whereby a manager closely observes and/or controls the work of his/her subordinates or employees.

Exam Probability: **Medium**

34. *Answer choices:*
(see index for correct answer)

- a. Micromanagement
- b. Counterproductive work behavior
- c. Discrimination based on hair texture
- d. Emotions in the workplace

Guidance: level 1

:: Dutch inventions ::

The Fairtrade certification initiative was created to form a new method for economic trade. This method takes an ethical standpoint, and considers the producers first.

Exam Probability: **High**

35. *Answer choices:*
(see index for correct answer)

- a. Dijkstra's algorithm
- b. Fairtrade

Guidance: level 1

:: Anti-capitalism ::

_____ is a range of economic and social systems characterised by social ownership of the means of production and workers' self-management, as well as the political theories and movements associated with them. Social ownership can be public, collective or cooperative ownership, or citizen ownership of equity. There are many varieties of _____ and there is no single definition encapsulating all of them, with social ownership being the common element shared by its various forms.

Exam Probability: **High**

36. *Answer choices:*
(see index for correct answer)

- a. Invisible Party
- b. Socialism
- c. Collectivist anarchism
- d. Communism

Guidance: level 1

:: ::

_____ is "property consisting of land and the buildings on it, along with its natural resources such as crops, minerals or water; immovable property of this nature; an interest vested in this an item of real property, buildings or housing in general. Also: the business of _____ ; the profession of buying, selling, or renting land, buildings, or housing." It is a legal term used in jurisdictions whose legal system is derived from English common law, such as India, England, Wales, Northern Ireland, United States, Canada, Pakistan, Australia, and New Zealand.

Exam Probability: **Low**

37. *Answer choices:*
(see index for correct answer)

- a. hierarchical
- b. similarity-attraction theory
- c. co-culture
- d. Real estate

Guidance: level 1

:: Production and manufacturing ::

_____ is a set of techniques and tools for process improvement. Though as a shortened form it may be found written as 6S, it should not be confused with the methodology known as 6S.

Exam Probability: **Medium**

38. *Answer choices:*
(see index for correct answer)

- a. Six Sigma
- b. Woodworking machine
- c. Nuffield Tools and Gauges
- d. Traditional engineering

Guidance: level 1

:: Parental leave ::

_____ , or family leave, is an employee benefit available in almost all countries. The term "_____" may include maternity, paternity, and adoption leave; or may be used distinctively from "maternity leave" and "paternity leave" to describe separate family leave available to either parent to care for small children. In some countries and jurisdictions, "family leave" also includes leave provided to care for ill family members. Often, the minimum benefits and eligibility requirements are stipulated by law.

Exam Probability: **High**

39. *Answer choices:*
(see index for correct answer)

- a. Motherhood penalty
- b. Pregnancy discrimination
- c. Maternity and Parental Leave, etc Regulations 1999
- d. Parental leave economics

Guidance: level 1

:: Natural gas ::

_____ is a naturally occurring hydrocarbon gas mixture consisting primarily of methane, but commonly including varying amounts of other higher alkanes, and sometimes a small percentage of carbon dioxide, nitrogen, hydrogen sulfide, or helium. It is formed when layers of decomposing plant and animal matter are exposed to intense heat and pressure under the surface of the Earth over millions of years. The energy that the plants originally obtained from the sun is stored in the form of chemical bonds in the gas.

Exam Probability: **Low**

40. *Answer choices:*
(see index for correct answer)

- a. Natural gas
- b. Twister Supersonic Separator
- c. Sour gas
- d. ISO 15971

Guidance: level 1

:: United States federal trade legislation ::

The _____ of 1914 established the Federal Trade Commission. The Act, signed into law by Woodrow Wilson in 1914, outlaws unfair methods of competition and outlaws unfair acts or practices that affect commerce.

Exam Probability: **Medium**

41. *Answer choices:*
(see index for correct answer)

- a. Bell Trade Act
- b. Section 22
- c. Federal Trade Commission Act
- d. Trading with the Enemy Act of 1917

Guidance: level 1

:: Leadership ::

_____ is a theory of leadership where a leader works with teams to identify needed change, creating a vision to guide the change through inspiration, and executing the change in tandem with committed members of a group; it is an integral part of the Full Range Leadership Model. _____ serves to enhance the motivation, morale, and job performance of followers through a variety of mechanisms; these include connecting the follower's sense of identity and self to a project and to the collective identity of the organization; being a role model for followers in order to inspire them and to raise their interest in the project; challenging followers to take greater ownership for their work, and understanding the strengths and weaknesses of followers, allowing the leader to align followers with tasks that enhance their performance.

Exam Probability: **Low**

42. *Answer choices:*
(see index for correct answer)

- a. Sex differences in leadership
- b. servant leader
- c. Love leadership
- d. Complex adaptive leadership

Guidance: level 1

:: ::

_____ was a philosopher during the Classical period in Ancient Greece, the founder of the Lyceum and the Peripatetic school of philosophy and Aristotelian tradition. Along with his teacher Plato, he is considered the "Father of Western Philosophy". His writings cover many subjects – including physics, biology, zoology, metaphysics, logic, ethics, aesthetics, poetry, theatre, music, rhetoric, psychology, linguistics, economics, politics and government. _____ provided a complex synthesis of the various philosophies existing prior to him, and it was above all from his teachings that the West inherited its intellectual lexicon, as well as problems and methods of inquiry. As a result, his philosophy has exerted a unique influence on almost every form of knowledge in the West and it continues to be a subject of contemporary philosophical discussion.

Exam Probability: **Medium**

43. *Answer choices:*
(see index for correct answer)

- a. similarity-attraction theory
- b. hierarchical
- c. functional perspective
- d. Aristotle

Guidance: level 1

:: ::

The _____ was a severe worldwide economic depression that took place mostly during the 1930s, beginning in the United States. The timing of the _____ varied across nations; in most countries it started in 1929 and lasted until the late-1930s. It was the longest, deepest, and most widespread depression of the 20th century. In the 21st century, the _____ is commonly used as an example of how intensely the world's economy can decline.

Exam Probability: **High**

44. *Answer choices:*
(see index for correct answer)

- a. cultural
- b. open system
- c. similarity-attraction theory

- d. corporate values

Guidance: level 1

:: ::

The American Recovery and Reinvestment Act of 2009, nicknamed the _____, was a stimulus package enacted by the 111th U.S. Congress and signed into law by President Barack Obama in February 2009. Developed in response to the Great Recession, the ARRA's primary objective was to save existing jobs and create new ones as soon as possible. Other objectives were to provide temporary relief programs for those most affected by the recession and invest in infrastructure, education, health, and renewable energy.

Exam Probability: **Medium**

45. *Answer choices:*
(see index for correct answer)

- a. process perspective
- b. corporate values
- c. empathy
- d. Recovery Act

Guidance: level 1

:: Supply chain management terms ::

In business and finance, _____ is a system of organizations, people, activities, information, and resources involved in moving a product or service from supplier to customer. _____ activities involve the transformation of natural resources, raw materials, and components into a finished product that is delivered to the end customer. In sophisticated _____ systems, used products may re-enter the _____ at any point where residual value is recyclable. _____ s link value chains.

Exam Probability: **Medium**

46. *Answer choices:*
(see index for correct answer)

- a. Widget
- b. Overstock
- c. Supply Chain

- d. Final assembly schedule

Guidance: level 1

:: Socialism ::

_____ is a label used to define the first currents of modern socialist thought as exemplified by the work of Henri de Saint-Simon, Charles Fourier, Étienne Cabet and Robert Owen.

Exam Probability: **High**

47. *Answer choices:*
(see index for correct answer)

- a. Sexualization
- b. Municipal socialism
- c. Utopian socialism
- d. Yellow socialism

Guidance: level 1

:: ::

In regulatory jurisdictions that provide for it, _____ is a group of laws and organizations designed to ensure the rights of consumers as well as fair trade, competition and accurate information in the marketplace. The laws are designed to prevent the businesses that engage in fraud or specified unfair practices from gaining an advantage over competitors. They may also provides additional protection for those most vulnerable in society. _____ laws are a form of government regulation that aim to protect the rights of consumers. For example, a government may require businesses to disclose detailed information about products—particularly in areas where safety or public health is an issue, such as food.

Exam Probability: **High**

48. *Answer choices:*
(see index for correct answer)

- a. interpersonal communication
- b. imperative
- c. levels of analysis
- d. Consumer Protection

Guidance: level 1

:: Labour law ::

An _____ is special or specified circumstances that partially or fully exempt a person or organization from performance of a legal obligation so as to avoid an unreasonable or disproportionate burden or obstacle.

Exam Probability: **Medium**

49. *Answer choices:*
(see index for correct answer)

- a. Undue hardship
- b. Emanation of the state
- c. Labor court
- d. Bharat Forge Co Ltd v Uttam Manohar Nakate

Guidance: level 1

:: ::

MCI, Inc. was an American telecommunication corporation, currently a subsidiary of Verizon Communications, with its main office in Ashburn, Virginia. The corporation was formed originally as a result of the merger of _____ and MCI Communications corporations, and used the name MCI _____ , succeeded by _____ , before changing its name to the present version on April 12, 2003, as part of the corporation's ending of its bankruptcy status. The company traded on NASDAQ as WCOM and MCIP . The corporation was purchased by Verizon Communications with the deal finalizing on January 6, 2006, and is now identified as that company's Verizon Enterprise Solutions division with the local residential divisions being integrated slowly into local Verizon subsidiaries.

Exam Probability: **Low**

50. *Answer choices:*
(see index for correct answer)

- a. WorldCom
- b. Character
- c. personal values
- d. surface-level diversity

Guidance: level 1

:: Law ::

_____ is a body of law which defines the role, powers, and structure of different entities within a state, namely, the executive, the parliament or legislature, and the judiciary; as well as the basic rights of citizens and, in federal countries such as the United States and Canada, the relationship between the central government and state, provincial, or territorial governments.

Exam Probability: **High**

51. *Answer choices:*
(see index for correct answer)

- a. Legal case
- b. Constitutional law

Guidance: level 1

:: ::

A _____ is an organization, usually a group of people or a company, authorized to act as a single entity and recognized as such in law. Early incorporated entities were established by charter. Most jurisdictions now allow the creation of new _____ s through registration.

Exam Probability: **High**

52. *Answer choices:*
(see index for correct answer)

- a. Corporation
- b. cultural
- c. co-culture
- d. functional perspective

Guidance: level 1

:: Business ethics ::

The _____ are the names of two corporate codes of conduct, developed by the African-American preacher Rev. Leon Sullivan, promoting corporate social responsibility.

Exam Probability: **Medium**

53. *Answer choices:*

(see index for correct answer)

- a. Sullivan principles
- b. Smart casual
- c. Terror-free investing
- d. The FCPA Blog

Guidance: level 1

:: Coal ::

_____ is a combustible black or brownish-black sedimentary rock, formed as rock strata called _____ seams. _____ is mostly carbon with variable amounts of other elements; chiefly hydrogen, sulfur, oxygen, and nitrogen. _____ is formed if dead plant matter decays into peat and over millions of years the heat and pressure of deep burial converts the peat into _____ . Vast deposits of _____ originates in former wetlands—called _____ forests—that covered much of the Earth's tropical land areas during the late Carboniferous and Permian times.

Exam Probability: **Low**

54. *Answer choices:*

(see index for correct answer)

- a. Vitrain
- b. Coldry Process
- c. Coalbed methane
- d. Hardgrove Grindability Index

Guidance: level 1

:: Types of marketing ::

_____ is an advertisement strategy in which a company uses surprise and/or unconventional interactions in order to promote a product or service. It is a type of publicity. The term was popularized by Jay Conrad Levinson's 1984 book _____.

Exam Probability: **High**

55. *Answer choices:*
(see index for correct answer)

- a. Customerization
- b. Global marketing
- c. Evangelism marketing
- d. Figure of merit

Guidance: level 1

:: United States federal defense and national security legislation ::

The USA _____ is an Act of the U.S. Congress that was signed into law by President George W. Bush on October 26, 2001. The title of the Act is a contrived three letter initialism preceding a seven letter acronym, which in combination stand for Uniting and Strengthening America by Providing Appropriate Tools Required to Intercept and Obstruct Terrorism Act of 2001. The acronym was created by a 23 year old Congressional staffer, Chris Kyle.

Exam Probability: **Low**

56. *Answer choices:*
(see index for correct answer)

- a. Export Administration Act
- b. USA PATRIOT Act

Guidance: level 1

:: ::

Revenge is a form of justice enacted in the absence or defiance of the norms of formal law and jurisprudence. Often, revenge is defined as being a harmful action against a person or group in response to a grievance, be it real or perceived. It is used to punish a wrong by going outside the law. Francis Bacon described revenge as a kind of "wild justice" that "does... offend the law [and] putteth the law out of office." Primitive justice or retributive justice is often differentiated from more formal and refined forms of justice such as distributive justice and divine judgment.

Exam Probability: **Low**

57. *Answer choices:*
(see index for correct answer)

- a. information systems assessment
- b. deep-level diversity
- c. Retaliation
- d. empathy

Guidance: level 1

:: Trade unions ::

A _____ was a group formed of private citizens to administer law and order where they considered governmental structures to be inadequate. The term is commonly associated with the frontier areas of the American West in the mid-19th century, where groups attacked cattle rustlers and gangs, and people at gold mining claims. As non-state organizations no functioning checks existed to protect against excessive force or safeguard due process from the committees. In the years prior to the Civil War, some committees worked to free slaves and transport them to freedom.

Exam Probability: **High**

58. *Answer choices:*
(see index for correct answer)

- a. Union dues
- b. National trade union center
- c. Vigilance committee
- d. Global Labour University

Guidance: level 1

:: Culture ::

_____ is a society which is characterized by individualism, which is the prioritization or emphasis, of the individual over the entire group. _____ s are oriented around the self, being independent instead of identifying with a group mentality. They see each other as only loosely linked, and value personal goals over group interests. _____ s tend to have a more diverse population and are characterized with emphasis on personal achievements, and a rational assessment of both the beneficial and detrimental aspects of relationships with others. _____ s have such unique aspects of communication as being a low power-distance culture and having a low-context communication style. The United States, Australia, Great Britain, Canada, the Netherlands, and New Zealand have been identified as highly _____ s.

Exam Probability: **Medium**

59. *Answer choices:*
(see index for correct answer)

- a. High-context
- b. Low-context culture
- c. Individualistic culture
- d. Intracultural

Guidance: level 1

Accounting

Accounting or accountancy is the measurement, processing, and communication of financial information about economic entities such as businesses and corporations. The modern field was established by the Italian mathematician Luca Pacioli in 1494. Accounting, which has been called the "language of business", measures the results of an organization's economic activities and conveys this information to a variety of users, including investors, creditors, management, and regulators.

:: Management accounting ::

An _____ is a classification used for business units within an enterprise. The essential element of an _____ is that it is treated as a unit which is measured against its use of capital, as opposed to a cost or profit center, which are measured against raw costs or profits.

Exam Probability: **High**

1. *Answer choices:*

(see index for correct answer)

- a. Investment center
- b. Construction accounting
- c. Chartered Institute of Management Accountants
- d. Activity-based management

Guidance: level 1

:: Corporate crime ::

_____ LLP, based in Chicago, was an American holding company. Formerly one of the "Big Five" accounting firms, the firm had provided auditing, tax, and consulting services to large corporations. By 2001, it had become one of the world's largest multinational companies.

Exam Probability: **High**

2. *Answer choices:*

(see index for correct answer)

- a. New England Compounding Center
- b. Corporate Manslaughter and Corporate Homicide Act 2007
- c. Holdings of American International Group
- d. Compass Group

Guidance: level 1

:: ::

The _____ or just chief executive, is the most senior corporate, executive, or administrative officer in charge of managing an organization especially an independent legal entity such as a company or nonprofit institution. CEOs lead a range of organizations, including public and private corporations, non-profit organizations and even some government organizations. The CEO of a corporation or company typically reports to the board of directors and is charged with maximizing the value of the entity, which may include maximizing the share price, market share, revenues or another element. In the non-profit and government sector, CEOs typically aim at achieving outcomes related to the organization's mission, such as reducing poverty, increasing literacy, etc.

Exam Probability: **High**

3. *Answer choices:*

(see index for correct answer)

- a. deep-level diversity
- b. information systems assessment
- c. co-culture
- d. Chief executive officer

Guidance: level 1

:: Competition (economics) ::

In taxation and accounting, _____ refers to the rules and methods for pricing transactions within and between enterprises under common ownership or control. Because of the potential for cross-border controlled transactions to distort taxable income, tax authorities in many countries can adjust intragroup transfer prices that differ from what would have been charged by unrelated enterprises dealing at arm's length. The OECD and World Bank recommend intragroup pricing rules based on the arm's-length principle, and 19 of the 20 members of the G20 have adopted similar measures through bilateral treaties and domestic legislation, regulations, or administrative practice. Countries with _____ legislation generally follow the OECD _____ Guidelines for Multinational Enterprises and Tax Administrations in most respects, although their rules can differ on some important details.

Exam Probability: **Medium**

4. *Answer choices:*
(see index for correct answer)

- a. Level playing field
- b. Leapfrogging
- c. Blindspots analysis
- d. Transfer pricing

Guidance: level 1

:: Notes (finance) ::

A _____, sometimes referred to as a note payable, is a legal instrument, in which one party promises in writing to pay a determinate sum of money to the other, either at a fixed or determinable future time or on demand of the payee, under specific terms.

Exam Probability: **Low**

5. *Answer choices:*
(see index for correct answer)

- a. Demand Note
- b. Capital note
- c. Promissory note
- d. Note issuance facility

Guidance: level 1

:: Banking terms ::

An _____ occurs when money is withdrawn from a bank account and the available balance goes below zero. In this situation the account is said to be "overdrawn". If there is a prior agreement with the account provider for an _____, and the amount overdrawn is within the authorized _____ limit, then interest is normally charged at the agreed rate. If the negative balance exceeds the agreed terms, then additional fees may be charged and higher interest rates may apply.

Exam Probability: **High**

6. *Answer choices:*
(see index for correct answer)

- a. Structural moving average model
- b. Universal Payment Identification Code
- c. Bank card
- d. Unbanked

Guidance: level 1

:: Marketing ::

_____ or stock is the goods and materials that a business holds for the ultimate goal of resale.

Exam Probability: **Medium**

7. *Answer choices:*
(see index for correct answer)

- a. Davie-Brown Index
- b. Product churning
- c. Bluetooth advertising
- d. Pink money

Guidance: level 1

:: Financial statements ::

In financial accounting, a _____ or statement of financial position or statement of financial condition is a summary of the financial balances of an individual or organization, whether it be a sole proprietorship, a business partnership, a corporation, private limited company or other organization such as Government or not-for-profit entity. Assets, liabilities and ownership equity are listed as of a specific date, such as the end of its financial year. A _____ is often described as a "snapshot of a company's financial condition". Of the four basic financial statements, the _____ is the only statement which applies to a single point in time of a business' calendar year.

Exam Probability: **Low**

8. *Answer choices:*
(see index for correct answer)

- a. Clean surplus accounting
- b. Financial statement
- c. Balance sheet
- d. Financial report

Guidance: level 1

:: Generally Accepted Accounting Principles ::

Financial statements prepared and presented by a company typically follow an external standard that specifically guides their preparation. These standards vary across the globe and are typically overseen by some combination of the private accounting profession in that specific nation and the various government regulators. Variations across countries may be considerable, making cross-country evaluation of financial data challenging.

Exam Probability: **High**

9. *Answer choices:*
(see index for correct answer)

- a. Earnings before interest, taxes, depreciation, and amortization
- b. French generally accepted accounting principles
- c. Generally Accepted Accounting Principles
- d. Engagement letter

Guidance: level 1

:: Real estate ::

An _____ is to, interest in, or legal liability on real property that does not prohibit passing title to the property but that may diminish its value. _____ s can be classified in several ways. They may be financial or non-financial. Alternatively, they may be divided into those that affect title or those that affect the use or physical condition of the encumbered property. _____ s include security interests, liens, servitudes, leases, restrictions, encroachments, and air and subsurface rights. Also, those considered as potentially making the title defeasible are _____ s, for example, charging orders, building orders and structure alteration. _____ : charge upon or claim against land arising out of private grant or a contract.

Exam Probability: **Low**

10. *Answer choices:*
(see index for correct answer)

- a. Open-Realty
- b. Encumbrance
- c. SIOR
- d. Future interest

Guidance: level 1

:: Financial ratios ::

_____ is a financial ratio that indicates the percentage of a company's assets that are provided via debt. It is the ratio of total debt and total assets.

Exam Probability: **Low**

11. *Answer choices:*
(see index for correct answer)

- a. Operating leverage
- b. Debt ratio
- c. Information ratio
- d. Accounting liquidity

Guidance: level 1

:: Value theory ::

Within philosophy, it can be known as ethics or axiology. Early philosophical investigations sought to understand good and evil and the concept of "the good". Today, much of _____ aspires to the scientifically empirical, recording what people do value and attempting to understand why they value it in the context of psychology, sociology, and economics.

Exam Probability: **High**

12. *Answer choices:*

(see index for correct answer)

- a. Value theory
- b. Paradox of value
- c. economic value
- d. Intrinsic theory of value

Guidance: level 1

:: Debt ::

A _____ is a party that has a claim on the services of a second party. It is a person or institution to whom money is owed. The first party, in general, has provided some property or service to the second party under the assumption that the second party will return an equivalent property and service. The second party is frequently called a debtor or borrower. The first party is called the _____, which is the lender of property, service, or money.

Exam Probability: **High**

13. *Answer choices:*

(see index for correct answer)

- a. Financial assistance
- b. Creditor
- c. Credit crunch
- d. Household debt

Guidance: level 1

:: Cash flow ::

In corporate finance, _____ or _____ to firm is a way of looking at a business's cash flow to see what is available for distribution among all the securities holders of a corporate entity. This may be useful to parties such as equity holders, debt holders, preferred stock holders, and convertible security holders when they want to see how much cash can be extracted from a company without causing issues to its operations.

Exam Probability: **Medium**

14. *Answer choices:*
(see index for correct answer)

- a. Propequity
- b. Discounted payback period
- c. Cash flow
- d. Free cash flow

Guidance: level 1

:: Accounting software ::

_____ is an accounting software package developed and marketed by Intuit. _____ products are geared mainly toward small and medium-sized businesses and offer on-premises accounting applications as well as cloud-based versions that accept business payments, manage and pay bills, and payroll functions.

Exam Probability: **Low**

15. *Answer choices:*
(see index for correct answer)

- a. Passport Software
- b. QuickBooks
- c. Gem Accounts
- d. MAS 90

Guidance: level 1

:: Free accounting software ::

A _____ is the principal book or computer file for recording and totaling economic transactions measured in terms of a monetary unit of account by account type, with debits and credits in separate columns and a beginning monetary balance and ending monetary balance for each account.

Exam Probability: **Medium**

16. *Answer choices:*
(see index for correct answer)

- a. HomeBank
- b. TurboCASH
- c. SQL-Ledger
- d. JGnash

Guidance: level 1

:: Partnerships ::

Articles of partnership is a voluntary contract between/among two or more persons to place their capital, labor, and skills into business, with the understanding that there will be a sharing of the profits and losses between/among partners. Outside of North America, it is normally referred to simply as a _____ .

Exam Probability: **High**

17. *Answer choices:*
(see index for correct answer)

- a. Revised Uniform Limited Partnership Act
- b. Partnership agreement
- c. Revised Uniform Partnership Act

Guidance: level 1

:: Generally Accepted Accounting Principles ::

_____ is a small amount of discretionary funds in the form of cash used for expenditures where it is not sensible to make any disbursement by cheque, because of the inconvenience and costs of writing, signing, and then cashing the cheque.

Exam Probability: **Medium**

18. *Answer choices:*

(see index for correct answer)

- a. Depreciation
- b. Petty cash
- c. Goodwill
- d. Operating profit

Guidance: level 1

:: United States Generally Accepted Accounting Principles ::

In a companies' financial reporting, _____ "includes all changes in equity during a period except those resulting from investments by owners and distributions to owners". Because that use excludes the effects of changing ownership interest, an economic measure of _____ is necessary for financial analysis from the shareholders' point of view

Exam Probability: **Medium**

19. *Answer choices:*

(see index for correct answer)

- a. Available for sale
- b. Accounting for leases in the United States
- c. Comprehensive income
- d. Impaired asset

Guidance: level 1

:: Tax reform ::

_____ is the process of changing the way taxes are collected or managed by the government and is usually undertaken to improve tax administration or to provide economic or social benefits. _____ can include reducing the level of taxation of all people by the government, making the tax system more progressive or less progressive, or simplifying the tax system and making the system more understandable or more accountable.

Exam Probability: **Low**

20. *Answer choices:*
(see index for correct answer)

- a. Tax shift
- b. Single tax
- c. Goods and services tax in Malaysia
- d. Tax reform

Guidance: level 1

:: ::

_____ is capital that is contributed to a corporation by investors by purchase of stock from the corporation, the primary market, not by purchase of stock in the open market from other stockholders. It includes share capital as well as additional _____.

Exam Probability: **Medium**

21. *Answer choices:*
(see index for correct answer)

- a. corporate values
- b. personal values
- c. levels of analysis
- d. Paid-in capital

Guidance: level 1

:: Budgets ::

_____ is a method of budgeting in which all expenses must be justified and approved for each new period. Developed by Peter Pyhrr in the 1970s, _____ starts from a "zero base" at the beginning of every budget period, analyzing needs and costs of every function within an organization and allocating funds accordingly, regardless of how much money has previously been budgeted to any given line item.

Exam Probability: **Medium**

22. *Answer choices:*

(see index for correct answer)

- a. Zero-based budgeting
- b. Operating budget
- c. Participatory budgeting
- d. Envelope system

Guidance: level 1

:: Accounting terminology ::

In accounting/accountancy, _____ are journal entries usually made at the end of an accounting period to allocate income and expenditure to the period in which they actually occurred. The revenue recognition principle is the basis of making _____ that pertain to unearned and accrued revenues under accrual-basis accounting. They are sometimes called Balance Day adjustments because they are made on balance day.

Exam Probability: **Low**

23. *Answer choices:*

(see index for correct answer)

- a. Cash flow management
- b. Enterprise liquidity
- c. Adjusting entries
- d. Statement of financial position

Guidance: level 1

:: Information systems ::

_____ are formal, sociotechnical, organizational systems designed to collect, process, store, and distribute information. In a sociotechnical perspective, _____ are composed by four components: task, people, structure, and technology.

Exam Probability: **High**

24. *Answer choices:*
(see index for correct answer)

- a. Urban and Regional Information Systems Association
- b. Improvement Support Systems
- c. Information systems
- d. Question Manager

Guidance: level 1

:: Generally Accepted Accounting Principles ::

_____ is a measure of a fixed or current asset's worth when held in inventory, in the field of accounting. NRV is part of the Generally Accepted Accounting Principles and International Financial Reporting Standards that apply to valuing inventory, so as to not overstate or understate the value of inventory goods. _____ is generally equal to the selling price of the inventory goods less the selling costs. Therefore, it is expected sales price less selling costs. NRV prevents overstating or understating of an assets value. NRV is the price cap when using the Lower of Cost or Market Rule.

Exam Probability: **Medium**

25. *Answer choices:*
(see index for correct answer)

- a. Net realizable value
- b. Net profit
- c. Cash method of accounting
- d. Deferral

Guidance: level 1

:: Television terminology ::

A nonprofit organization, also known as a non-business entity, _____ organization, or nonprofit institution, is dedicated to furthering a particular social cause or advocating for a shared point of view. In economic terms, it is an organization that uses its surplus of the revenues to further achieve its ultimate objective, rather than distributing its income to the organization's shareholders, leaders, or members. Nonprofits are tax exempt or charitable, meaning they do not pay income tax on the money that they receive for their organization. They can operate in religious, scientific, research, or educational settings.

Exam Probability: **High**

26. *Answer choices:*
(see index for correct answer)

- a. multiplexing
- b. Not-for-profit
- c. nonprofit
- d. Satellite television

Guidance: level 1

:: ::

The U.S. _____ is an independent agency of the United States federal government. The SEC holds primary responsibility for enforcing the federal securities laws, proposing securities rules, and regulating the securities industry, the nation's stock and options exchanges, and other activities and organizations, including the electronic securities markets in the United States.

Exam Probability: **Low**

27. *Answer choices:*
(see index for correct answer)

- a. Securities and Exchange Commission
- b. information systems assessment
- c. cultural
- d. empathy

Guidance: level 1

:: ::

A _____ is a fund into which a sum of money is added during an employee's employment years, and from which payments are drawn to support the person's retirement from work in the form of periodic payments. A _____ may be a "defined benefit plan" where a fixed sum is paid regularly to a person, or a "defined contribution plan" under which a fixed sum is invested and then becomes available at retirement age. _____ s should not be confused with severance pay; the former is usually paid in regular installments for life after retirement, while the latter is typically paid as a fixed amount after involuntary termination of employment prior to retirement.

Exam Probability: **High**

28. *Answer choices:*

(see index for correct answer)

- a. Pension
- b. open system
- c. functional perspective
- d. corporate values

Guidance: level 1

:: Generally Accepted Accounting Principles ::

In accounting, an economic item's _____ is the original nominal monetary value of that item. _____ accounting involves reporting assets and liabilities at their _____ s, which are not updated for changes in the items' values. Consequently, the amounts reported for these balance sheet items often differ from their current economic or market values.

Exam Probability: **Medium**

29. *Answer choices:*

(see index for correct answer)

- a. Revenue recognition
- b. French generally accepted accounting principles
- c. Long-term liabilities
- d. Operating income before depreciation and amortization

Guidance: level 1

:: Accounting ::

It is the period for which books are balanced and the financial statements are prepared. Generally, the _____ consists of 12 months. However the beginning of the _____ differs according to the jurisdiction. For example, one entity may follow the regular calendar year, i.e. January to December as the accounting year, while another entity may follow April to March as the _____ .

Exam Probability: **Medium**

30. *Answer choices:*

(see index for correct answer)

- a. Accounting period
- b. Accounting records
- c. Professional services networks
- d. Accountant General

Guidance: level 1

:: Manufacturing ::

_____ s are goods that have completed the manufacturing process but have not yet been sold or distributed to the end user.

Exam Probability: **Medium**

31. *Answer choices:*

(see index for correct answer)

- a. Ppc cycle
- b. Manufacturing operations management
- c. Flexible manufacturing system
- d. Factory Physics

Guidance: level 1

:: Options (finance) ::

A _____ bond is a type of bond that allows the issuer of the bond to retain the privilege of redeeming the bond at some point before the bond reaches its date of maturity. In other words, on the call date, the issuer has the right, but not the obligation, to buy back the bonds from the bond holders at a defined call price. Technically speaking, the bonds are not really bought and held by the issuer but are instead cancelled immediately.

Exam Probability: **High**

32. *Answer choices:*
(see index for correct answer)

- a. Callable
- b. Covered call
- c. Options writing
- d. LEAPS

Guidance: level 1

:: Commercial crimes ::

_____ is the act of withholding assets for the purpose of conversion of such assets, by one or more persons to whom the assets were entrusted, either to be held or to be used for specific purposes. _____ is a type of financial fraud. For example, a lawyer might embezzle funds from the trust accounts of their clients; a financial advisor might embezzle the funds of investors; and a husband or a wife might embezzle funds from a bank account jointly held with the spouse.

Exam Probability: **Medium**

33. *Answer choices:*
(see index for correct answer)

- a. Embezzlement
- b. Credit card hijacking
- c. Bait-and-switch
- d. Price gouging

Guidance: level 1

:: Basic financial concepts ::

In finance, maturity or _____ refers to the final payment date of a loan or other financial instrument, at which point the principal is due to be paid.

Exam Probability: **High**

34. *Answer choices:*

(see index for correct answer)

- a. Leverage cycle
- b. Maturity date
- c. Eurodollar
- d. balloon payment

Guidance: level 1

:: Asset ::

In accounting, a _____ is any asset which can reasonably be expected to be sold, consumed, or exhausted through the normal operations of a business within the current fiscal year or operating cycle. Typical _____ s include cash, cash equivalents, short-term investments, accounts receivable, stock inventory, supplies, and the portion of prepaid liabilities which will be paid within a year. In simple words, assets which are held for a short period are known as _____ s. Such assets are expected to be realised in cash or consumed during the normal operating cycle of the business.

Exam Probability: **High**

35. *Answer choices:*

(see index for correct answer)

- a. Current asset
- b. Asset

Guidance: level 1

:: ::

_____ is the consumption and saving opportunity gained by an entity within a specified timeframe, which is generally expressed in monetary terms. For households and individuals, " _____ is the sum of all the wages, salaries, profits, interest payments, rents, and other forms of earnings received in a given period of time."

Exam Probability: **High**

36. *Answer choices:*
(see index for correct answer)

- a. Income
- b. corporate values
- c. Character
- d. co-culture

Guidance: level 1

:: Debt ::

A _____ is a monetary amount owed to a creditor that is unlikely to be paid and, or which the creditor is not willing to take action to collect for various reasons, often due to the debtor not having the money to pay, for example due to a company going into liquidation or insolvency. There are various technical definitions of what constitutes a _____ , depending on accounting conventions, regulatory treatment and the institution provisioning. In the USA, bank loans with more than ninety days' arrears become "problem loans". Accounting sources advise that the full amount of a _____ be written off to the profit and loss account or a provision for _____ s as soon as it is foreseen.

Exam Probability: **Medium**

37. *Answer choices:*
(see index for correct answer)

- a. Consumer debt
- b. Medical debt
- c. Bad debt
- d. Internal debt

Guidance: level 1

:: Stock market ::

_____ is a form of corporate equity ownership, a type of security. The terms voting share and ordinary share are also used frequently in other parts of the world; "_____" being primarily used in the United States. They are known as Equity shares or Ordinary shares in the UK and other Commonwealth realms. This type of share gives the stockholder the right to share in the profits of the company, and to vote on matters of corporate policy and the composition of the members of the board of directors.

Exam Probability: **High**

38. *Answer choices:*
(see index for correct answer)

- a. Size premium
- b. Mosaic theory
- c. Pattern day trader
- d. Alternative display facility

Guidance: level 1

:: United States federal income tax ::

Under United States tax law, the _____ is a dollar amount that non-itemizers may subtract from their income before income tax is applied. Taxpayers may choose either itemized deductions or the _____, but usually choose whichever results in the lesser amount of tax payable. The _____ is available to US citizens and aliens who are resident for tax purposes and who are individuals, married persons, and heads of household. The _____ is based on filing status and typically increases each year. It is not available to nonresident aliens residing in the United States. Additional amounts are available for persons who are blind and/or are at least 65 years of age.

Exam Probability: **Medium**

39. *Answer choices:*
(see index for correct answer)

- a. The New Spirit
- b. Free File Alliance
- c. Standard deduction
- d. Rabbi trust

Guidance: level 1

:: Loans ::

In finance, a _____ is the lending of money by one or more individuals, organizations, or other entities to other individuals, organizations etc. The recipient incurs a debt, and is usually liable to pay interest on that debt until it is repaid, and also to repay the principal amount borrowed.

Exam Probability: **Medium**

40. *Answer choices:*
(see index for correct answer)

- a. Loan
- b. Private student loan
- c. Loan agreement
- d. Bullet loan

Guidance: level 1

:: Accounting in the United States ::

_____ refers to a Memorandum of Understanding signed in September 2002 between the Financial Accounting Standards Board, the US standard setter, and the International Accounting Standards Board. The agreement is so called as it was reached in Norwalk.

Exam Probability: **High**

41. *Answer choices:*
(see index for correct answer)

- a. Norwalk Agreement
- b. Association of Certified Fraud Examiners
- c. Federal Accounting Standards Advisory Board
- d. Other postemployment benefits

Guidance: level 1

:: Production and manufacturing ::

_____ consists of organization-wide efforts to "install and make permanent climate where employees continuously improve their ability to provide on demand products and services that customers will find of particular value." "Total" emphasizes that departments in addition to production are obligated to improve their operations; "management" emphasizes that executives are obligated to actively manage quality through funding, training, staffing, and goal setting. While there is no widely agreed-upon approach, TQM efforts typically draw heavily on the previously developed tools and techniques of quality control. TQM enjoyed widespread attention during the late 1980s and early 1990s before being overshadowed by ISO 9000, Lean manufacturing, and Six Sigma.

Exam Probability: **Low**

42. *Answer choices:*
(see index for correct answer)

- a. Joint product
- b. Digital materialization
- c. Engineering validation test
- d. Enterprise control

Guidance: level 1

:: Economics terminology ::

A corporation's share capital or _____ is the portion of a corporation's equity that has been obtained by the issue of shares in the corporation to a shareholder, usually for cash. "Share capital" may also denote the number and types of shares that compose a corporation's share structure.

Exam Probability: **Low**

43. *Answer choices:*
(see index for correct answer)

- a. Capital stock
- b. payee
- c. Currency trading
- d. economic profit

Guidance: level 1

:: Insolvency ::

_____ is the process in accounting by which a company is brought to an end in the United Kingdom, Republic of Ireland and United States. The assets and property of the company are redistributed. _____ is also sometimes referred to as winding-up or dissolution, although dissolution technically refers to the last stage of _____ . The process of _____ also arises when customs, an authority or agency in a country responsible for collecting and safeguarding customs duties, determines the final computation or ascertainment of the duties or drawback accruing on an entry.

Exam Probability: **Medium**

44. *Answer choices:*
(see index for correct answer)

- a. Preferential creditor
- b. Debt consolidation
- c. Liquidator
- d. United Kingdom insolvency law

Guidance: level 1

:: Management accounting ::

_____ is accounting which tracks the costs and revenues by "job" and enables standardized reporting of profitability by job. For an accounting system to support _____ , it must allow job numbers to be assigned to individual items of expenses and revenues. A job can be defined to be a specific project done for one customer, or a single unit of product manufactured, or a batch of units of the same type that are produced together.

Exam Probability: **Low**

45. *Answer choices:*
(see index for correct answer)

- a. Direct material usage variance
- b. Job costing
- c. Standard cost
- d. Constraints accounting

Guidance: level 1

:: Management accounting ::

In finance, the _____ or net present worth applies to a series of cash flows occurring at different times. The present value of a cash flow depends on the interval of time between now and the cash flow. It also depends on the discount rate. NPV accounts for the time value of money. It provides a method for evaluating and comparing capital projects or financial products with cash flows spread over time, as in loans, investments, payouts from insurance contracts plus many other applications.

Exam Probability: **High**

46. *Answer choices:*
(see index for correct answer)

- a. Dual overhead rate
- b. Factory overhead
- c. Net present value
- d. Managerial risk accounting

Guidance: level 1

:: Accounting in the United States ::

The _____ is the internal audit profession's most widely recognized advocate, educator, and provider of standards, guidance, and certifications. Established in 1941, the IIA today serves more than 200,000 members from more than 170 countries and territories. IIA's global headquarters are in Lake Mary, Fla., United States.

Exam Probability: **Low**

47. *Answer choices:*
(see index for correct answer)

- a. Institute of Internal Auditors
- b. Uniform Certified Public Accountant Examination
- c. Positive assurance
- d. Statements on Auditing Procedure

Guidance: level 1

:: Password authentication ::

A _____ , or sometimes redundantly a PIN number, is a numeric or alpha-numeric password used in the process of authenticating a user accessing a system.

Exam Probability: **Low**

48. *Answer choices:*

(see index for correct answer)

- a. Personal identification number
- b. PBKDF2
- c. Password-authenticated key agreement
- d. Password notification email

Guidance: level 1

:: ::

A tax is a compulsory financial charge or some other type of levy imposed upon a taxpayer by a governmental organization in order to fund various public expenditures. A failure to pay, along with evasion of or resistance to _____ , is punishable by law. Taxes consist of direct or indirect taxes and may be paid in money or as its labour equivalent.

Exam Probability: **Low**

49. *Answer choices:*

(see index for correct answer)

- a. deep-level diversity
- b. Taxation
- c. open system
- d. Character

Guidance: level 1

:: Management accounting ::

_____ is a managerial accounting cost concept. Under this method, manufacturing overhead is incurred in the period that a product is produced. This addresses the issue of absorption costing that allows income to rise as production rises. Under an absorption cost method, management can push forward costs to the next period when products are sold. This artificially inflates profits in the period of production by incurring less cost than would be incurred under a _____ system. _____ is generally not used for external reporting purposes. Under the Tax Reform Act of 1986, income statements must use absorption costing to comply with GAAP.

Exam Probability: **High**

50. *Answer choices:*
(see index for correct answer)

- a. activity based costing
- b. Throughput accounting
- c. Investment center
- d. Certified Management Accountants of Canada

Guidance: level 1

:: ::

An _____ is a systematic and independent examination of books, accounts, statutory records, documents and vouchers of an organization to ascertain how far the financial statements as well as non-financial disclosures present a true and fair view of the concern. It also attempts to ensure that the books of accounts are properly maintained by the concern as required by law. _____ ing has become such a ubiquitous phenomenon in the corporate and the public sector that academics started identifying an " _____ Society". The _____ or perceives and recognises the propositions before them for examination, obtains evidence, evaluates the same and formulates an opinion on the basis of his judgement which is communicated through their _____ ing report.

Exam Probability: **Medium**

51. *Answer choices:*
(see index for correct answer)

- a. interpersonal communication
- b. process perspective

- c. Audit
- d. levels of analysis

Guidance: level 1

:: Management accounting ::

"_____ s are the structural determinants of the cost of an activity, reflecting any linkages or interrelationships that affect it". Therefore we could assume that the _____ s determine the cost behavior within the activities, reflecting the links that these have with other activities and relationships that affect them.

Exam Probability: **Low**

52. *Answer choices:*
(see index for correct answer)

- a. Management control system
- b. Institute of Certified Management Accountants
- c. Cost driver
- d. Inventory valuation

Guidance: level 1

:: Business law ::

The expression " _____ " is somewhat confusing as it has a different meaning based on the context that is under consideration. From a product characteristic stand point, this type of a lease, as distinguished from a finance lease, is one where the lessor takes residual risk. As such, the lease is non full payout. From an accounting stand point, this type of lease results in off balance sheet financing.

Exam Probability: **Low**

53. *Answer choices:*
(see index for correct answer)

- a. Operating lease
- b. Country of origin
- c. Ordinary resolution
- d. Bulk sale

Guidance: level 1

:: Generally Accepted Accounting Principles ::

A _____ , in accrual accounting, is any account where the asset or liability is not realized until a future date , e.g. annuities, charges, taxes, income, etc. The deferred item may be carried, dependent on type of _____ , as either an asset or liability. See also accrual.

Exam Probability: **Medium**

54. *Answer choices:*
(see index for correct answer)

- a. Deferral
- b. Generally accepted accounting principles
- c. Income statement
- d. Cost pool

Guidance: level 1

:: Inventory ::

In business and accounting/accountancy, _____ or continuous inventory describes systems of inventory where information on inventory quantity and availability is updated on a continuous basis as a function of doing business. Generally this is accomplished by connecting the inventory system with order entry and in retail the point of sale system. In this case, book inventory would be exactly the same as, or almost the same, as the real inventory.

Exam Probability: **High**

55. *Answer choices:*
(see index for correct answer)

- a. GMROII
- b. Inventory bounce
- c. Perpetual inventory
- d. Consignment stock

Guidance: level 1

:: Accounting terminology ::

Accounts are typically defined by an identifier and a caption or header and are coded by account type. In computerized accounting systems with computable quantity accounting, the accounts can have a quantity measure definition.

Exam Probability: **Medium**

56. *Answer choices:*

(see index for correct answer)

- a. Fair value accounting
- b. General ledger
- c. Chart of accounts
- d. Total absorption costing

Guidance: level 1

:: Management accounting ::

_____ s are costs that change as the quantity of the good or service that a business produces changes. _____ s are the sum of marginal costs over all units produced. They can also be considered normal costs. Fixed costs and _____ s make up the two components of total cost. Direct costs are costs that can easily be associated with a particular cost object. However, not all _____ s are direct costs. For example, variable manufacturing overhead costs are _____ s that are indirect costs, not direct costs. _____ s are sometimes called unit-level costs as they vary with the number of units produced.

Exam Probability: **High**

57. *Answer choices:*

(see index for correct answer)

- a. Variable cost
- b. Hedge accounting
- c. Relevant cost
- d. Responsibility center

Guidance: level 1

:: Organizational theory ::

Decentralisation is the process by which the activities of an organization, particularly those regarding planning and decision making, are distributed or delegated away from a central, authoritative location or group. Concepts of _____ have been applied to group dynamics and management science in private businesses and organizations, political science, law and public administration, economics, money and technology.

Exam Probability: **Low**

58. *Answer choices:*
(see index for correct answer)

- a. Sociogram
- b. Team Service Management
- c. Organizational change fatigue
- d. Decentralization

Guidance: level 1

:: Project management ::

In economics, _____ is the assignment of available resources to various uses. In the context of an entire economy, resources can be allocated by various means, such as markets or central planning.

Exam Probability: **Low**

59. *Answer choices:*
(see index for correct answer)

- a. Resource allocation
- b. ISO 21500
- c. Feature-driven development
- d. Graphical Evaluation and Review Technique

Guidance: level 1

INDEX: Correct Answers

Foundations of Business

1. : Preference

2. c: Brainstorming

3. a: Credit

4. b: Buyer

5. : Labor relations

6. a: Alliance

7. a: Schedule

8. : Fraud

9. : Sharing

10. c: Accounts receivable

11. c: Cash flow

12. c: Management

13. a: Sexual harassment

14. b: Arbitration

15. d: Shareholders

16. c: Number

17. : Revenue

18. d: Publicity

19. c: Finance

20. c: Diagram

21. a: Marketing

22. d: Capital market

23. d: Productivity

24. : Currency

25. b: Chart

26. d: Gross domestic product

27. a: Market share

28. d: Exchange rate

29. d: Strategy

30. d: Integrity

31. d: Money

32. b: Risk

33. b: Initiative

34. : Availability

35. d: Corporation

36. d: Contract

37. b: Error

38. a: Consumer Protection

39. a: Business process

40. : Solution

41. c: Planning

42. : Working capital

43. a: Total quality management

44. a: Land

45. c: Duty

46. d: Advertising

47. a: Quality management

48. : Foreign direct investment

49. d: Technology

50. c: System

51. a: Perception

52. d: Affirmative action

53. d: Cash

54. b: Strategic alliance

55. d: Entrepreneurship

56. b: Officer

57. d: Corporate governance

58. a: Property rights

59. c: Audience

Management

1. a: Feedback

2. c: Case study

3. b: Supply chain

4. d: Transactional leadership

5. b: Interview

6. : Project manager

7. c: Certification

8. a: Inventory

9. c: Decentralization

10. a: Mass customization

11. : Creativity

12. b: Shareholder

13. d: Span of control

14. a: Situational leadership

15. c: Recruitment

16. b: Quality management

17. b: Business plan

18. : Overtime

19. : Human capital

20. d: Perception

21. b: Social loafing

22. b: Budget

23. : Halo effect

24. c: Linear programming

25. d: Theory X

26. c: Learning organization

27. d: Distance

28. d: Industrial Revolution

29. b: Job description

30. : Project

31. : Job analysis

32. a: Leadership

33. d: Supply chain management

34. a: Bureaucracy

35. a: Explanation

36. b: Product design

37. a: Small business

38. c: Self-assessment

39. b: Vertical integration

40. d: Joint venture

41. a: Offshoring

42. : Time management

43. b: Individualism

44. a: Senior management

45. b: Export

46. a: Management process

47. c: Choice

48. b: E-commerce

49. : Criticism

50. : Code

51. a: Size

52. c: Trade agreement

53. d: Subsidiary

54. : Project team

55. b: Glass ceiling

56. c: Training

57. d: Job enlargement

58. b: Performance appraisal

59. : Sexual harassment

Business law

1. a: Money laundering

2. a: Insurable interest

3. c: Regulation

4. a: Testimony

5. c: Incentive

6. : First Amendment

7. a: Antitrust

8. d: Advertisement

9. c: Committee

10. d: Foreign Corrupt Practices Act

11. b: Void contract

12. b: Petition

13. d: Affirmative action

14. a: Personnel

15. b: Charter

16. b: Good faith

17. b: Firm

18. : Res ipsa

19. b: Fair use

20. c: Bailee

21. a: Dividend

22. d: Relevant market

23. b: Board of directors

24. c: Undue influence

25. a: Trespass

26. a: Common carrier

27. a: Shares

28. a: Property

29. b: Comparative negligence

30. : Sole proprietorship

31. c: Forgery

32. a: Garnishment

33. b: Wire fraud

34. c: White-collar crime

35. d: Fraud

36. : Securities Act

37. c: World Trade Organization

38. d: Contract Clause

39. : S corporation

40. a: Federal Arbitration Act

41. b: Industry

42. b: Insurance

43. c: Mens rea

44. b: Social responsibility

45. b: Duress

46. a: False imprisonment

47. a: Beneficiary

48. b: Mortgage

49. b: Private law

50. a: Fee simple

51. d: Interest

52. c: Probate

53. b: Punitive damages

54. d: Aid

55. b: Security agreement

56. d: Manufacturing

57. b: Environmental Protection

58. c: Economic espionage

59. b: Disparagement

Finance

1. b: Put option

2. c: Management accounting

3. : Sole proprietorship

4. c: Public Company Accounting Oversight Board

5. a: Convertible bond

6. : Current ratio

7. c: Risk premium

8. : Operating leverage

9. a: Historical cost

10. b: Manufacturing overhead

11. b: Dividend yield

12. c: Gross profit

13. b: Technology

14. d: Amortization

15. : Accounts receivable

16. : Variable Costing

17. c: Standard deviation

18. : Debtor

19. b: Cost

20. b: Debit card

21. c: Discounting

22. b: Pension

23. a: Finance

24. : Yield curve

25. : Retirement

26. a: Internal control

27. d: Bank account

28. d: Investment

29. a: Exercise

30. a: Indenture

31. a: Total cost

32. a: Operating expense

33. b: Inventory turnover

34. d: Money market

35. c: Internal Revenue Service

36. b: Bank statement

37. b: Industry

38. d: Conservatism

39. b: Municipal bond

40. d: Limited liability

41. b: INDEX

42. d: Property

43. d: Bank

44. b: Normal balance

45. d: Advertising

46. : Corporation

47. b: Capital asset

48. c: Accounting method

49. b: Face

50. c: Cash equivalent

51. c: Primary market

52. a: Callable bond

53. a: Capital stock

54. : Board of directors

55. c: Compound interest

56. b: Receipt

57. c: Shares

58. d: Cost accounting

59. b: Accrued liabilities

Human resource management

1. c: Whistleblower

2. a: Departmentalization

3. b: Trainee

4. a: Globalization

5. a: Xerox Corporation

6. c: Piece rate

7. b: Functional job analysis

8. : Hazard

9. b: Adaptive

10. c: Salary

11. c: Authoritarianism

12. : Grievance

13. a: Impasse

14. : Independent contractor

15. c: Featherbedding

16. d: Ingratiation

17. : Officer

18. c: Competitive advantage

19. c: Cross-training

20. a: Drug test

21. c: Assessment center

22. : Recruitment advertising

23. : Exit interview

24. a: Socialization

25. a: Resignation

26. b: Strategic planning

27. c: Survey research

28. d: Human capital

29. : Employee handbook

30. b: Work ethic

31. a: National Labor Relations Act

32. b: Workplace bullying

33. b: Theory Z

34. : Brainstorming

35. b: Body language

36. c: Evaluation

37. b: Prevailing wage

38. c: Executive officer

39. c: American Federation of Government Employees

40. d: Distance learning

41. d: UNITE HERE

42. c: Social loafing

43. a: Workforce

44. d: National Institute for Occupational Safety and Health

45. : Absenteeism

46. d: Control group

47. b: Workforce planning

48. b: E-HRM

49. : Sweatshop

50. a: Age Discrimination in Employment Act

51. : Labor union

52. d: Proactive

53. a: Predictive validity

54. a: Worker Adjustment and Retraining Notification Act

55. d: Job rotation

56. a: Rating scale

57. d: Criterion validity

58. : New Deal

59. : Material safety data sheet

Information systems

1. c: Master data

2. c: Information governance

3. a: Utility computing

4. a: Text mining

5. d: Gmail

6. c: Downtime

7. c: Interactivity

8. a: Infrastructure

9. a: Social shopping

10. d: Supplier relationship management

11. c: Data link

12. a: Accessibility

13. c: Output device

14. c: Total cost of ownership

15. c: World Wide Web

16. d: Web content

17. : Analytics

18. b: Consumerization

19. : User interface

20. c: Random access

21. : Wiki

22. : Open source

23. d: Star

24. : Yelp

25. b: Joint application design

26. : Web analytics

27. b: Data center

28. b: Credit card

29. : Business intelligence

30. d: Internet

31. : Authentication

32. b: Web mining

33. c: Relational database

34. d: Mobile commerce

35. c: Information literacy

36. d: Supply chain

37. b: Chief information officer

38. b: Data redundancy

39. b: Google Docs

40. : Data warehouse

41. b: Enterprise search

42. a: Global Positioning System

43. a: ICANN

44. d: Verisign

45. : Netflix

46. a: Health Insurance Portability and Accountability Act

47. : Network management

48. c: Electronic funds transfer

49. a: Database

50. a: System software

51. a: Business rule

52. a: Disaster recovery plan

53. c: Information overload

54. a: Business analytics

55. d: Information management

56. c: Wide Area Network

57. d: Interoperability

58. d: Knowledge management

59. c: Blog

Marketing

1. : Stock

2. a: Life

3. d: Direct selling

4. : Department store

5. c: Bottom line

6. d: Marketing strategy

7. d: Mission statement

8. a: Price war

9. c: Concept testing

10. a: Federal Trade Commission

11. b: Market research

12. : Census

13. b: Investment

14. b: Household

15. a: Raw material

16. a: American Express

17. d: Question

18. c: Creative brief

19. c: Preference

20. c: Google

21. c: Product differentiation

22. c: Inventory

23. b: Logistics

24. : Business Week

25. c: Reseller

26. b: Advertising agency

27. c: Target market

28. : Sherman Antitrust Act

29. a: Market share

30. : Data warehouse

31. b: Advertising

32. a: Cost

33. : Demand

34. a: Reinforcement

35. a: Communication

36. a: Customer service

37. d: Commodity

38. d: Quantitative research

39. c: Data collection

40. c: Logo

41. b: Mass media

42. d: Sales promotion

43. d: Clayton Act

44. b: Brand loyalty

45. c: Supply chain

46. b: Infomercial

47. d: Consumer Protection

48. d: Value proposition

49. c: Standing

50. b: Supermarket

51. : Partnership

52. d: Research and development

53. c: Patent

54. a: Business model

55. : Social networking

56. : Shares

57. a: Loyalty program

58. c: Exploratory research

59. d: Star

Manufacturing

1. b: Consortium

2. : Milestone

3. d: EFQM

4. c: Asset

5. c: Product differentiation

6. c: Inventory

7. c: Kanban

8. c: Certification

9. b: Credit

10. b: Sensitivity analysis

11. c: Process management

12. d: E-procurement

13. a: Cash register

14. : Stakeholder management

15. a: Production schedule

16. d: Perfect competition

17. d: Expediting

18. b: DMAIC

19. d: Sequence

20. d: Quality assurance

21. b: Steel

22. d: Economic order quantity

23. : Assembly line

24. c: Kaizen

25. : E-commerce

26. d: Raw material

27. b: Supply chain risk management

28. : Resource allocation

29. : Gantt chart

30. c: Customer

31. b: Capacity planning

32. a: Inspection

33. d: Scope statement

34. a: Heat exchanger

35. c: Estimation

36. c: Authority

37. b: Downtime

38. c: Licensed production

39. b: Turbine

40. c: Purchasing

41. : Forecasting

42. : Rolling

43. : Heat treating

44. b: Water

45. d: Process flow diagram

46. d: Solution

47. b: Manufacturing

48. b: Minitab

49. a: Scientific management

50. d: Thomas Register

51. a: Steering committee

52. : Quality audit

53. c: ROOT

54. b: Material requirements planning

55. b: Supply chain network

56. a: Reflux

57. a: Zero Defects

58. c: Reorder point

59. b: Quality policy

Commerce

1. b: Electronic commerce

2. b: Recruitment

3. : Cost structure

4. d: Security

5. b: Disintermediation

6. b: Logo

7. : Lease

8. : Exchange rate

9. b: E-procurement

10. d: Property

11. d: Consortium

12. c: Productivity

13. b: Semantic

14. b: Market research

15. a: Economic regulation

16. d: Shopping cart

17. b: Logistics Management

18. a: Computer security

19. b: Supply chain management

20. : Excite

21. : Walt Disney

22. : Graduation

23. : Hearing

24. b: Collaborative filtering

25. d: Insurance

26. d: Forward auction

27. b: Board of directors

28. a: Automation

29. b: Advertisement

30. c: Commodity

31. c: Supranational

32. : Anticipation

33. c: Consumer-to-consumer

34. d: Micropayment

35. b: Asset

36. c: Committee

37. : Optimum

38. b: Real estate

39. : Import

40. d: Consideration

41. b: Adoption

42. b: Management team

43. : Tariff

44. b: Strategic plan

45. b: Mass production

46. : Payment system

47. : Subsidy

48. c: Reverse auction

49. c: Expense

50. b: Investment

51. c: Trial

52. c: Marketspace

53. a: Raw material

54. b: Market share

55. c: Lycos

56. d: Labor union

57. : Commerce

58. a: Statutory law

59. b: Netflix

Business ethics

1. a: Edgewood College

2. a: Electronic waste

3. b: Corporate social responsibility

4. c: Working poor

5. d: Protestant work ethic

6. c: Lead

7. d: Sustainable

8. b: Occupational Safety and Health Administration

9. c: Consumerism

10. b: Tobacco

11. : Pollution Prevention

12. : East Germany

13. b: Madoff

14. a: Building

15. b: Statutory law

16. d: Reputation

17. a: ExxonMobil

18. c: Organizational culture

19. d: Toxic waste

20. b: Community development financial institution

21. b: Urban sprawl

22. b: Authoritarian

23. c: Locus of control

24. a: Exxon Valdez

25. d: Clayton Act

26. c: Solar power

27. c: Corporate citizenship

28. d: Pyramid scheme

29. : Consumer Financial Protection Bureau

30. d: Human nature

31. a: Cultural relativism

32. a: Affirmative action

33. d: Trojan horse

34. a: Micromanagement

35. c: Fair Trade Certified

36. b: Socialism

37. d: Real estate

38. a: Six Sigma

39. : Parental leave

40. a: Natural gas

41. c: Federal Trade Commission Act

42. : Transformational leadership

43. d: Aristotle

44. : Great Depression

45. d: Recovery Act

46. c: Supply Chain

47. c: Utopian socialism

48. d: Consumer Protection

49. a: Undue hardship

50. a: WorldCom

51. b: Constitutional law

52. a: Corporation

53. a: Sullivan principles

54. : Coal

55. : Guerrilla Marketing

56. c: Patriot Act

57. c: Retaliation

58. c: Vigilance committee

59. c: Individualistic culture

Accounting

1. a: Investment center

2. : Arthur Andersen

3. d: Chief executive officer

4. d: Transfer pricing

5. c: Promissory note

6. : Overdraft

7. : Inventory

8. c: Balance sheet

9. c: Generally Accepted Accounting Principles

10. b: Encumbrance

11. b: Debt ratio

12. a: Value theory

13. b: Creditor

14. d: Free cash flow

15. b: QuickBooks

16. : Ledger

17. b: Partnership agreement

18. b: Petty cash

19. c: Comprehensive income

20. d: Tax reform

21. d: Paid-in capital

22. a: Zero-based budgeting

23. c: Adjusting entries

24. c: Information systems

25. a: Net realizable value

26. b: Not-for-profit

27. a: Securities and Exchange Commission

28. a: Pension

29. : Historical cost

30. a: Accounting period

31. : Finished good

32. a: Callable

33. a: Embezzlement

34. b: Maturity date

35. a: Current asset

36. a: Income

37. c: Bad debt

38. : Common stock

39. c: Standard deduction

40. a: Loan

41. a: Norwalk Agreement

42. : Total quality management

43. a: Capital stock

44. : Liquidation

45. b: Job costing

46. c: Net present value

47. a: Institute of Internal Auditors

48. a: Personal identification number

49. b: Taxation

50. : Variable Costing

51. c: Audit

52. c: Cost driver

53. a: Operating lease

54. a: Deferral

55. c: Perpetual inventory

56. c: Chart of accounts

57. a: Variable cost

58. d: Decentralization

59. a: Resource allocation

CPSIA information can be obtained
at www.ICGtesting.com
Printed in the USA
LVHW031341301019
635717LV00009B/1126/P